NO S
LEFT
BEHIND

AVOIDING

THE GREAT

COLLEGE

RIP-OFF

MARC SCHEER

Common Courage Press, Monroe Maine

Copyright 2008 © by Marc Scheer
All rights reserved

Cover art by Matt Wuerker
Cover design by Matt Wuerker and Erica Bjerning
Typesetting by www.EssexGraphix.com

Library of Congress Cataloging-in-Publication Data is available from publisher on request.

ISBN 13 paper: 9781567513783
ISBN 13 hardcover: 9781567513790

Common Courage Press
P.O. Box 702
121 Red Barn Road
Monroe, ME 04951

207-525-0900
fax: 207-525-3068

www.commoncouragepress.com
info@commoncouragepress.com

First printing
Printed in Canada

This publication is designed to provide competent and reliable information regarding the subject matter covered. However, it is sold with the understanding that the author and publisher are not engaged in rendering legal, financial, or other professional advice. Laws and practices often vary from state to state and if legal or other expert assistance is required, the services of a professional should be sought. The author and publisher specifically disclaim any liability that is incurred from the use or application of the contents of this book.

While the author has made every effort to provide accurate telephone numbers and Internet addresses at the time of publication, neither the publisher nor the author assumes any responsibility for errors, or for changes that occur after publication. Further, the author and publisher have no control over and do not assume responsibility for third-party websites or their content.

In Loving Memory of
Harry Josephs
Gertrude and Philip Meyer
Rose and Arthur Scheer
Libby and George Alderman
Alan Miller
Sonia and Hillel Lawsky
Anna and Irving Rothenberg

ACKNOWLEDGMENTS

First and foremost, thank you to Greg Bates, the best publisher and editor in the world, for his dedication, encouragement, mentoring, excellent feedback, and faith. His assistance led to vast improvements in the quality of my writing, and every author would be lucky to work with him.

Next, thank you to those who provided technical suggestions, including Louise Litt, Lauren Davis, Ronald Ehrenberg, Phil Graves, Laura Perna, Jennifer Washburn, and Devon Lynch. I'm also grateful to Google for its excellent research tools. And I have much appreciation for those whose work provided me with additional inspiration, motivation and focus, including Bruce Springsteen, Derek Jeter, Mariano Rivera, Damon Lindelof, Carlton Cuse, J.J. Abrams, and the radio stations of WXPK (107.1), WBLS (107.5), WRKS (98.7), and WQCD (101.9).

Finally, thank you to all of my friends and family, who provided significant encouragement during the writing process. Specific shout-outs to Cousins Eve and Brad; Cousins Jamie and Alley; Rugby David; VRed; VFitz; Richie; Gregg; Dmitry; Cousin Adam; and Herb and Sue. Thanks to Mike, Pam, and Lauren for their emotional and technical support. Also, much thanks to Daniel Marc, *il eximius fabbro*, for his good will and valuable suggestions. In addition, I am grateful for the influence of Harry 7, who read early drafts, mentored me on the art of writing persuasively, and always believed in my abilities. Special gratitude to Mom for her devotion and sacrifice, and to Dad for his encouragement and pride. Additional thanks to Phantom Danger for his superb companionship. And much love to Heather, whose assistance, dedication, patience, and faith were critical during the completion of this project.

"In all affairs it's a healthy thing now and then to hang a question mark on the things you have long taken for granted."
—Bertrand Russell

CONTENTS

Chapter 1 1
Exploitive Colleges and Desperate Graduates

Chapter 2 15
Colleges Gone Wild—*How Colleges Use Marketing to Maximize Their Profits*

Chapter 3 53
Distasteful College Services

Chapter 4 66
Dire Education—*Do Students Get the Instruction They Pay For?*

Chapter 5 94
The Real Cost & Value of College—*Getting the Most for Your Money*

Chapter 6 118
Attention Shoppers! *The Hidden Costs of "Financial Aid" and How to Make the Discounts Work for You*

Chapter 7 142
Avoiding the College Debt Trap

Chapter 8 165
Got Value? *Choosing an Appropriate College*

Chapter 9 194
Getting More for Less—*Saving Money While Enrolled*

Chapter 10 208
Til Debt Do Us Part—*Managing Debt After Leaving School*

Chapter 11 221
Greedy Grad Schools—*Avoiding More Bad Deals*

Appendix A 244
Success Without College—*An Appendix for the Adventurous*

Appendix B **254**
Putting Colleges to the Test—*Twenty-Five Questions Before You Enroll*

Appendix C **257**
Winning the College Gamble—*Online Resources for Success*

References 266

Index 325

About the Author 342

TOP 10
MYTHS ABOUT COLLEGE

1. A college degree is worth about $1 million (or more) over a lifetime.

2. College graduates are financially "set for life."

3. Colleges have very little money and need every penny they can get.

4. Colleges are committed to giving their students a good education.

5. Colleges provide students with excellent career preparation.

6. Colleges give their students the support they need in order to graduate.

7. Prestigious and expensive colleges provide a better education and better career advantages than other colleges.

8. All kinds of financial aid are safe for students.

9. Graduate school always leads to an excellent pay-off for students.

10. People have to go to college to get a "college education."

CHAPTER 1

EXPLOITIVE COLLEGES AND DESPERATE GRADUATES

College is supposed to be an investment that guarantees a student's success—but this is no longer true. Of course, at its best, a college education can help students gain skills, develop important friendships, and learn new things about themselves and the world. A college degree can also provide employment advantages, making it easier for graduates to get hired and receive better salaries and better jobs (on average).[1]

> **Myth: College graduates are financially "set for life."**

The problem is that, despite new discounts at a handful of colleges, too many students receive a disappointing college payoff, paying high prices and borrowing large amounts of money in exchange for low-quality instruction and low starting salaries. A number of recent books, articles, and research studies have shown that the college investment is very risky, including *Generation Debt*, by Anya Kamenetz; *Strapped*, by Tamara Draut; and "Thirty and Broke," by *BusinessWeek*.

Consider this:
- Prices for classes at some colleges now top $100 per hour.[2] The real total cost of college paid by each student averages almost $100,000 (for four years), including costs for tuition, lost income, student loan interest, and all other expenses.[3]

- Almost seven out of ten college graduates leave school with student loan debt.[4] The average borrower now owes $23,000 in student loans and $3,000 in credit card debt when they leave school,[5] and many owe much more. In addition, average student debt has more than doubled since just 1993 (an increase of about 60% after considering inflation).[6]

- Dropping out of college is surprisingly common: more than one out of three college students drop out of school within six years after they start,[7] and more than 600,000 college students drop out of four-year colleges every year.[8] Dropouts have an especially tough time, stuck with a double whammy of high college debt bills and low salaries.

- Most college graduates don't even obtain the initial career success they hope for. Several studies show that many college students are unrealistically optimistic, expecting to earn 45% more than they actually will when they graduate, an overestimate of about ten thousand dollars.[9] In fact, college grads often receive starting salaries of only about $31,000 or less.[10] Also, in 2004, more than one million college graduates were unemployed.[11] And more than one out of three recent college graduates have jobs that don't require a college degree.[12] Since it's common for college students to pay high costs and receive disappointing payoffs, the average high school graduate has more money than the average college graduate for about the first 15 years after high school.[13]

- Since their college loans are so high and their salaries are so low, nearly half of college borrowers leave school with an "unmanageable student loan debt," or high bills take up more than about 10% of their salaries.[14] In addition, one out of ten borrowers must use more than 20% of their salaries to pay for their loans.[15]

- When their first student loan bill arrives, one out of three student loan borrowers are surprised at how the high the bill is. Also, more than one out of three graduates of four-year colleges who have student loan debt are unprepared to pay their first loan bill when they receive it. And four out of ten recent graduates of four-year colleges who used loans and receive a monthly bill have difficulty making their monthly loan payments.[16]

- About half of recent student loan borrowers regret taking out as much money in loans to pay for college as they did, and many believe their education was not worth the amount of student loan debt they built up.[17]

- As tuition prices and student loan debts skyrocket, the number of 18 to 24 year olds filing for bankruptcy has doubled, while the number of people under age 26 who filed has tripled.[18] Hundreds of thousands of young people now declare bankruptcy every year, including over 100,000 people under the age of 25, and more than 400,000 people aged 25-34.[19] Since so many students leave school with so much debt, it's likely this contributes to the large number of bankruptcies among young adults.

- High college costs and low salaries (or unemployment) make it difficult for many students to set up their lives after they leave school. Therefore, every year, more young people become "boomerang kids,"[20] returning to live at home with their families. Specifically, there are now

6 million more young people (ages 18-34) living with their parents than there were in the year 1970![21] And more than six out of ten college students move back in with their parents after graduation.[22] This arrangement is often more long-term than people realize: in mid-2006, almost half of 2005 college graduates were still living at home.[23]

- Due to high college costs, one out of five student loan borrowers choose to give up their career dreams and seek higher-paying jobs, just so they will have an easier time paying off their student loans.[24] Also, borrowers are more likely than non-borrowers to leave low-paying jobs they enjoy because they can't repay their loans.[25] Repayment is especially difficult for new graduates who work in important public service careers like teaching, social work, or public interest law.[26]

- College costs often make it difficult for grads to buy other things they want, and meet other personal goals. For example, four out of ten recent graduates (44%)[27] say they put off buying a home because of their student loans (up from 25% in 1991).[28] Also, more than one out of ten recent graduates (14%) say they delayed marriage due to their student loans (up from 7% in 1991),[29] and three out of ten recent graduates (28%)[30] say they delayed having children due to their student loans (up from 12% in 1991).[31] In addition, college students often lose out on hundreds of thousands of dollars because they can't afford to start saving for retirement as soon as they leave school; more than half of borrowers (55%) say college debt has delayed their retirement savings.[32]

- Graduates who can't afford to repay their debts often

ruin their "credit rating," making it even more difficult, or more expensive, for them to buy things, obtain housing, and get hired by employers.[33]

- Many graduate students don't do much better, often borrowing even more money, but then still receiving low salaries when they leave school. Many graduate school alumni even have trouble finding jobs within their fields of study.[34]

- Finally, high costs prevent many people from obtaining a formal college or graduate education. Each year, nearly half of all college-qualified, low- or moderate-income high school graduates—over two hundred thousand students—do not go to college because they can't afford the high costs.[35] Lower-income students are also more likely to drop out of college.[36] The evidence shows that many talented students are held back by high education costs, and not by a lack of academic ability: seven out of ten high-scoring low-income students <u>do not</u> get college degrees (71%).[37] In addition, about four out of ten college graduates don't go to graduate school just because they can't afford it.[38] In this way, many deserving students are denied the opportunity to attend—and finish—higher education programs.

THE EMOTIONAL DAMAGE CAUSED BY HIGH COLLEGE COSTS

Since college costs are often so high, and college payoffs are often relatively poor, it shouldn't be too surprising that many college students and graduates feel sad, worried, and overwhelmed. Specifically, half of recent four-year graduates feel "stressed out" due to their student loan debt,[39] four out of ten feel "depressed" due to the debt, and three-quarters of graduates with college debt say that it has been difficult for them to pay back what they owe.[40] In some ways, college graduation is a mixed blessing, because it often marks students' official entrance into "Generation Debt."

Two students in particular, Sean Moyer and Mitzi Pool, represent the worst-case college scenarios: these two students took their own lives due to the debt they built up in college.[41] Sean, a National Merit Finalist and University of Oklahoma student, was 22 years old and had more than $12,000 in credit card debt when he died. Sean's mother says that just one week before his suicide, Sean told her that he "had no idea how to get out of his financial mess and didn't see much of a future for himself." Sean's mom continues: "He said he was in debt and didn't know how it happened. He thought he was a failure."[42] And: "I have no doubt that [Sean's debt] played a significant part in his [death]." Around the same time, Mitzi, an 18-year old student at the University of Central Oklahoma, also committed suicide, with $2,500 in credit debt and "her checkbook and [debt] bills spread out on her bed."[43] Although these students' deaths may have been caused by more than just money, it's tragic that debt played any role at all in this situation.

The student debt problem is magnified by the fact that colleges are significantly responsible for students' hardship and pain. As Mitzi's mother points out, "[Mitzi] got a hold of these credit cards on campus."[44] In addition, colleges often include expensive loans within the "financial aid packages" that they offer to their students. Although colleges may not want their students and graduates to get hurt from debt, the harm is incidental to what they do want: money.

LOOKING INSIDE COLLEGES' PIGGY BANKS

Exactly how much money do schools have? Although colleges present themselves as non-profit organizations that need every dollar to survive, and some colleges are struggling, many colleges have much more money than people are led to believe.

> **Myth: Colleges have very little money and need every penny they can get.**

In fact, in January 2007, there were 62 colleges and universities that <u>each owned over $1 billion</u> in cash and other financial investments,[45] including:

- Harvard University ($29 billion),
- Yale University ($18 billion),
- Stanford University ($14 billion),
- University of Chicago ($5 billion),
- Emory University ($5 billion),
- Northwestern University ($5 billion),
- Washington University in Saint Louis ($5 billion),
- Duke University ($4 billion),
- Rice University ($4 billion),
- University of Notre Dame ($4 billion), and
- Williams College ($1 billion).

And it's not only private colleges that are rich. Plenty of public colleges are also extremely wealthy, and 18 of them each owned at least $1 billion in 2006, including:

- University of Texas system ($13 billion),
- University of California ($6 billion),

- University of Michigan ($6 billion),
- University of Minnesota ($2 billion),
- University of North Carolina at Chapel Hill ($1 billion), and
- Penn State University ($1 billion).[46]

This means that the wealthiest colleges have an average of $331,000 <u>per student</u>.[47]

Of course, not every college is a billionaire, but many private and public colleges have hundreds of millions of dollars in their "endowment funds," or investment and savings accounts. Specifically, the median total college endowment value is about $72 million, and 334 colleges have over $100 million.[48] The average college has $35,000 in its endowment fund for <u>each</u> of its full-time students.

The problem is that, although many colleges are rich, the vast majority don't use enough of their wealth to help students with scholarships and grants. Instead, colleges hold on to almost all of their endowment money, investing it and making more money from it. For example, even though wealthy colleges obtain annual investment returns as high as 20%,[49] and average annual returns of about 9-11%,[50] many colleges spend less than 5% of their total endowments each year,[51] including wealthy schools like Williams College, Harvard University, Yale University, Princeton University, Stanford University, the University of California, Grinnell College, Swarthmore College, and Amherst College.[52] In this way, colleges tend to spend a very small portion of their investment income, while never actually spending the original donations they receive! Meanwhile, schools' endowment funds keep growing in size, as the schools also raise their prices, lure their students into borrowing crippling amounts of money, and ask for more money in donations—which also increases students' pain. A number of colleges have even announced plans to <u>each</u> raise more than $1 billion in new donations, and some intend to raise more than $3 billion, including Harvard, the University of Pennsylvania, Cornell, Yale, the University of Virginia, Stanford, and Columbia.[53] Colleges often say that they can't spend more of their endowment money, because they have to save it in case of a "rainy day," when their money runs low—but for the students and graduates suffering under the weight of tuition-induced debt, it's already pouring.

ADMINISTRATE AND GROW RICH

While students and graduates struggle financially, colleges' top employees get rich (and get large salary raises every year that are much higher than inflation[54]). What makes their high salaries particularly outrageous is that the college 'educators' who get paid the most, including top professors, are often the ones who spend the least time actually teaching students (as explained in Chapter 4).

For example, college deans, who are in-charge of schools' specific departments, commonly receive more than $100,000 per year.[55] Also, top-level professors, who tend to spend most of their time conducting research projects instead of teaching, receive an average salary of $136,689 per year at private schools (and up to $177,400 at prestigious private schools like Harvard University), and an average salary of $106,495 per year at public schools (and up to $133,200 at prestigious public schools like the University of California).[56]

And college presidents, who usually focus most of their energy on fundraising instead of education, often receive some of the highest salaries. The median annual salary for private college presidents is over $500,000 per year, while public college presidents receive a median salary of

$374,846.[57] In fact, 112 college presidents receive more than $500,000 per year, including those at 42 public schools like the University of Michigan and Rutgers University.[58] And a few private college presidents are paid more than $1 million per year,[59] while the public University of Delaware gives its president an annual salary of $979,571.[60] College presidents are supposed to be public servants, especially at both public and private non-profit schools, but many of them receive more money than the President of the United States!

On top of high salaries, upper-level college employees also receive many expensive perks. Specifically, high-level professors receive "tenure," which basically guarantees their jobs (and their big salaries), for just about as long as they want to show up—even if they are not doing a very good job. Also, professors are allowed to use their schools' facilities for free (such as health clubs), and send their children to almost any college and graduate school for free.[61] In addition, colleges often pay for their presidents to live in mansions, ride in expensive cars, and play at country clubs.[62] Finally, colleges also spend large amounts of money on health and retirement benefits for their executives and professors (including multi-million-dollar retirement payouts to their presidents).

Education is supposed to be a noble profession, a labor of love carried out by modestly-paid but dedicated faculty in non-profit institutions focused on one goal: educating the next generation. For many instructors, especially public high school teachers and low-level college instructors, that's an accurate description. And there's nothing wrong when educators manage to earn a decent salary—they deserve it. But are college presidents really worth a cool million, or even half million? Wealthy schools think they are, especially since the presidents help to obtain and protect their millions—or billions. However, when it comes to helping students to obtain a valuable education at an affordable price, these presidents (and other top college employees) are often an expensive liability.

Colleges also display a focus on profitability by giving high salaries to the employees who aren't directly involved in education at all. For example, 35 colleges give salaries of more than $1 million to the coaches of their sports teams (including the University of Alabama, which signed its football coach to a contract of $32 million over 8 years),[63] and many other college coaches receive annual salaries worth hundreds of thousands of dollars.[64] In addition, some of the highest paid people in all of American education are the people who manage schools' endowment funds; in 2003, Harvard gave $35 million to <u>each</u> of the people that managed its endowment money.[65] Although these kinds of workers may deserve high salaries because they help generate significant wealth for colleges, the problem is that colleges don't use enough of these profits to improve their educational services or reduce students' costs.

In a 2006 *New York Times* Op-Ed article called "A Little Learning is An Expensive Thing," William Chase, the former president of Emory University and Wesleyan University, makes several statements that illustrate how colleges and college employees tend to focus on financial profit rather than affordability or customer satisfaction. He begins the article by saying, "When I was a college president, I was never able to give incoming freshmen the honest talk I wanted to," and he continues with a long list of truths he admits he should have communicated to new students. Chase's actual confessions include the following statements: "The next time we'll see each other is when you graduate;" "…a good many of you won't finish [your degrees] on time;" due to expensive student loans, "…many of you [will] begin your adult lives…in serious debt;" "I am [overpaid];" "I take home more money at [this college] than [almost] anyone else;" "My pay is about five times greater than an average faculty member's;" "I'm thought of as the chief executive of the university and chief executives get paid a lot in America;" and "[This college] could save some money by paying me less." At the end of his article, Chase highlights finances one more time: "I welcome you all—[including] those who will waste their dollars [here]…"

HOW COLLEGES GET AWAY WITH IT

Unfortunately, college students often suffer because colleges (and banks) take advantage of them for profit. After all, colleges are fully responsible for setting their own high prices, for strongly encouraging students to borrow too much, and for using a variety of manipulative strategies to get as much money as possible (as explained extensively throughout the rest of this book). In particular, colleges leverage their admissions systems, their prices, their financial aid systems, and the government donation system, in order to get more money. At the same time, colleges increase their profits by surprisingly neglecting their educational services (as described extensively in Chapter 4).

These techniques seem to work for colleges, because many of them are rich and few of them go out of business: only about 5 private colleges close up every year (out of 1,600 total private colleges in the country).[66] However, these techniques are not helpful for students, graduates, and taxpayers, who often get tricked into spending too much. The reality is that colleges are aggressive businesses, and students and taxpayers are their exploited customers.

Ultimately, schools get away with their profiteering because so many people want to go to college: almost nine out of ten Americans (87%) believe that a college education has become as important as a high school diploma once was;[67]

half of Americans believe that a four-year college degree is essential for success;[68] and many other Americans believe that a two-year degree is essential. In addition, more than six out of ten American parents of high school students believe that it's "absolutely necessary" for their children to have a college degree,[69] three-quarters of parents (74%) say that it is likely that their children will go to college,[70] and most teenagers expect to go to college.[71]

In this way, colleges are guaranteed to have millions of customers each year, no matter what they charge. Specifically, two out of three high school graduates go to college,[72] more than 17 million students are currently enrolled,[73] and millions more enroll each year. In addition, student applications and enrollments are rising for most colleges,[74] allowing them to continue their profitable schemes.

AVOIDING THE GREAT COLLEGE RIP-OFF
"Caveat discipulus": let the student beware!

The main problem is that many students don't realize they have a bad deal until it is too late, after they have paid high expenses and been saddled with crippling debt. Going to college is supposed to be part of the "American Dream," but these days it often leads to an "American Nightmare." When colleges feed their greed by charging high prices, encouraging high debt, and favoring profit over education, many people are burdened with high costs, and almost no sucker—or victim—is left behind.

However, as described earlier, college degrees can also provide some important advantages, especially for obtaining good jobs, so the key for students is to get a degree while avoiding dangerous pitfalls and disappointments. The good news is that there are many things that <u>all</u> students can do to protect themselves, reduce their risk, avoid college traps, and put the odds of the college gamble in their favor. College is a financial investment, and the following chapters offer information for students and graduates about how to get the most for their money. The tips begin in the next chapter, with an examination of the extensive catalog of strategies that schools use to increase their income, usually at students' and taxpayers' expense.

CHAPTER 2

COLLEGES GONE WILD
How Colleges Use Marketing to Maximize Their Profits

"Universities share one characteristic with compulsive gamblers and exiled royalty: there is never enough money to satisfy their desires."

—Derek Bok,
president of Harvard University,
in *Universities in the Marketplace,* 2003

In their aggressive search for profits, schools exploit students' desire for a college degree by using a wide variety of strategies to increase students' costs. However, students who understand these strategies may be able to get better deals. It can be helpful for students to act cautiously even before they get to college, because colleges begin to target students as they decide which schools to apply to.

TWISTING THE RATINGS SYSTEM

Students often use college ratings and rankings to decide which schools to apply to and attend, but schools tend to tamper with these systems in order to increase their earnings and get students to enroll. One of the most popular ratings systems—and most tampered with—is the one distributed every year by *U.S. News and World Report*,[75] but many other magazines and books also feature college descriptions, evaluations, and judgments. These kinds of systems imply that higher-rated schools are better for students, but this is inaccurate—especially since schools manipulate the systems to try to get better scores than they actually deserve.

First, college ratings like those of *U.S. News and World Report* are especially tainted because the schools provide the information that their own rankings are based on![76] How can anyone trust a ratings system that allows the schools to basically rate themselves? Robert Woodbury (former chancellor of the University of Maine), and Arthur Rothkopf (president of Lafayette University) say that many schools use this opportunity to report false and deceptive data, so that they can look better and get better ratings.[77] For example, some schools improve their ratings by changing their class sizes at different times of the year.[78] Also, *The Wall Street Journal* reports that many colleges report fake data about the amount of donations they receive, in order to improve their overall ratings.[79] In addition, schools like Franklin and Marshall College and Emory University have unfairly rejected excellent and qualified students, while also accepting students who had less impressive credentials,[80] just because this helped the schools to improve their ratings, rankings, and profits (because schools are penalized in the ratings for accepting talented students who then enroll somewhere else).

Ratings and rankings also can't be trusted because they have little to do with whether a college is really good or not. For example, college ratings are often based on criteria like how much money a school receives or spends, how much money a school's professors receive, the number of research professors at the school, how many students were rejected for admission, and what workers at other schools supposedly think of the school ("peer ratings")[81]—but none of these things really have much to do with whether students receive a good and valuable education. In fact, although peer ratings can determine 25% of a school's score, these ratings are often inaccurate because the peer raters don't know enough about the schools they rate.[82] And college ratings usually <u>don't</u> include important educational criteria like teaching quality, or important student results like the amount of student learning, or average salaries for graduates. A recent study by Education Sector determined that 95% of a college's rating tends to be based on the school's fame, fortune, and exclusivity, which have relatively nothing to do with the school's educational effectiveness or its impact on students.[83] Even worse, Michele Tolela Myers, the president of Sarah Lawrence College, recently accused *U.S. News & World Report* of preparing to publish false data about her school in its rankings.[84] Specifically, Myers accused the publication of threatening to unfairly assign the school a low (and fake) average SAT score, just because the school does not require its applicants to take the SAT admissions exam, preferring to judge applicants on other criteria. Bob Schaeffer, public education director for the National Center for Fair and Open Testing, says, "The *U.S. News* policy of fabricating data for colleges…is both unfair and unethical," and that this strategy "further undermines the credibility of the magazine's already widely criticized rankings."[85]

People also shouldn't expect college ratings to be very helpful because students at the same school often take different classes, and then later obtain varying salaries. In addition, different students need different kinds of training, so a school's rating usually has little to do with whether the school will be a good fit for a particular student. Therefore, differences in rankings often don't mean much for students.

Although college ratings aren't usually that important for student success, schools continue to manipulate them because many people trust them. Higher-rated colleges can charge higher prices—and get people to pay them. While students probably don't attend schools just because the schools have good ratings, a good rating can create some valuable publicity for a school, and be a great marketing tool, leading to more applicants, prestige, and money. For example, from 1994 to 2003, Washington University in St. Louis jumped from 20th place to 9th place on the list of top colleges—and doubled its number of student applications, from 10,000 to 20,000. The reverse is also true: Yale University experienced a drop in applications when its ratings dropped.[86] However, when students make college decisions, they should probably approach college ratings and rankings with caution.

LEGAL MANIPULATION

The college ratings and rankings system is just one example of the portfolio of marketing techniques that schools use to increase their revenue, just like other businesses. Marketing is so pervasive, important, and valuable to colleges that a large number of them spend $1,000 <u>or more</u> on marketing, advertising, and recruiting for <u>each and every one</u> of their first-year students, including seven out of ten private colleges, and one out of ten public colleges.[87] Some colleges even spend as much as $5,000 per student on marketing.[88]

The phrase "enrollment management" has been used to describe all of the ways that colleges manipulate their marketing, recruitment, admissions, pricing, and financial aid systems, in order to maximize their income.[89] To coordinate all of their marketing efforts, schools have special departments that are devoted to "recruitment" and "enrollment." In addition, schools hire special companies to help them develop sophisticated marketing strategies.[90] Specifically, more than 125 colleges and universities have used the services of the marketing company named J.M. Lord & Associates, Inc. to help them target students, including Cornell University,

Columbia University, the University of Central Florida, the University of Massachusetts, and the University of Saint Louis.[91] Also, more than 300 colleges have used the marketing services of a company called Lipman Hearne.[92] In addition, many colleges hire enrollment management consulting companies, such as Noel-Levitz, or Maguire Associates.[93] Finally, the American Marketing Association hosts conferences about "The Marketing of Higher Education," for college admissions, recruitment, and enrollment departments,[94] and the American Association of Collegiate Registrars and Admissions Officers (AACRAO) hosts enrollment management conferences for college administrators.[95]

Many colleges also conduct market research studies to analyze students and learn how to get their money. For example, more than half of the colleges and universities in the United States have used the services of Primary Research Group, a company that specifically focuses on market research studies for colleges and college-related companies.[96] In addition, Hobsons partnered with Harris Interactive in 2005 to offer "CollegePulse," a market research study that is sold to colleges and other organizations that want to target and recruit students.[97]

In their effort to attract as many students as possible, colleges get creative in their marketing efforts.[98] In one extreme example, Beaver College recently changed its name to Arcadia University, after completing a market research process to pick a new name that would be more popular.[99] Many colleges also create slick brochures that focus on their atmosphere and facilities,[100] and they often construct (or renovate) attractive buildings like dormitories, gymnasiums, and arts centers that have little to do with the quality of the education that students receive. Some of the schools that have recently done this include the University of Akron, Ohio Stare University, Cleveland State

University, Youngstown State University, Boston University and the University of Michigan.[101] And these tactics work for colleges: the University of Massachusetts received a 10% boost in student applications after opening a new student center, and the University of Akron attracted 67% more visitors to campus after opening its new student center.[102] In addition, Penn State University has featured its students in magazine fashion spreads, allowed MTV to film a reality show on its campus, and developed ways to target high school students online.[103] Consultant Eric Sickler says that his marketing company "routinely encourage[s] [colleges] to [use] audacious marketing strategies and tactics."[104]

Colleges also send their "recruitment officers" to high schools and college fairs around the world, just to make sure that as many students as possible receive their marketing messages. These officers meet one-on-one with students to try to convince them to attend—but these officers are simply marketers in disguise. In addition, colleges often encourage high school guidance counselors to promote their schools, and some colleges even provide the counselors with free trips to visit the schools. For example, in April 2005, Emory University spent $8,000 to fly in about 10 high school guidance counselors from the Pacific Northwest region for this kind of promotional session.[105]

The main problem is that all of these kinds of promotional activities can encourage students to attend colleges that are too expensive, or not a good fit for them. Colleges' extensive marketing system makes it very difficult for students to know exactly which information—and which people—they can trust.

MARKETING MADNESS

The NCAA college basketball championship tournament that occurs every spring is often called "March Madness"—but a better title would be "Marketing Madness." Many people admire and respect college sports, because they think that these activities are more "pure" than professional sports where athletes play for a paycheck—but college sports are a sophisticated business and publicity strategy, not a hobby. Since college sports often attract students and donations, sports are one of schools' most successful marketing tools.

College sports are big business, and schools profit from their sports in many ways, including ticket sales, sales of food and drinks, broadcasting of games and advertising, prize money when they win games, and corporate or alumni sponsorship. It's common for individual schools to each receive millions of dollars every year directly from their sports programs, including schools like Syracuse University, Xavier University, Providence University, Wake Forest University, St. Joe's University, Gonzaga University, and Baylor University.[106] Many schools even require their season-ticket holders to make annual donations of $100-$1,000 per seat (on top of ticket costs); this donation requirement generates at least $10 million per year for the University of Michigan, and about $7 million per year for the University of Kansas.[107]

Sports teams also help schools to sell their merchandise, such as shirts and hats: colleges sold $10 billion worth of merchandise in 2001,[108] including over $800 million worth of items with college insignia (logos or pictures) on them.[109] And individual schools get a big piece of the merchandise pie: in 2001, the University of Kansas received $780,000 just from "royalties," or sales commissions, on its merchandise.[110] Also, Northwestern University sold $600,000 in merchandise after it won the Big Ten football championship in 1995 and played in the Rose Bowl, a ten-fold increase from its $60,000 in merchandise sales the year before.[111] To increase their piece of the pie, colleges are happy to sell almost anything with their name on it, including wine,[112] and school pictures that people can download onto their cell phones.[113] In fact, since schools make so much money from their merchandise, more than 180 colleges and universities have hired the Collegiate Licensing Company to prevent anyone else from selling school logo merchandise without paying a licensing fee.[114] While it might be admirable for a cash-starved elementary school to hold a bake sale to raise money, college sports (and college merchandise) have a different theme: profit to the maximum extent.

Also, sports generate additional massive profits for colleges by attracting student applicants and enrollees—and schools that have more famous and popular teams get more applicants. One study found that more students apply to colleges as their football teams improve.[115] This is exactly what happened at Boston College, when it experienced a 28% rise in student applications in the two years after its very successful 1984 football season.[116] And Georgetown University experienced a 45% increase in applications from 1983-1986, right after its men's basketball team appeared in the 1982, 1984, and 1985 championship games.[117]

Gonzaga University presents a more recent example of this phenomenon: as Gonzaga's sports program improved from 1998 to 2004, the school's total student enrollment went up from 4,800 students to 6,100 students, and donations went up from $9.1 million to $17.1 million during the same time.[118] In addition, the number of students in Gonzaga's freshman class grew by 65% from 1997 to 2003, and Gonzaga received twice as many student applications.[119]

Even just one sports season can boost a college's profile

enough to generate large increases in student applications. In 2006, George Mason University leveraged its most successful basketball season by blasting recruitment messages to 50,000 SAT superstars and 250,000 other prospective students, telling them: "If you remain interested in attending a world-class university with one HECK of a basketball team, we urge you to complete your application [for admission]."[120] In fact, it doesn't even matter if a college's teams win or lose their contests; according to standard marketing theory, "all publicity is good publicity," because colleges stay in the spotlight by participating in sports. Although sports are not the only factor in a student's college decision, they can play a major role.

Some colleges report that they lose money from their sports programs, but many of these schools are not telling the whole truth. As a marketing tool, sports bring in large amounts of money in many different ways. When the full financial benefits of college sports are calculated, including tuition payments and other money spent by students who are attracted by the schools' sports programs, as well as money donated by people who are fans of the sports teams, and the amount of merchandise sold, it's obvious that sports programs are very profitable for colleges. Even Gonzaga University's president admits that "certainly well over 50% of [Gonzaga's] application rise [after 1998]" came from publicity that is "attributable in great part to basketball."[121] Successful businesses often expect to spend money on advertising, to help sell their products, and colleges often profit tremendously from using sports as an advertising tool. So it makes sense for most colleges to spend money on sports—and it's misleading for these schools to complain that sports are costly for them.

In fact, sports are so financially important to colleges that they often manage their sports programs unethically. Specifically, colleges often break athletic rules during recruitment and the athletic season,[122] reward their athletes with admissions advantages and improper payments, [123] and allow their athletes to cheat on exams or take suspiciously easy classes.[124] Even many of the most prestigious colleges give significant admissions advantages to most of their athletes in prominent sports (including all 8 Ivy League schools).[125] And colleges often give full scholarships to their athletes, even though many of them never graduate; only about half of male college basketball and football players ever finish their degrees,[126] and African-American athletes tend to have much lower graduation rates than white athletes.[127]

In addition, colleges' sports programs often put their non-athletes at-risk, because college sports tend to be associated with dangerous behavior. For example, at least 15 major universities have had a sports-related riot in recent years, including the University of Connecticut, the University of Minnesota, Ohio State University, University of Maryland, Purdue University, and West Virginia University.[128] Also, college sports fans are more likely to binge drink than non-fans,[129] and almost half of students at sports schools are significantly disrupted or assaulted by students who drink.[130]

Even worse, colleges enroll a number of athletes that pose an actual physical danger to other students. Specifically, college athletes have recently been accused of breaking the law at schools such as the University of Colorado, Baylor University, Brigham Young University, Rutgers University, University of Miami, University of Wisconsin, West Virginia University,[131] Arizona State University,[132] University of Connecticut,[133] and Michigan State University, where football players were suspected of planting three bombs near student housing.[134] In fact, one study estimates that one out of every three sexual assaults on college campuses are perpetrated by student athletes.[135] Also, college athletes are more likely than non-athletes to binge drink and have academic, behavior, and legal problems.[136] And a number of athletes report being hazed by their teammates and coaches, including being forced to drink dangerous levels of alcohol.[137]

It's important to note that most college athletes are upstanding citizens, but too many of them are not, and colleges unfortunately often allow or encourage them to misbehave. Margaret Soltan, an English professor at George Washington University, summarizes common college sports criticisms in the following way: "…almost every major sports program in this country's universities is stewing in some mix of bogus coursework, endemic plagiarism, diploma mill admits, risible graduation rates, and team thuggery—and that's just the players. Add [millionaire] drunk coaches crashing their cars all over town; meddling and corrupt alumni boosters subsidizing luxury boxes in new stadiums with massively overpriced tickets and names honoring the local bank; trustees averting their eyes as students tailgate their way to the emergency room; and presidents disciplining on-field rioters by ever so lightly spanking their bottoms, and you get a problem difficult to ignore."[138] Despite all of these problems, college professors rarely speak out against their schools' sports programs.[139] And colleges allow all of these misbehaviors in the name of profit.

COLLEGE ADMISSIONS FOR SALE

Just as colleges twist their sports programs in order to get more money, they also often twist the admissions process to get students to pay high prices.

First, colleges require students to pay expensive application fees,[140] often as much as $50-$75 at schools like the University of Maryland, the University of Texas, the University of North Carolina, New York University, and the University of Miami.

When students apply to several colleges, these fees easily add up to hundreds of dollars per student. Therefore, students tend to apply to a limited number of colleges, and this gives schools a major advantage by restricting price competition among them. Banks have used a similar strategy, requiring their customers to pay application fees for things like mortgage loans, which reduced banks' competition and allowed them to keep their prices high—a dirty trick, but colleges use it well. High application fees also allow colleges to screen out low-income students, and to identify the students who are most ready and willing to pay their high prices.

Colleges also make things more difficult for less wealthy students by using potentially biased admissions criteria like lengthy applications, standardized test scores, essays, recommendations, and interviews. These criteria tend to favor wealthy students, who can afford the expensive instruction, tutoring, and professional assistance for their applications that allow them to excel on these criteria. In addition, admissions tests like the SAT and ACT have been criticized for being biased against low-income students, females, and racial minorities.[141] And these admissions criteria often don't identify the most talented students: many researchers have found that the SAT and ACT are not very good at identifying the students who will do the best in college (or after).[142] Even Kurt Landgraf, the chief executive officer of ETS, the company that creates the SAT, barely achieved an average score on the test (he scored 1060 out of 1600),[143] so many top colleges would not accept him if he applied for admission today.

The evidence shows that colleges tend to favor admissions criteria that allow them to receive more money (even if these criteria put talented students at a disadvantage)—and colleges seem to obtain extra money just by making their admissions process more complicated. The psychological theory of "cognitive dissonance" explains that, when people have to work hard to get something, they tend to value it more. In this way, the difficult, lengthy, time-consuming, and costly college admissions process can "trick" students into becoming more devoted, dedicated, and committed toward their schools...and more willing to spend money.

Even worse, colleges often allow wealthy students to literally buy their admission. In the most extreme example, it's been estimated that colleges will accept students whose parents donate $20,000-$50,000 (or more).[144] This kind of behavior makes a mockery of the admissions process by often favoring wealth over talent.[145] In addition, colleges often accept the children of alumni (codeword: "legacy admissions"), or the children of wealthy or influential people (codeword: "developmental admits"), even if the students are not very intelligent, hard-working, or gifted, because the colleges believe these admissions will lead to high donations. This kind of "affirmative action for rich people" happens all the time at schools like Duke University, Harvard University, Stanford University, University of Michigan, Princeton University, University of Pennsylvania, Notre Dame University, and Emory University.[146]

Suki Park's son seems to represent a typical casualty of the current college admissions system: after several Ivy League colleges rejected him, despite his superb 1560 SAT score and high rank within his high school class, Mrs. Park said, "I was naïve...I thought college admissions had something to do with academics."[147] In short, college acceptances are for sale, and schools often manipulate the admissions process by accepting the students that will allow them to make the most money. On the other hand, the good news is that the second half of this book presents some strategies that students of all income levels can use to bypass college roadblocks and obtain degrees that are both valuable and affordable.

STICKER SHOCK

"Economists report that a college education adds many thousands of dollars to a man's lifetime income—which he then spends sending his son to college."
—Bill Vaughn

It's clear that students need to be cautious and not allow colleges to discourage them, or trick them into spending too much. And, as the quotation above humorously (or tragically) implies, college costs have gotten so high that they can significantly cut in to the financial benefits of a degree.

How high? Specifically, in 2007-08, the average "sticker price," or advertised full price, for tuition and fees at four-year private colleges was $23,712 per year, and the average sticker price for tuition and fees at four-year public colleges was $6,185 per year.[148] However, prices for just tuition and fees are more than $35,000 per year at private colleges like George Washington University, the University of Richmond, Sarah Lawrence College, Kenyon College, Vassar College, Bucknell University, Bennington College, Columbia University, Wesleyan University, Trinity College, and Colgate University.[149] And the top 20 most expensive public colleges each charge over $10,000 for one year of tuition and fees for "in-state" students, or students who live within their states.[150] Of course, it must be noted that "one college year," is actually only about 8 months; summer classes cost extra.

Colleges also boost their profits by charging high prices for food, housing, and other services. For example, during the 2007-08 school year, the total one-year sticker price at private colleges was $32,307 (including food and housing), and the total one-year sticker price at public colleges was $13,589, meaning that eight months of room and board were $8,595 at the average private school, and $7,404 at the average public school.[151] And students usually can't avoid expensive college housing and food, because schools usually require their students to live on-campus and purchase a "meal plan" (this is especially true for first-year students).

At these prices, it's common for colleges to charge at least $3,000 per student for just one class. It's also common for colleges to have 200 students per class—meaning that one class can easily bring in $600,000 for a school ($3,000 x 200)! And just one large class that has 500 students—like those at Cornell University, the University of Minnesota, the University of Massachusetts, and Temple University[152]—can bring in over $1 million!

In addition, these prices also often come out to more than $100 an hour, for each student, for every hour that a student is in class. For example, during the 2007-08 school year, Colgate University charged a total of $48,710 for only eight months of attendance.[153] When this amount is divided by 34 weeks of classes, and 12 hours of class per week, classes cost $119 per hour, per student. And for the many full-time students who only take 10 hours of class per week, the cost is $143 per hour, per student. These hourly prices include housing and food costs, since Colgate and other schools require their first-year students to purchase these expensive services, and many students go out-of-town for college (while parents still often maintain and pay for a room for them at home). Therefore, when students at Colgate University miss a 90-minute class because they oversleep, in some ways their nap costs them between $179 and $215. Since private tutors only cost $30-$50 an hour, colleges charge prices that are much higher than the cost of a personalized education.

Colleges also make things more difficult for students by raising their high prices by a large amount every year, just to increase their profits. In fact, colleges have discovered that they can obtain more students just by raising their prices![154] Specifically, students tend to think that more expensive schools are better, and colleges raise their prices to take advantage of this perception and increase their income. For example, Ursinus College increased its freshman class by 35% after raising its prices.[155] In addition, some college presidents have admitted that their schools increased their prices just to increase their profits: William Cooper, president of the University of Richmond, specifically says that he and his administrators increased tuition by 27% in 2005 because, by maintaining their lower tuition prices, they were "leaving money on the table," and they didn't want to be "the cheap school" anymore.[156] And Russell Osgood, president of Grinnell College (the wealthiest liberal arts college, with almost $1.5 billion in its endowment), says that he and his administrators raised their tuition price by 15% because the school had "been motoring along for about 20 years at a tuition figure and fees that was about 10 percent below the average for our [competitors], and…being lower [wasn't] doing great things for us."[157]

This attitude helps to explain why colleges tend to raise their prices even when they are rich, and even when they receive large donations—and why wealthy colleges tend to charge higher prices than schools that are less wealthy.[158] Specifically, colleges increased their prices faster than inflation from 1981-2003,[159] and by 6-10% (double or triple the rate of inflation) in each of the years 2004, 2005, 2006, and 2007 (on average).[160] Even after adjusting for general inflation, tuition and fees have gone up a total of 54% at public 4-year colleges, and 33% at private 4-year colleges, over just the past ten years.[161] In fact, even after adjusting for inflation <u>and</u> subtracting financial aid, students at both public and private colleges still pay "net prices" for tuition, room, and board that are much higher than they were just ten years ago (30% and 27% higher, respectively).[162]

Although a race for revenue may be accepted in the business world, colleges are supposed to have more of an ethical duty to resist this trend (especially since both public <u>and</u> private colleges receive financial gifts from the government). When colleges race each other for financial profit, students are the ones who lose out.

Students have protested against rising costs at many colleges, including Columbia University and Yale University,[163] but schools continue to feed their money hunger by raising their prices at rates that are nearly impossible to handle. In short, college prices are out of control.

WANT FEES WITH THAT?

Outrageous prices for tuition, housing, and food are just the tip of the "college cost iceberg." Schools increase the burden by requiring students to pay for many extra fees that can cost hundreds or thousands of dollars more, including: <u>activity fees</u> (even if students don't participate in the activities); <u>athletic fees</u> (even if students don't use the gym or go to the sporting events); <u>parking fees</u>; <u>internship fees</u> (which can easily cost thousands of dollars, even if the internships are off-campus and the school has little or no involvement); <u>class fees</u> (for special equipment or services); <u>credit card fees</u> (for students who pay their school bills with a credit card at schools like the University of Pittsburgh, Temple University, and Penn State University);[164] <u>technology or administrative fees</u> (which recently increased from $50 to $100 per year at the University of Maryland);[165] and <u>construction fees</u> for new campus buildings (usually hundreds of dollars per student, per year,[166] and can be as high as $1,000 at schools like the University of

Colorado).[167] Construction fees are especially excessive since students usually leave their schools before the buildings that they have paid for are constructed.[168] Even worse, schools often "quadruple-dip," paying for their new buildings with construction fees, donations, increases in tuition, and other student fees.[169]

In addition, colleges charge expensive fees when students drop out of a class within the first few weeks of the semester. For example, Indiana University keeps all of a student's money when the student drops the class after just the fourth week.[170] In this way, students can be charged thousands of dollars for the equivalent of as little as 10 to 12 hours of actual class time. These high penalties increase the danger of the college gamble for students.

Colleges' fees seem to never end: many schools also charge for things like "state fees," "media fees," "late fees" when a student registers for classes late or pays a bill late, and, of course, "graduation fees" that all students must pay in order to get their degrees (at a price of up to $160 each, plus cap and gown payment for students who attend the ceremony).[171] Colleges also raise their fees and add new fees every year, and some schools, such as the University of Maryland, even charge fees before they know how they will use the money![172]

Although all colleges require students to pay fees, and students should not necessarily avoid or switch schools just because of expensive fees, savvy students may be able to seek out schools that will cost them less.

AID AS THEFT: THE TRICKS COLLEGES USE TO "HELP" STUDENTS PAY FOR THEIR EDUCATION

Many students are able to reduce their costs by using scholarships and grants to help pay for college, but colleges often encourage students to pay most of their bills with large amounts of cash and loans. In addition, although financial aid is supposed to lower students' expenses and make college more affordable for them, colleges often manipulate the financial aid system to trick students into paying more. Here are some of the tricks that students and families should understand:

Trick #1: Inappropriate Meetings About Pricing

First, it's been discovered that 23 of the top colleges in the country met with each other once every year for 35 years—in order to restrict the amount of financial aid students could receive (including M.I.T. and the eight schools of the Ivy League: Brown, Columbia, Cornell, Dartmouth, Harvard, Pennsylvania, Princeton, and Yale). At these meetings, colleges would share information with each other about their student applicants, and all schools would agree to offer a student the exact same financial aid package of loans, scholarships, and grants.[173]

In the early 1990s, the U.S. Department of Justice ruled that these "price-fixing" meetings were illegal, because the meetings allowed colleges to get extra money from students by unfairly reducing competition among schools, and preventing students from getting the best deals. The colleges appealed this legal decision, unwilling to acknowledge that their actions were harmful for students, even though the schools admitted that they used the meetings to avoid accepting low-income students.[174] Unfortunately, this particular legal ruling didn't solve the problem: colleges have given out even less financial aid to needy students since the ruling was handed down.[175] And a set of 28 wealthy private colleges, called the "568 Group," are still legally allowed to talk with each other about financial aid and coordinate their aid policies.[176] Colleges often claim to be places of "higher learning," where proper ethics are taught, but they often don't follow their own teachings.

Trick #2: Exploiting Students' Enthusiasm
Many colleges also use students' enthusiasm to take advantage of them. More than half of colleges are more likely to accept a student if the student shows interest in attending,[177] and a big reason for this is that schools know that enthusiastic students will be willing to pay higher prices. These students are easy targets.

Therefore, colleges often track students' interest in attending, including whether students have visited the schools, or contacted the schools with any special calls, letters, or essays.[178] Some colleges are even able to measure students' interest by obtaining information that students provide to the College Board about their most preferred colleges when they take their SAT and ACT admissions exams (the ACT and College Board sell this information to colleges).[179] Then, colleges offer less favorable financial aid packages to the students who are most interested in attending.[180] Kalman Chany, a financial aid consulting firm president, and author of *Paying for College Without Going Broke,* says that schools use this kind of "financial aid leveraging" to get more money from students.[181]

Trick #3: The "Early Decision" Trap
"Early decision" college admissions programs are usually presented as something that helps students, but schools often use these programs to again exploit students' enthusiasm and swindle them. On one hand, the early decision college application and admissions process can be useful for students, because students who use this process may be able to find out quickly if the schools will accept them, and they may be able

to have a better chance of getting accepted to the schools of their choice. Also, these students may only have to apply to one school (so they save time and money by not having to fill out other applications).

However, the downside of early decision is rarely advertised: colleges usually force these students to attend the schools,[182] if accepted, no matter the cost—so the schools often offer weak financial aid packages to these students. David Hawkins, director of Public Policy at the National Association for College Admission Counseling, agrees that early decision programs "[help] colleges register as many 'full-paying' students as possible,"[183] or students who do not receive any scholarships or grants. This strategy can be punishing for low-income or middle class students, who may be pressured to spend more than they can afford.

Trick #4: When An Offer of Admission is Really a Rejection in Disguise

Although many colleges say that they use a system of "need-blind" admissions, accepting and rejecting applicants based solely on the applicants' academic talent, and not on the applicants' need for financial aid, this claim is not totally true. In fact, one of the most hidden secrets in the college admissions system is that some colleges specifically offer horrible financial aid packages to low-income students, in order to discourage them from ever enrolling.[184] This strategy is called "admit-deny," and it often works to either prevent low-income students from enrolling, or to make life so difficult for them after they enroll that they incur the high costs but then have to drop out.

Trick #5: Deceptively Meeting Students' Financial Need

Even when colleges actually want their admitted students

to enroll, they still often meet their students' financial need by encouraging the students to borrow unaffordable amounts of money, instead of providing adequate scholarships and grants. And, as described throughout this book, many students dangerously follow colleges' encouragement, borrowing much more than they can afford.

Trick #6: The Scholarship and Grant Aid Illusion

Amazingly, colleges also often make students' scholarships and grants worthless. Emily Brandon, a student at the University of Rochester, and Mike Sirianni, a student at Ithaca College, both applied for and received scholarships for college from organizations outside their colleges—and they were both stunned when their schools did not use their scholarships to lower their costs.[185] These students learned that colleges almost never use money from "outside" scholarships or grants to lower the amount of money students must pay or borrow, thus preventing students from saving any money. Instead, colleges usually subtract students' outside scholarships or grants from the scholarship or grant money that they were going to give the students anyway. Sirianni complains: "Students that spend the time to get the [special outside] scholarships are treated no differently from those who don't bother to get them...I went out there, did the extra work, and brought income into the school from an outside source...why shouldn't I be able to use that money?"[186] In this way, colleges often use outside grants and scholarships to help themselves, but not to help students.

Trick #7: Preferential Profiteering

Colleges also often use another version of "financial aid leveraging," called "preferential packaging,"[187] to get wealthy students to pay full-price, or close to it. For example, colleges convince these students to pay their high prices by giving the students "perks" like small discounts, vacations, dinners with the school president, or money to conduct research projects. In this way, schools give out relatively inexpensive prizes in order to obtain much larger amounts of money from students.

Amazingly, colleges even benefit from this strategy by providing wealthy students with "merit aid" discounts, instead of giving this money to less wealthy students as "need-based aid."[188] In fact, colleges have recently vastly increased scholarships for students from families earning $100,000 or more per year, while neglecting scholarship increases for students from families earning $40,000 or less.[189] Even the top 50 public colleges recently increased aid to rich families by eight times more than aid to low-income families.[190]

In general, colleges often use financial aid leveraging with all students in a very manipulative way, guided by pricing techniques that are very similar to the ones used by aggressive businesses such as credit card companies.[191] In fact, many colleges use strategies developed from a popular airline industry book called *Revenue Management: Hard-Core Tactics for Market Domination*. Specifically, colleges often work with experts to obtain and analyze extensive personal data about their applicants, including financial data from credit-reporting agencies like Equifax. Colleges then use these analyses to predict exactly what kind of aid package a student might accept, often offering as few discounts as possible, for both wealthy and low-income students.

The evidence shows that these strategies are very effective for colleges; specifically, some colleges have used these techniques to increase their revenue by as much as 162%, or increase their enrollment of full-paying students by 60-70%. Therefore, many colleges actively encourage their administrators to use these strategies, especially by awarding lucrative bonus payments to administrators who meet certain performance targets—and by firing administrators who fail to meet the revenue and prestige goals.

Trick #8: The Pricing "Bait and Switch" Trap: Using Aid to Raise Students' Costs After They Enroll

To make as much money as possible, colleges also often change students' financial aid packages significantly from year-to-year. Many students expect to receive the same financial aid package during every year that they are in school, including scholarships and grants that do not have to be paid back—but schools often surprise students by giving them much worse financial aid packages each year.

The trick is that colleges do not usually guarantee financial aid packages for more than one year at a time. Instead, schools often disappoint students by taking away some scholarships or grants from one year to the next, or increasing the cash that the students must pay, or the hours that the students must work. Even worse, it's common for colleges to encourage students to borrow much more money each year, such as at least $3,500 for their first year, $4,500 for their second year, and $5,500 for every year after their second year. In short, colleges lure students with teaser starting prices, but then corner students into paying much higher costs than they planned.

Trick #9: Devious Debt Deals

To get even more money, colleges also develop special deals with banks that improperly take advantage of their students. For example, during the next few years, the 250 largest universities in the U.S. will accept a total of about $5 billion from banks, in exchange for allowing banks to market and advertise financial services and credit cards on their campuses, including within dorms.[192] The University of Maryland alone received $8 million for this kind of deal.[193]

Some colleges even allow credit card companies to buy their way into the classroom, where they can "sponsor" class content and projects that encourage students to sign up for cards.[194] Catherine Cummings, vice president of consumer affairs for one of the largest card companies, says, "…simply having students see [our brand] name at the end of a presentation is a very powerful one-on-one association…," and youth marketer Tony Sgro adds that these programs introduce "college students to [credit card brands] at a deep level, which helps build general loyalty [to credit card brands]."[195]

A large number of colleges also receive millions by selling the names and addresses of their students, alumni, and employees to credit card companies,[196] including the University of Tennessee ($16.5 million), the University of Michigan ($14 million), Michigan State University ($14 million),[197] and the University of Oklahoma ($13 million).[198] Many colleges also get a percentage of the money that their students spend with these cards.[199] Some schools have smaller, but still lucrative, deals with credit card companies; for example, Brigham Young University received about $70,000 from credit card companies for allowing the companies to advertise at the school's bookstore.[200]

Due to these deals, the average college student receives eight credit card applications during their first week of college,[201] and 25 credit card offers every semester.[202] To get students to sign up, companies offer gifts, catchy slogans, misleading "0% interest rates," and even free meals.[203] And eight out of ten students who sign up for credit cards say that they sign up just to get the free gifts.[204]

As exposed in the news media throughout 2007, colleges also have special deals with student loan lenders, including "kickback" payments that allow each school to receive an extra million dollars each year for providing them with student customers.[205] Some schools that have benefited from this arrangement include Michigan State University, Case Western Reserve University, Wayne State University, Seton Hall University, Harding University, Austin College, UCLA,[206] and the University of Nebraska.[207] In addition, many colleges accept payments and gifts from the lenders they promote on their "preferred lender lists" for students.[208] At least one college financial aid administrator even added a lender to a "preferred list" after accepting a free Caribbean vacation from the lender![209] Also, many colleges only include one lender on their "preferred" list, which can discourage students from shopping around for the best deals.[210] The problem is that, when colleges promote lenders that allow them to increase their profits, they may promote lenders that are more expensive, increasing students' costs.

Many colleges also make extra money by becoming lenders themselves.[211] By giving loan money directly to students through "school-as-lender" programs, these colleges often obtain several million extra dollars each year (again, often through kickbacks from banks[212]). Craig Munier, the financial aid director for the University of Nebraska-Lincoln, admits that his school started lending money to students so that the school could make extra money. Although this lending program has been relatively small in the past, federal lending increased from $155 million at 22 schools in 1994 to $1.5 billion at 64 schools in 2004, and 100 colleges provided these kinds of student loans in 2005.[213] The top 5 college lenders in 2006 were: Nova Southeastern University ($392 million lent to students); University of Phoenix ($214 million); Webster University ($103 million); University of Pennsylvania ($94 million); and Michigan State University (which is a public school; $92 million).[214] And 64 universities applied to become new lenders in 2006, including public schools like Oklahoma State University, University of Illinois, University of Maryland, University of Minnesota, University of Pittsburgh, and University of Vermont.[215]

Colleges that lend money often become aggressive debt collectors when students and graduates don't pay their loan bills, by taking them to court (even when the borrowers have little or no income), refusing to release their transcripts (preventing the borrowers from attending other schools and obtaining jobs), and charging penalty fees up to 66% of the original loan balance.[216] For example, Northeastern University and Boston University each file an average of 200 lawsuits each year to collect money from their former students, most of whom have low incomes.[217] Elizabeth Warren, Harvard Law professor, says that it's especially inappropriate for colleges to sue struggling students because colleges receive many government gifts and are supposed to "serve the public good."[218]

In fact, all of these college debt deals and behaviors are dangerous and somewhat unethical, because they allow colleges to increase their income by encouraging students to borrow too much or pay expensive interest rates. Many colleges even own valuable shares of stock in educational loan companies, further benefiting from their students' debt![219] Although students are responsible for taking colleges' advice and borrowing unaffordable debt, colleges are the ones who set the prices and policies, develop the "financial aid offers" stacked with loans, and take advantage of students' trust.

Even worse, colleges often encourage unaffordable debt among many students who don't understand what they are signing up for. For example, more than half of college students don't know how to evaluate complex math tasks, such as understanding credit cards,[220] and many college students also don't understand financial issues, including credit.[221] Although Yale University receives money from credit card companies, Yale's dean of undergraduate admissions and financial aid, Richard Shaw, admits: "I am particularly concerned about [students] being targeted [for credit cards]. Many of these students have never used a credit card before, and have no experience managing their finances. Only after the use and the running up of the bills have they realized what they've gotten themselves into."[222] Debbie Alford, a student who filed for bankruptcy in her junior year, says: "My debt was a huge cloud hanging over me. I felt ashamed…but I should never have been able to get all those cards at such a young age. When you're 18, you think you know what you're doing with finances, but you really don't."[223] One research study even declared that credit card marketing "poses a greater threat [to college students] than alcohol or sexually transmitted diseases."[224]

Since colleges directly benefit by acting like "debt-pushers," colleges hold much responsibility for the student fallout. This is especially true since colleges even encourage high debt for students who have low salaries or are on-track to receive low salaries when they graduate. Under this pressure, even students and families who hope to remain debt-free often fall victim to common college debt traps; Anya Kamenetz, author of *Generation Debt*, says, "When you have to borrow money to [enroll in] college, just as you take your first step toward independence, already you are a debtor. And it changes your psychology. For a lot of people, it is a rationalization that makes it much easier for them to [then also] owe on credit cards."[225]

THE "FOUR-YEAR" TRAP

Colleges also maximize their income by benefiting from the requirement that each student must complete at least four years of school for a bachelor's degree, no matter what subject the student studies. Even students who take classes over the summer must still take the equivalent of four years of classes.

Of course, students should be required to complete a certain number of classes before receiving a college degree, but there's no proof that "four years" is the magic amount of time that any student needs for a college education about any subject. It's hard to believe that any and every subject can be learned, mastered, and completed in exactly four years, regardless of a student's individual ability. While it's possible that past students needed four years of college so that they could have time to develop physically and emotionally, many of today's college students are over the age of 21, and many others don't need extra time to develop. But the required four-year time period for a bachelor's degree keeps the money flowing in to schools.

> **Myth: College students only pay costs for four years of college (or less).**

Many colleges also increase their income by making students pay for more than four years of expenses. For example, there's new evidence that some schools have added more class requirements for students, making it nearly impossible for students to complete their degrees within 4 years—and helping schools to obtain even more money.[226] Some colleges also make students take remedial classes, without warning them in advance that these classes will require extra costs and will not count toward their degrees. In addition, many schools don't offer enough space in their required classes, forcing students to attend college for a longer time (and pay more money), including Dartmouth University,[227] University of North Carolina at Chapel Hill,[228] George Washington

University,[229] the University of Connecticut,[230] and Oakland University in Michigan.[231] Noah Morgan, a junior at Wayne State University, says that, at his school, "It's so hard to get [the] classes that allow students to graduate in four years."[232] And many colleges won't allow students to transfer class credits from other schools, forcing these students to take more classes and spend more money.[233] Finally, some colleges also discourage students from taking classes over the summer, by not providing enough financial aid for these classes, while other colleges actually require students to complete summer classes[234] (in addition to their regular four years of classes), adding to students' costs, and preventing them from working in summer jobs and internships.

Although some students are slowed from finishing college due to their own individual academic, financial, personal, or family problems, standard college policies force many students to take six years to complete four years of coursework, often leading to a "six-year trap" for students—but six years of profits for schools. Specifically, one out of five students at four-year colleges (21%) take five or six years to graduate.[235] As described later, students may be able to cut some of their college costs by enrolling in schools that allow them to finish their degrees as quickly as possible.

DONATIONS AND DECEPTIONS

Colleges also use classic marketing techniques to encourage people to donate as much money as possible—even when the schools are already rich. For example, wealthy Williams College trains its fundraisers with a handbook that features instructions for money-raising strategies like "Writing a Winning [Donation Request] Letter," "Making a Successful [Donation Request] Phone Call," and "Convincing [a Donor] to Support Williams."[236] One section of the Handbook even lists specific fundraising tricks, such as: asking people to donate more money than they donated the previous year; telling people how much money their classmates have donated; asking people to donate more money so that their graduating class can "beat" another graduating class; asking people to double their usual donation; and asking people to increase their gift if it is the 10th or 20th anniversary of their graduation. Each year, many schools also send their students and alumni a list of all the people who donated money during the prior year, with specific information about exactly how much money each person donated. Schools hope this information will encourage more donations. Many schools, including Williams College, also encourage their fundraisers to say that the schools would not be able to continue offering their educational services if they didn't receive donations. In short, rich colleges hope to get more money by convincing people that they're poor.

In addition, many colleges aggressively target their alumni by digging up personal information about them, enabling the schools to contact the alumni and ask for large donations. A number of schools have access to their graduates' school histories (including the activities they were involved in, and what years they graduated), donation histories, and other personal data, including Iowa State University, DeSales University, University of Puget Sound, Muhlenberg College, Cedar Crest College, Lehigh University, University of Georgia, and Moravian College.[237] Colleges also use public records databases to learn things like: how much their graduates paid for their homes (and how much the homes are currently worth), how much money their graduates earn, whether their graduates donate money to other organizations,[238] whether their graduates have gotten married, and whether their graduates have changed addresses.

Of course, some people enjoy donating money to schools—and these are just the kind of easy targets that colleges are looking for. On the other hand, some people are not fooled by colleges' tricks; these people have stopped giving donations to schools, because they are upset that schools do not use enough of the donations to help students. Many people think it's a waste to give money to wealthy schools that will just use it to make their administrators rich, give financial aid to wealthy students, spend it on unnecessary projects that don't improve students' education, or allow it to just sit in their endowment funds (and increase their already excessive wealth)—all while they also increase their tuition prices. Professor Roger Kaufman of Smith College says: "[Isn't] there a point where [colleges] are so rich [that they] don't need to have all these capital fund drives?"[239] Lee Arnold, a long-time university fund-raiser, recently stopped performing this role, saying "I could no longer in good conscience solicit my classmates to feed [the school's] insatiable [financial] appetite."[240] And, in 2003, Christine Mann, of the Princeton class of 1980, wrote to her classmates and said: "When there are so many people starving in the world, so many dying for lack of basic medical care, so many American children living in poverty, so many local schools closing arts and music programs for lack of funds, the University's boundless appetite for cash seems more than ever like naked greed."[241]

Many donors are also angry because they believe that colleges are not keeping their promises. For example, the Robertson family, heirs to the A&P supermarket wealth, recently filed suit against Princeton University for allegedly misusing their 1961 donation of $35 million (worth $650 million today). William Robertson says: "We have been mugged, and we want justice."[242] Unfortunately, there's usually no way for people to ensure how their college donations will be used; schools often force their donors to make "unrestricted" donations that can be used in any ways the schools want.

The evidence shows that colleges use a range of manipulative techniques to obtain "donation jackpots." And colleges often accumulate these jackpots relatively quickly: Yale University raised $1.7 billion in non-government donations from just 1992-1997[243] (approximately $340 million per year), and Tufts University collected $609 million in non-government donations from just 1995-2002 (approximately $87 million per year).[244] In 2006 alone, colleges and universities received a total of $28 billion in non-government donations, and more than 20 colleges each received more than $200 million (including the University of Wisconsin-Madison, a public school).[245] In fact, colleges accept almost any kind of donation, as long as it has financial value, including artwork, stocks and bonds, real estate, and life insurance policies. Since fundraising is serious business, many colleges tend to use large numbers of fundraisers, and offer financial bonuses based on fundraisers' success in convincing people to donate. For example, Stanford University employed 300 full-time fundraisers in 2006,[246] and both public and private colleges provided their fundraising administrators with an average base salary of $153,200 in 2002-03 (in addition to bonus payments).[247]

EXPLOITING LOWER-LEVEL WORKERS FOR PROFIT

Although many colleges are rich (and provide valuable rewards to their high-level employees), they often take advantage of many of their lower-level workers in order to increase their profits. Specifically, many colleges give poor salaries and benefits (or no benefits at all) to their lower-level employees, such as groundskeepers, janitors, food-service workers, research assistants, teaching assistants, and part-time or low-level instructors. For example, in 2006, most janitors at the University of Miami were living at or close to the poverty level, with many earning just $11,000 per year with no health benefits for full-time work of 35-40 hours per week[248] (despite the University's high tuition prices, and its pledged obligation "to provide an exemplary environment and opportunities for every individual"[249]). In addition, colleges often give salaries of only $2,000 per class (on average) to their non-tenured instructors,[250] with no benefits like health insurance, even though the schools often receive tens of thousands of dollars per class from students' tuition and fees. And colleges often exploit their athletes by not giving them official and reasonable salaries, or health and disability insurance,[251] even though the schools require the athletes to participate in long practices, maintain busy travel schedules, and endure hectic game schedules—and schools make millions of dollars from their athletes' efforts. Finally, a large amount of college merchandise is made in "sweatshops," where employees work long hours, receive very low salaries, and endure poor working conditions.[252]

YOUR MONEY AT WASTE: HOW ALL AMERICANS GET TRICKED

Unfortunately, colleges don't just take advantage of students, their families, private donors, and their own employees; many colleges also exploit the government—and therefore all Americans. Although government spending for higher education is essential in order to maintain quality and ensure access for students of all income groups, colleges tend to abuse this system.

Gifts from the government pay off in a big way for colleges. For example, both public <u>and</u> private colleges receive "tax breaks," which allow most schools to save millions of dollars by <u>not</u> paying any tax money to the government (even though many schools are rich and profitable, and most other businesses must pay taxes). In addition, many colleges receive gifts of money and land from the government, whether the schools are public, private, non-profit, or for-profit. The government also provides large amounts of money for university research projects, even though many schools conduct projects that have little practical value, or the schools improperly use this money for non-research activities (and under-pay their student researchers).[253] Also, the government gave more than $2 billion to colleges in 2003 for "earmarks," or special projects, such as a $2.5 million planetarium at The University of North Carolina-Chapel Hill.[254] And schools benefit when the government spends billions of dollars to help students at all colleges pay for their student loans. Specifically, in 2003, schools obtained a large amount of the $90 billion that the federal government spent on college and graduate school education.[255]

The government also creates laws that help colleges obtain even more millions—even though the laws also allow colleges to neglect taxpayers. One such law is the Bayh-Dole Act, passed in 1980, which allows schools to receive money for their research patents, or discoveries. In the years 2000[256] and 2003[257] alone, this deal allowed colleges to obtain a total of <u>one billion dollars</u> each year in licensing fees from the patents that they owned. For example, in 2002, Columbia University obtained more than $155 million from its research patents,[258] and other schools have also received over $100 million each from their patents.[259] Michael Mandl, Emory University's executive vice president for finance and administration, confirms the high profitability of college research by saying, "Right now, Emory...has a pipeline [of research discoveries that] many companies would envy."[260] Unfortunately, the Bayh-Dole Act also allows schools to keep their research discoveries secret,[261] even though government and taxpayer gifts paid for most of these discoveries in the first place, and the discoveries could help save people's lives if they were shared more freely. In fact, as of 2006, taxpayers were blocked from obtaining access to the results of research studies that were paid for with their tax dollars.[262]

To encourage the government to give them these kinds of lucrative deals, both private <u>and</u> public colleges (non-profit <u>and</u> for-profit) use lobbyists, or people who try to influence politicians in their favor by giving them money and gifts,[263] including free trips and vacations.[264] Specifically, 336 private non-profit colleges spent money on political lobbying in 2006, as did 265 public 4-year colleges, 80 community colleges, and several for-profit colleges.[265] Several dozen colleges also registered as new lobbyists in 2006.[266] In addition, colleges and related organizations have more than 200 lobbying groups to represent them,[267] including large powerful groups like the American Council on Education, the National Collegiate Athletic Association, and the American Association of University Professors. In short, just as other major industries use lobbying to exert their influence with politicians—including Big Tobacco, Big Oil, Big Pharma, and Big Auto—Big College utilizes lobbying for its own benefit as well.

Lobbying is legal, but college organizations have an unfair advantage over students and taxpayers, because they have much more money to spend. In contrast, students and their families only have four small organizations to represent their interests and help them: The United States Student Association (www.usstudents.org/main.asp), College

Parents of America (www.collegeparents.org), the State Public Interest Research Groups (www.pirg.org; www.studentpirgs.org), and the Project on Student Debt (www.projectonstudentdebt.org).

And when colleges swindle the government, then all Americans are swindled, since the government gets its money and resources from all American citizens—even from people who don't go to college. Although students and taxpayers are supposed to be represented by the government officials they have elected, lobbying encourages politicians to help colleges and organizations instead of students. In this way, colleges use political lobbying as just another marketing technique that allows them to profit from their customers. Therefore, although the government can create some positive changes in the college system, students and taxpayers can't depend on politicians to make college more affordable for them.

• • •

The evidence shows that colleges are highly profitable businesses that use a number of aggressive techniques to get large amounts of money from their customers. A frustrated blogger named "Matt" recently summarized the dangers that students need to look out for: "…I can't forgive [a college] that behaves like a [con] artist during the admissions process, a used car dealer during the financial aid process, and a loan shark during the years immediately after graduation…but then, years later when I finally reassemble the remnants of the life they shattered in my early 20's and start making real money, wants me to think of them as a charity."[268]

However, when students understand the typical college dangers, then they can get the degrees they need while avoiding the traps, regardless of their income level. To get the best deals, it can be helpful for students to wonder exactly what they're getting for their money. Too often, the answer is: not enough. Colleges' distasteful food and housing services are explored in the next chapter.

CHAPTER 3

DISTASTEFUL COLLEGE SERVICES

In their aggressive search for profits, colleges often force their students to pay for all kinds of high-priced services they either don't need or could get elsewhere if they were allowed to do so. Students especially need to watch out for college housing and food scams.

ROOM AND GORED:
THE COLLEGE HOUSING SCAM

Since colleges often require their first-year students to live on-campus, housing is an important factor in students' decisions about where to go to college,[269] and it's also an important marketing tool for schools. Unfortunately, student housing is also often part of the Great College Rip-off.

> **Myth: On-campus housing is less expensive than off-campus housing.**

First, it's common for colleges to charge prices for their housing that are much higher than prices for off-campus housing. For example, in 2007-08, the University of Miami, in Florida, charged students about $970 per month for 100-square foot rooms that they did not share with anyone else.[270] Instead of living on-campus, Miami students could have rented average 600-square-foot one-bedroom apartments close to the school for about $1,000 a month, so on-campus housing is almost six times more expensive than off-campus housing at UM ($9.70 per square foot on-campus vs. $1.67 per square foot off campus)! Miami students who shared their on-campus rooms with one other person did not get a much better deal, each paying about $720 a month to split 200 square feet of space ($7.20 per square foot for their half of the room, per person, which is four times as much as off-campus housing). Actually, on-campus housing is an even worse deal, because students can share large off-campus apartments, getting about three times as much space for about two-thirds of the price (about $500 each, per month). As described earlier, even public colleges set high prices for housing: for example, the University of Florida charges more for its on-campus rooms[271] than it would cost students to live in larger off-campus apartments.

On the other hand, students who live on-campus save some money, because they usually don't have to pay for rent or utilities when school is not in session (and students are not at school)—but colleges swindle them at all other times of the year. Also, on-campus housing offers some advantages because it's often furnished, it's located close to school resources, and it usually includes telephone, television, Internet, and utilities, but these features may not be worth the high costs (including expensive parking fees). In addition, on-campus housing is often a poor value because it usually doesn't offer important features like sinks, toilets, showers, laundry machines or kitchens in students' rooms; students often must walk down the hall to cook, wash their hands, go to the bathroom, or shower in "gang bathrooms"[272] that they share with everyone else who lives on their floors.

In short, colleges' prices for on-campus housing should not be as high as they are, particularly because schools have the opportunity to use an "economy of scale," that should allow them to offer housing at much lower prices than typical market rates. This is especially true since colleges have a large, guaranteed market of first-year student tenants, making it possible for them to build and rent for less than other landlords can. Also, unlike other landlords, schools receive valuable tax discounts for their housing.[273] In light of these advantages, the fact that colleges charge many times more than the market rate for student housing is staggering.

> **Myth: On-campus housing is more helpful than off-campus housing.**

On-campus housing also usually doesn't give students many academic advantages. Several studies have found that living on-campus does not help students get better grades, or study more often.[274] This shouldn't be too surprising, since on-campus housing often doesn't give students much space or privacy, and it can be noisy or distracting. Besides, on-campus housing won't magically provide students with good study habits; students who are poor studiers will perform poorly in their classes, no matter where they live.

Also, most schools, including Harvard University,[275] Emory University, and the University of Miami, don't give their students much time to move into, or out of, their on-campus dorms. For example, colleges usually don't let students move into the dorms until a couple of days before classes start, and then schools also force students to move out of the housing within 24 hours after their last exam at the end of the semester. Since students must move in, unpack, and pack up while classes are in session, this policy takes valuable time and effort away from studying during important parts of the school year.

> **Myth: On-campus housing is safer than off-campus housing.**

On-campus housing is also often not as safe as people think it is. For example, according to the U.S. Department of Education, there are over 3,000 assaults on college campuses each year (including 1,000 within residence halls), and over 2,000 incidents of violent or intimidating robberies (including 300 within residence halls).[276] However, college campuses are often even more dangerous than this, because a recent government study suggests that two-thirds of colleges and universities illegally under-report the actual amount of crime that takes place on their campuses.[277] Colleges also <u>do not</u> perform background criminal checks on their students, although these checks could help to keep some dangerous students off their campuses (or at least out of student housing).[278] And, as mentioned in Chapter 2, dangerous sports-related riots, that often include fires, also occur on many college campuses.[279]

In fact, students who live on-campus may have a greater chance of being exposed to a fire than students who live off-campus. An average of 1,700 fires occur in college dormitories and fraternity/sorority houses every year.[280] In addition, The Center for Campus Fire Safety reports that, between January 2000 and August 2005, 75 people died in student housing fires.[281] And, in 2000, Seton Hall University experienced the worst school dormitory fire in history when 3 students were killed, and almost 60 others were hurt.[282]

Although many colleges have strict fire safety standards, including the use of alarms, extinguishers, and fire drills, many colleges <u>do not</u> have basic safety measures in place. For example, The Center for Campus Fire Safety reports that many colleges do not have dormitory sprinklers;[283] as of 2007, more than half of the students living in college dorms in Iowa were not protected in this way.[284] Unfortunately, many states do not legally require colleges to have sprinklers in their residence halls or fraternity/sorority houses,[285] and many colleges only add dorm sprinklers <u>after</u> someone on their campus dies in a housing fire.[286] Even when colleges are required by law to install safety measures, many of them neglect to fulfill their duties. For example, although colleges <u>are</u> legally required to have fire alarms, the U.S. Fire Administration reports that, in the late 1990s, 7% of dorms that had fires did not have fire alarms.[287] Considering the high prices that colleges charge for their housing, if not a desire to keep their students as safe as possible, colleges should have basic safety features in their dormitories, whether required by law or not.

UNHAPPY MEALS: THE COLLEGE FOOD SCAM

Students also need to understand the pricing and quality of their colleges' food services.

Myth: College food is inexpensive.

One of colleges' most devious strategies involves encouraging students to pay for more meals than they actually eat. Specifically, colleges often require their students to pre-pay for a certain number of meals by buying the schools' "meal plans"—but schools have figured out that their students usually only eat about 60-70% of the meals that they purchase. So, students who buy a "10-meals-per-week plan" only eat 6 or 7 meals per week. For example, in January 2004, 1,200 out of 1,600 first-year students at Duke University did not show up for breakfast meals, even though most of these students had paid for breakfast.[288] In fact, the University of Massachusetts,

Rutgers University, and James Madison University admit that they call this strategy the "Missed Meal Factor,"[289] and use it to obtain as much money from students as possible, particularly by not giving any refunds for the meals students miss.

When the missed meal factor is considered, exactly how much do colleges make students pay for each meal that they actually eat? Let's figure it out. The University of Miami, in Florida, charged students $2,011 per semester in 2007-08 for a 20-meals-per-week plan[290] (for a 14-week semester, not counting holidays or breaks). This comes out to about <u>$10 per meal</u>, since most students on a 20-meal plan only eat 14 of the 20 meals each week. And students at this school who only bought the 5-meal plan got an even worse deal, paying about <u>$18 per meal</u> ($874 per semester,[291] but only eating about 3-and-a-half meals per week). As mentioned earlier, prices aren't any better at public colleges: the University of Florida charges $1,635 per semester (plus tax) for 19 meals per week,[292] and since students on this plan usually only eat 13 meals per week, the cost easily comes out to about $9 per meal. At these prices, on-campus meals cost much more than off-campus meals (especially for breakfast and lunch).

By depending on students to miss meals, colleges try to make it seem like students are getting more for their money than they really are. The University of Massachusetts admits the deception: "The prices of the meal plans take into account the missed-meal factor. If the students did eat all the meals on their meal plans, the prices of the meal plans would be [even] higher."[293] However, Colin Megill, a student at the University of Connecticut, believes that this is not fair and says, "[The school] should...figure out a meal plan that both gives us what we pay for and charges us what we're able to pay."[294]

While it's true that students have some responsibility to

figure out this misleading deal on their own and spend less on college food, schools often require students to buy the plans, and schools tend to use some tricky marketing techniques to get students to spend more. For example, colleges charge lower prices per meal in their 10-meal plans than their 5-meal plans, but the 10-meal plans cost students much more overall (especially when they don't eat all the meals they've paid for). Colleges also charge high prices for the other food they sell on-campus, such as candy and frozen yogurt, maintaining the trend of college food being more expensive than the exact same food that is sold off-campus.[295]

Colleges' high prices for food are especially egregious because, just as with their housing services, schools can benefit from an "economy-of-scale" for their food services. Unlike restaurants, colleges can predict their costs and demand for food much more accurately, since they have a stable and captive audience, and a guaranteed pre-paid income from their customers. Therefore, colleges should be able to offer meals at much lower prices than off-campus restaurants. Also, while restaurants must charge enough to make a profit, most colleges are supposed to be non-profit institutions that, at least theoretically, do not have to earn more than they spend on their food services. For these reasons, on-campus food prices should be less, or at least equal, to off-campus food prices.

> **Myth: Colleges offer food that students enjoy eating.**

Unfortunately, many colleges don't even serve good food; although meal plans are very expensive, many students are unhappy with the food they get, complaining that it's low-quality, or just doesn't taste good.[296] For example, Trevor Behar, a student at N.C. State University, says, "The food is just plain unenjoyable."[297] His classmate, Bryon Harrington, adds, "I don't even eat dinner at the cafeterias anymore; I can't stand the food there, so I usually just pick up something [elsewhere]."[298] When Jared Duke, a student at the University of Illinois, lived on campus, he often ate cereal for dinner because he didn't like the other food that was served. Duke stopped eating the school's food when he moved off-campus, and says: "The meals in the dining hall were just not good."[299] And Vicky Volvovski, a student at the University of Wisconsin-Madison, says that the school's meal plan forced her "to choose from the same monotonous things everyday."[300] These feelings are common across the nation: The Princeton Review recently collected college food ratings from more than 100,000 students, and only 17 out of 200 schools rated an "A-" or better.[301]

> **Myth: The food that colleges sell to students is healthy and safe.**

It's often said that college students gain 15 pounds during their first year in school,[302] and this rumor is not far from the truth. Specifically, a recent research study found that new college students gain an average of five pounds per semester, and much of this gain is due to the "all-you-can-eat" buffets and "junk food" that colleges serve.[303]

Colleges are somewhat responsible for this weight gain because much of the food they serve is high in fat and sugar. For example, Ohio University serves 283,737 lbs of French fries, 40,530 lbs of hamburgers, and 61,290 lbs of chicken nuggets every year.[304] The registered dietician at the University of Pennsylvania, Kasis Burton, admits that the school's dining halls offer "a lot of sweets."[305] In addition, colleges offer many unhealthy food options in vending machines and on-campus "convenience" stores,[306] and most colleges in the United States have a fast-food franchise restaurant on their campuses, such as McDonald's, Burger King, or Pizza Hut.

On-campus food is not only unhealthy; it's also sometimes unsafe. On November 3, 1998, more than 50 students at the University of Pennsylvania developed nausea, vomiting, diarrhea, fevers and headaches after eating at one of the school's main dining halls. Local physicians determined that these illnesses were probably caused by food served by the University.[307] And in the New York City area, half of college cafeterias that were inspected had at least one health code violation between 2003-2004, and some were in danger of being shut down by the Board of Health.[308] Student Jared Duke adds: "The fruit they offered in the dining hall was questionable at best...so I'd have a sugar cereal for dinner because the regular food was so bad."[309]

Of course, colleges offer some healthy foods, and students have some responsibility for selecting the food that they eat, but schools paint students into a corner. In addition to the fact that colleges often force students to buy the meal plans, there are many times when colleges only offer unhealthy food options on-campus; this is particularly true after 5 p.m. on weekdays, or all day on weekends (especially while the meal plan cafeterias are closed). During these times, people can usually only get food on-campus from unhealthy fast food franchises, vending machines, or convenience stores. Also, a number of colleges allow their students to use their pre-paid meal plan dining dollars to eat at unhealthy off-campus fast-food restaurants, such as Domino's Pizza—but these schools don't allow their students to also use their dining dollars in the same way at healthier off-campus restaurants.[310]

The prevalence of unhealthy food on college campuses just continues the trend of schools favoring financial profit over the welfare of their students. For example, colleges can greatly increase their food sales just by bringing famous fast-food franchises to their campuses. Food and beverage corporate sponsorship deals are also often a cash cow for schools: the University of Vermont recently completed an agreement that will allow them to receive more than $4 million from Coca-Cola for allowing Coke to provide all of the drinks in the school's vending machines and dining halls.[311]

And colleges' deals extend to much more than just food: many schools increase their revenue by running ads for gambling, liquor stores, and bars within their newspapers, TV shows, and radio shows. Specifically, ads for bars sometimes take up 20% of a college newspaper's advertising[312]—even though many college students are not old enough to legally drink alcohol. Many colleges also get large amounts of money from alcohol advertising during their sporting events.[313]

WHATEVER HAPPENED TO CUSTOMER SERVICE?

Although colleges often impose a punishing combination of high prices and poor services on students, many colleges also make it difficult for students to complain about the services they receive. Most successful businesses have "customer service departments," so that their customers can contact them with questions, comments, and complaints, but many colleges are not interested in providing assistance to their customers. Although colleges have departments that focus on donations, recruiting, and admissions, and colleges frequently contact students directly about these kinds of financial issues, most colleges don't have customer service departments, and don't call or write to students just to offer help.

In fact, far from customer service, colleges often engage in what can only be called "customer punishment." For example, most colleges won't let a student register for classes, receive grades, receive transcripts, graduate, or receive his or her diploma, unless the student has paid all of his or her school bills—including school parking and library fines! Schools such as Boston College, Emory University, the University of Florida, Miami University of Ohio, Michigan State University, and the University of Virginia use this strategy to put their students on "financial hold."[314] The University of Virginia clearly spells out this policy in their "orientation guide" for students: "Did you know that you are not allowed to graduate until you have settled your account? This includes paying outstanding parking tickets and overdue library fees!"[315] This policy is hard to believe, especially since colleges receive so much money from students and other sources, but students confirm that schools really enforce this strategy; Peggy O'Neill says: "I got a letter from the [college] dean saying that, unless I paid my overdue library book charges, I couldn't graduate."[316]

Unfortunately, colleges often get away with offering poor services, because they have a consistent flow of customers. Few students leave schools and transfer to other schools due to poor customer service, and it's easy for many schools to replace the students that leave. In this way, colleges can charge high prices for low-quality services, even if their students or other customers are not happy. Professor Murray Sperber, of Indiana University, says that colleges support a system of "beer and circus," or parties and sports, to help distract students from the fact that they often don't get what they pay for.[317]

Actually, some colleges try to actively and preemptively discourage their customers from contacting them. For example, in 2005, Colgate University (annual full cost of attendance = $48,710) gave parents a flyer and lectures to try to convince them that students should deal with their problems on their own.[318] When parents now call Colgate to report complaints and get information, the school tells them to have their children call instead. Colgate's executives explain this policy by saying that the policy is meant to help students become "functioning, autonomous" people, and that the policy gives students the opportunity to learn "accountability and responsibility." But the truth is that Colgate is not really interested in solving students' complaints; in a notice to its employees, Colgate recently wrote: "We will not solve problems for students because it robs students of an opportunity to learn." This shows that Colgate may be the one who is most guilty of avoiding accountability and responsibility, since this policy allows the school to avoid making the effort to resolve its customers' complaints. The end result is that Colgate prevents its customers from having the opportunity to receive the costly services that they pay for.

Colgate's Dean of Student Affairs, Jim Terhune, justifies Colgate's policies by saying, "What [students are] paying for is an education, not a [hotel] room, and sometimes that education is uncomfortable"[319]—but Dean Terhune totally misses the point. Although guests are not required to stay in a hotel, Colgate requires its first-year students to live in its student housing and purchase its meal plans. Actually, Colgate requires its first-year students to purchase its most expensive housing and meal plans.[320] In addition, even if an education is sometimes "uncomfortable," as Dean Terhune suggests, students are paying a high price for that education, and therefore they have the right to express their disappointment with the services they receive. After all, aren't colleges supposed to be one of the places in the country where "free speech" is most protected, and the fight for justice is most respected?

In fact, although Colgate discourages parents from voicing their opinions, Colgate also uses many strategies to actively encourage parents to give money to the school, including a page on its website that specifically focuses on college financing plans for parents;[321] the page also features requests for donations to the school's "Parent's Fund."[322] Of course, some people can be described as "helicopter parents,"[323] who hover over their children, acting in an overbearing or bullying manner, and becoming too involved in their lives—but that doesn't give permission for schools like Colgate to ignore all of their customers' complaints, many of which are legitimate and justified.

College is much more important than a hotel room, and Colgate and other schools are able to charge extremely high prices exactly for this reason. Since schools aggressively ask for, and receive, so much money from students and parents, and since schools enjoy profiting from their customers' high expectations, it's arrogant, unreasonable, and insulting for colleges to get upset when parents and students try to put their mouths where their money is. When colleges encourage their customers to spend large amounts of money, and then discourage them from complaining about the poor services they receive, colleges seem to be saying: just shut up and pay.

• • •

So, it's important for students to watch out for the many profitable schemes that colleges use—and it's just as important for students to wonder if they will get what they came for in the first place: a good education. As usual, students can get the best deals by fully understanding what kinds of services they can expect to receive. Although college degrees can be valuable, the next chapter shows that schools often deliver poor-quality instruction, skills training, and knowledge to many of their students.

CHAPTER 4

DIRE EDUCATION
Do Students Get
the Instruction They Pay For?

College degrees can help students get higher salaries and better jobs, but many students also want to receive good instruction. Although colleges often require students to pay high prices, many schools are surprisingly not very dedicated to providing an excellent education.

YOU CALL THIS A COLLEGE EDUCATION?

First, colleges often force students to take a large number of classes they don't want, especially classes that have little practical value. For example, students must usually take classes called "general requirements," but many of these classes have nothing to do with students' individual interests, or the specific careers that students want to pursue. Therefore, some Kansas State University students say: "[general requirements are a] waste of…time and money," and "there are too many required classes that [feature information] we will never use," as well as "[the classes don't] really teach skills," and the school "requires [students to take] classes that…shouldn't be required…based on the career path that [students] have chosen."[324] In addition, recent graduates from Eastern Illinois University say "[general requirement] classes…keep you in school as long as possible," and "I still cannot see the benefit [of general requirement classes] to this day."[325] Even Stephen A. Mitchell, chair of the folklore and mythology program at

Harvard University, says that it "break[s] your heart" when students are forced to enroll in classes they'd rather not take.[326]

> **Myth: If it's a "college education," it must be good.**

Although schools should have the freedom to create a helpful curriculum for students, and students can benefit from being exposed to topics they have little interest in, the curriculum at most colleges is not practical and relevant enough, or considerate enough of students' individual goals and passions. In fact, several authors reveal that colleges may even push certain classes on students just to make sure that every department in the school has some students taking its classes (and not because the required classes are particularly helpful for students).[327]

To improve its educational services, Harvard University is seriously considering some curriculum changes that would give its students much more control in choosing classes.[328] But Harvard and most other colleges still have a long way to go before they create the kind of curriculum that students want and need, especially since every college offers a completely unique curriculum, or set of classes.

> **Myth: Colleges are committed to giving their students a good education.**

Colleges also offer many suspicious "electives," or classes that students can choose to take. Although these classes may be interesting for some students, and schools should have the freedom to teach controversial topics, it's surprising that some of these classes count toward a college degree. For example, Muhlenberg College and Indiana University offer a course on "Religions of Star Trek," Georgetown University offers "Star Trek and Philosophy," Duke University has "Campus Culture and Drinking," Williams College presents "Shopping: Desire, Compulsion and Consumption," and Carnegie Mellon University has "American Golf: Pastime or the People's Game."[329]

Although students aren't required to take these kinds of electives, colleges often waste their instructors by allowing them to teach these classes, when they could be teaching more relevant classes instead. After all, as described in Chapter 2, many colleges don't offer enough space in their required classes. Noah Morgan, a junior at Wayne State University, says, "I see fewer professors teaching the [required] courses students need [in order to graduate]."[330]

In fact, while colleges allow instructors to teach irrelevant classes, and force students to take irrelevant classes, and shut out students from important classes, colleges over-crowd their more popular classes (making these classes less effective). For example, in Fall 2002, the University of Houston had three classes with at least 500 students and 44 classes with 301 to 500 students.[331] Even some classes at Harvard University have "200 to 500 students or more."[332] David Laude, the University of Houston's associate dean for undergraduate education (who also teaches chemistry at the school), says that large classes are nothing new: "I've been teaching general chemistry courses within a 500-seat lecture hall [since 1993]."[333] Not all big classes are bad for students, but large classes usually restrict discussion and personal interaction between students and instructors, leading to a lower level of student engagement, and a higher likelihood of students dropping out of college altogether.[334]

"REAL PROFESSORS DON'T TEACH"

Many college students expect to receive excellent instruction, but they are often disappointed. Amazingly, many colleges actually <u>discourage</u> their professors from teaching.

> **Myth: College students receive instruction from professors who teach full-time.**

Students expect to be taught by professors in college, but college professors don't spend much time teaching students. In fact, recent U.S. Department of Education studies found that college instructors only spend an average of 10 hours per week in the classroom teaching students,[335] and other sources say that it's common for colleges to require "full-time" professors to teach within classrooms for only 6 to 16 hours per week.[336] Many instructors are also not available for students outside the classroom; it's common for professors to only be available in their offices to speak with students for 1-3 scheduled hours per week, often at inconvenient times.[337] In addition, many professors teach much less, or not at all, during fall, winter, spring, and summer breaks.

In fact, colleges often allow their highest-level (and highest paid) professors to spend the least time teaching college students.[338] For example, four out of ten high-level professors don't teach college classes at 4-year schools that offer graduate programs,[339] and high-level instructors only spend 3-5 hours per week interacting with college students in classrooms.[340] A recent *Inside Higher Ed* article stated: "the norm in higher education is that when professors [take on various responsibilities], their reward is to have their teaching load reduced."[341] In addition, many professors increase their income by completing "consulting" projects outside of their schools,[342] further diverting them from teaching. And some professors spend their time writing books—which they then require their students to buy, allowing them to receive extra royalty payments.[343]

> **Myth: Colleges encourage their professors to focus on teaching.**

The problem is that many colleges are more committed to conducting research projects than teaching. For example, schools only give top rewards—including high salaries, great benefits, promotions, valuable retirement plans, and "tenure"—to professors who complete research projects and publish their results.[344] Tenure is the most valuable reward, because it basically allows professors to keep their positions (including high salaries and benefits) for as long as they want, even if they're not doing a good job; tenured professors usually can't be fired.[345] Also, colleges allow tenured professors to take sabbaticals of six or twelve months; during this time, professors don't have to teach, and they can work on research projects—or go on vacation—instead.[346]

As usual, colleges' commitment to research can be explained by their quest for wealth. Colleges tend to focus on research over teaching because they use research projects to get extra money, prestige, publicity, and top ratings. And, since a college's reputation depends so much on research, even the most respected schools tend to focus on research over teaching.

However, colleges' commitment to a research-based tenure system hurts students. For example, colleges that use a tenure system have larger classes than schools that don't use a tenure system.[347]

> **Myth: Professors' top priority is to teach students.**

Even worse, the tenure system deters good teaching. Yahya Rahmat-Samii, chair of the electrical engineering department at UCLA, says, "Indirectly there is a pressure [for professors to conduct research], especially for younger faculty for promotion."[348] Also, Roger Bohman, a UCLA instructor, says, "Teaching is not held in such high esteem [at UCLA]," and Bowman thinks that UCLA students don't receive enough attention from instructors.[349] Marc Kubasak, also an instructor at UCLA, admits: "I have to give up the teaching to do the research."[350] And a tenured (but anonymous) Ivy League professor was glad that he didn't win the "Teacher of the Year" award until he was almost retired: "Lucky for me, I was on my way out; it would have hurt my career if I won that kind of award [earlier]."[351] Another (anonymous) professor at a respected school puts it more bluntly: "I do anything to avoid [students]; real professors don't teach undergraduates."[352]

Since professors' top rewards are based on research, it shouldn't be too surprising that professors tend to focus on research over just about any other professional task. In fact, due to the tenure system, colleges seem to attract professors who aren't that interested in teaching: only one out of three professors say that teaching is their main professional interest.[353] And some professors specifically try to work at schools that will allow them to teach fewer classes.[354] Therefore, students and taxpayers help pay for the high salaries of professors who don't provide many direct educational services. Unfortunately, the focus on research over teaching is very widespread at colleges; seven out of ten colleges use a tenure system.[355]

> **Myth: Professors improve their teaching skills by conducting research projects.**

Some people try to justify colleges' focus on research over teaching by saying that professors can improve their teaching skills by conducting research projects—but this assertion is inaccurate. In fact, the people who support this view are usually the ones who benefit most from the tenure system, like professors and college administrators. For example, Clemson University President James Barker says that research helps him and his fellow professors "to make ourselves better teachers," because research helps faculty understand new discoveries in their fields.[356] Yahya Rahmat-Samii, of UCLA, also says "[Professors who conduct research] are typically more exciting teachers for students."[357] And Peofilo Ruiz, UCLA history department chair, says: "You cannot be a good teacher unless you do research…"[358]

However, several large scientific studies have shown that these opinions are wrong; research skills actually have little to do with good teaching. For example, one analysis reviewed 2,600 studies about research and teaching, and found that there is not much of an association between research and teaching skills,[359] and another analysis found similar results,[360] suggesting that good researchers are not necessarily good teachers. Also, a smaller study looked at 200 colleges and found that when professors focus on research, students are unhappy and they learn less.[361]

It makes sense that conducting research has little to do with good teaching; after all, professors who spend time on research have less time to spend on teaching (or preparing to teach). Also, being a good researcher and being a good teacher often involve very different skills. In addition, most professors complete research projects on very specific topics, so their research doesn't help them to teach classes that focus on general topics. Besides, professors don't have to complete research projects of their own to learn about new developments in their fields; they can just read the research journals that report on other peoples' new research results.

WHO TEACHES THE STUDENTS?

If professors don't teach students, then who does? Lafayette University's Provost, June Schlueter,[362] and Mitch Vogel, president of the University Professionals of Illinois,[363] confirm that colleges across the country use part-time instructors, instead of full-time instructors; this is yet another bait-and-switch trick that allows colleges to increase their profits. The most common part-time college instructors are called "adjuncts," who may have graduate degrees, or "teaching assistants" (T.A.s), who are usually graduate students. Specifically, in 2001-02, 45% of college instructors were part-timers, up from 33% in 1987,[364] and there are now over 400,000 part-time college teachers.[365]

Part-time instructors have a large amount of teaching responsibility. John Curtis, director of research at the American Association of University Professors, says that, although T.A.s used to just help out full-time instructors, it's now "more and more common that graduate students [teach] courses on their own."[366] For example, T.A.s now teach about half the classes at schools like University of California-Berkeley, University of Washington, Ohio State University, and the University of Massachusetts,[367] and part-timers also often teach more than half of the freshman and sophomore classes in Florida's public colleges.[368] Even Ivy League schools, such as Columbia University, Princeton University, and Yale University, use hundreds, if not thousands of T.A.s.[369] Larry Summers, recent president of Harvard, admits that, even at Harvard, "a growing fraction of teaching and grading [is] done by graduate students."[370]

In some ways, students are lucky to be taught by part-time instructors. First, teaching is often the main academic focus for adjuncts, and they spend little or no time on research: part-time instructors focus on teaching during 89% of their work schedules.[371] Also, part-time instructors can have a better general knowledge of their fields than tenured professors, who are often very specialized. This is especially true because, as described above, tenured professors tend to focus on very specific research topics, and part-timers who have recently graduated from school can have a more up-to-date general knowledge of their fields.

On the other hand, colleges don't pay their part-time instructors enough, so these instructors struggle to be helpful for students. Specifically, while colleges give top rewards to professors who focus on research and neglect teaching, colleges often give poor salaries, no benefits, and no sabbatical privileges to their part-time instructors. For example, more than six out of ten English and foreign language adjuncts were recently paid only $1,200 to $2,500 for each class that they taught.[372] And, in 1999, seven out of ten English departments gave no health, retirement, or life insurance benefits at all to their part-time instructors.[373] Even Jonathan Loesburg, American University's former literature chairperson, admits: "I'm authorized to pay an adjunct here to teach a course something like around $2,000 [with no benefits at all, and] that seems to me on the face of it exploitative."[374] In addition, colleges usually only hire part-time instructors for one year at a time,[375] and Perry Robinson, deputy director of higher education for the American Federation of Teachers, says that colleges can refuse to renew the contracts of part-time instructors at any time for just about any reason,[376] even if they have taught for five or six years at one school.[377]

Therefore, although part-time instructors may have skill and passion for teaching, a number of factors make it difficult for them to focus on working with students. First, since they usually receive limited work hours and poor compensation, "part-timers" often have to work at more than one school. In addition, those who are lucky to piece together a full-time schedule between several schools often receive much less than full-time compensation. Also, some instructors who work at more than one school have trouble traveling between schools, and then show up late to the classes they are supposed to teach, or miss these classes altogether.[378] And part-timers understandably say that schools' one-year contracts are stressful for them,[379] because they don't know if they will be retained or fired. It doesn't help that many colleges don't give any office space to their part-timers. Finally, T.A.s, who are usually graduate students, often have to take their own classes and conduct their own research projects, so they can't completely focus on their teaching duties.

DIRE EDUCATION

Since colleges tend to focus on research over teaching, and often use part-time instructors, it shouldn't be too much of a surprise that college instructors are often not very good.

> **Myth: College instructors are good teachers.**

Although many college instructors are dedicated, knowledgeable, interesting, easy-to-understand, helpful, caring, or inspiring—too many instructors are not. In his book called *ProfScam*, Charles Sykes says that a large number of college instructors use ineffective teaching strategies, such as: reading directly from a textbook or their old notes, focusing on their very specific interests (instead of broader knowledge), encouraging informal discussions about random topics that have little educational value, or displaying a lack of preparation.[380] And a number of students agree with Sykes; for example, one anonymous student recently posted this message on a website that features ratings of college instructors: "You don't really need to go to [this instructor's] class, because [the instructor] follows the book right down to the words."[381] Also, on a college blog, a recent poster named "Supergenius" described having bad college instructors who taught straight from the textbook, using the same teaching materials that they had been using for years.[382] In many cases, students would learn more information than they do in their classrooms just by reading books.

In addition, although colleges often allow students to rate their instructors, colleges usually don't use these ratings to get rid of the bad instructors. Actually, the ratings system <u>can</u> get non-tenured instructors fired—"If you don't get good evaluations [as a non-tenured instructor], it doesn't matter how else you do," says Tom Dickson, associate professor of journalism at Southwest Missouri State University[383]—but colleges usually don't fire tenured professors who get bad ratings. Notre Dame student Lance Gallop says that one of his tenured professors told his class: "It doesn't matter what you put on the [student evaluations]. It doesn't matter if you say that I am a bad teacher. I have tenure."[384]

Many college instructors have also figured out how to "trick" students into giving them good ratings. For example, several recent studies show that instructors get better student evaluations just by making classes easier, giving out high grades, and being good performers/entertainers[385]—and many instructors take advantage of the system in these ways. Since the ratings system doesn't accurately evaluate college teaching and learning, and schools usually don't use the ratings to get rid of bad teachers, student evaluations are often a sham.

Unfortunately, colleges even drive out some of their best instructors. Specifically, the tenure system encourages good instructors who are not tenured to leave their schools, because the schools don't compensate them properly. Dennis Jerz, Associate Professor at Seton Hill University in Pennsylvania, says that it's common for "students to protest the loss of their favorite teacher," because "teachers who were rated highly in the classroom and who were well-liked by students...[leave after being] denied tenure because they didn't meet the [research] requirements."[386] Some non-tenured instructors who have excellent teaching skills are also directly fired by colleges.

Myth: College instructors communicate effectively.

Some students at American colleges never find out if their professors have good teaching skills—because their professors don't speak proper English. A recent editorial in the University of Central Florida's newspaper said that instructors' poor language skills are a problem all across the country, noting that "...the number one problem with taking classes [is that] sometimes you can't understand the professor; you have no idea what the professor is saying due to his [or her] thick accent or [unfamiliar way of speaking]."[387] Students have also expressed similar complaints at many other schools, including Ohio State University,[388] University of California-Berkeley, University of Michigan, and Brooklyn College.[389] And one researcher in North Dakota has received "dozens" of language complaints from students.[390] Susan Sarwack, director of

OSU's Spoken English program, says that she receives many cultural complaints from students, including complaints about one instructor who would not answer students' questions in class because doing so was not common in the instructor's native culture.[391] Although many colleges provide educational training to their foreign instructors, and require instructors to pass an English test, many students complain that the instructors' spoken English is still not good enough, and administrators acknowledge that some inadequate instructors pass the exams.[392] Some foreign instructors also admit that adapting to American students is very challenging; Min Liu, an instructor at North Dakota State University, says that if she had known how difficult it was to teach in the United States, she "wouldn't have come here."[393]

On the other hand, some people believe that foreign instructors provide students with helpful exposure to new cultures, including Dean Richard Beeman of the University of Pennsylvania, Donald Rubin, a professor at the University of Georgia, and Julie Bloom, a Berkeley student—but even Dean Beeman admits that some foreign instructors shouldn't be teaching in the classroom.[394] Students are customers and have a right to receive a high-quality education, and instructors' language and cultural differences can be a significant barrier to students' learning. In fact, George Borjas, a researcher at Harvard University, says that students don't do as well in classes taught by foreign instructors.[395]

Therefore, to try to protect students, Rep. Bette Grande has introduced a new law that would allow North Dakota students to withdraw from their classes, with no financial or academic penalties, if their instructors do not speak an acceptable level of English.[396] This law may be very beneficial, but it won't solve the real problem: ensuring that instructors have good language skills. Also, there are some classes that students can't drop, because they need the classes for their careers, or to graduate. And no similar laws have been proposed yet to help protect students in other states.

> **Myth: College instructors are open to all perspectives.**

Many students and parents also complain that college instructors try to impose their own political beliefs on their students. Specifically, three out of ten students (29%) at the top 50 colleges say that they have to agree with their instructors' political or social views to get good grades in their classes.[397] Students also complain that some instructors don't acknowledge or respect any political opinions but their own.[398]

In contrast, some critics say that reports of instructor persecution are exaggerated because the studies that have produced these results have not properly represented all students.[399] In addition, the president of the American Association of University Professors, Roger Bowen, says that instructors' political beliefs don't have much of an impact on their teaching.[400] However, even if the exact percentage of unhappy students is open to debate, it's clear that a large number of students are upset about the way their professors treat them. It's also clear that a number of these complaints are justified; for example, Missouri State University recently completed an out-of-court settlement with a student who sued the school after being required to write and sign a letter to politicians endorsing adoption rights for gay people.[401]

In 2001, one student's mother was upset to find out that the University of California-San Diego required her son to write a report about, as she puts it, "the [harmfulness] of the white race."[402] This mother then created a website (www.noindoctrination.org) where students can post complaints about instructors who pressure students to support their views, as well as complaints about instructors who prevent students from expressing opinions that conflict with their own.[403] As of 2005, students at more than 1,000 colleges had posted complaints on this site.

On the other hand, due to recent student complaints, many instructors feel like they are victims of a "witch hunt," or a movement to unfairly monitor and silence them.[404] In some ways, these instructors are right; it's important for all instructors to enjoy "freedom of speech," with the ability to openly discuss their opinions and express their beliefs, without fear of punishment. After all, learning about new perspectives may be more valuable for students than learning about perspectives that are already familiar. Also, it's insulting to think that students are easily "brainwashed," and can't come to their own conclusions.

However, students must also be allowed to enjoy these same rights; it's important for students: to be welcome in any class they want to take, to be permitted to express their personal opinions and disagreements in their classes without getting punished, and to get graded based on the quality of their work (and not based on how much they agree with their instructors). Anne Neal, president of the American Council of Trustees and Alumni, says: "The classroom should be a place where students are free to explore different points of view. [Students] should not feel they will be penalized if they think for themselves."[405] Students should also have the opportunity to easily know which classes present a biased perspective, and what that bias is. In short, it seems that colleges and graduate schools need to work harder to make sure that both instructors and students are able to enjoy their freedoms in an appropriate way.

> **Myth: Celebrity professors enhance student education.**

Even colleges' most famous professors tend to be unhelpful for students, because they often teach the least. "Visiting professors," who only work at a school for a short time, enjoy a particularly extreme combination of high salaries and light teaching loads. For example, the University of North Florida paid Archbishop Desmond Tutu $76,800, plus free use of a home, a personal assistant, and an office on campus for one semester,[406] and he only taught one class to the University's students.[407] In addition, Princeton University pays some of its visiting professors $59,000 per semester, just to teach only one class of 18 students for 3 hours a week—and these professors are allowed to bring in guest speakers to teach for them![408]

Colleges like to hire famous professors because they can help the schools to receive large amounts of publicity and money.[409] But, since these professors are very expensive and don't teach much, the vast majority of students and taxpayers don't directly benefit from them. If colleges were truly committed to providing a good education to as many of their students as possible, they would instead hire instructors who would teach full-time and instruct a larger number of students.

> **Myth: The college grading system accurately measures and represents true student learning.**

If college education is so disappointing, then why do many students get good grades? The answer is that many colleges often use a "grade inflation" system, giving out high grades to most students. Several studies support this idea by showing that colleges give out much higher grades today than they have in the past.[410] In fact, a number of schools are now trying to reduce the number of high grades they award, including Princeton University, Harvard University, Stanford University, Dartmouth University, Boston University, and Arizona State University[411]—virtually admitting that they have used a "grade inflation" system and have improperly given out too many high grades.

Although many college students are brilliant, and many students deserve the high grades they receive, it makes sense that colleges might try to enhance their students' grades. After all, a college wouldn't look very impressive (or be able to attract new students) if many of its current students were getting bad grades. In addition, instructors who want to focus on research but still satisfy their students might give out high grades, because then students might not complain about the poor instruction they receive. For better or worse, students tend to appreciate easier classes. However, the grade inflation system allows some colleges to continue to provide an inferior education.

THE COURSEWORK "BAIT AND SWITCH" TRAP

Colleges also sometimes forbid their students from enrolling in the academic programs they most expected to complete. For example, Emory University doesn't accept students into their business program until after they complete two years of general classes.[412] This means that students who want to study business can complete two full years of work at Emory, get rejected from the business school, and then have to pick another major or transfer to another college that will allow them to study business. The same situation occurs at the University of Iowa, where, after completing two years of classes, 2,000 students then compete with each other for only 1,300 spots in the school's business program.[413] Many colleges also forbid their students from taking practical classes, like business classes, outside their "majors," or areas of academic focus.[414]

In addition, the *Wall Street Journal* reports that some colleges now limit the number of their students who are allowed to "study abroad," in other countries (or the colleges require students to pay unexpected extra fees for these programs).[415] But students usually don't find out if they will be allowed to participate in the study abroad programs—or how much these programs will cost them—until they apply for the programs during their sophomore or junior years.

Both of these strategies are unfair to students because colleges accept several years of payments before telling their students that they can't obtain the educational experiences they expected when they first enrolled. Many colleges also unfairly restrict students' study abroad options, limiting them to only those programs that provide the schools with kickbacks; these deals can increase students' costs, and reduce their educational options.[416]

COLLEGES TO STUDENTS: WE DON'T CARE HOW MUCH YOU PAID US FOR AN EDUCATION—YOU'RE ON YOUR OWN

All of the evidence in this chapter shows that the college education system has some major problems, and student Lance Gallop is fed up.[417] Gallop thinks that if faculty can't teach well, or don't want to teach, then colleges shouldn't force them to teach: "In fact do not even ALLOW them to teach." Gallop continues: "We pay an almost unthinkable amount of money and spend a tremendous amount of time in pursuit of a quality education. To force us to endure terrible professors is disrespectful of our dignity as learners.

[Colleges] have no right to subject us to low-quality teachers. We deserve better, and we demand it."

To a certain extent, colleges even admit that they don't provide a good education for their students. For example, many public and private schools tell their students where to find additional outside private tutoring that will cost extra money for the students, including Penn State University,[418] the University of Arizona,[419] Boise State University,[420] Clemson University,[421] Wayne State University,[422] California State University,[423] and Western Washington University.[424] Although many college students need extra tutoring because they don't learn enough in college, private tutors can easily add hundreds or thousands of dollars to students' already-steep education costs.

Colleges may think they're being helpful by telling students where to find private tutors, but colleges' real message to their customers is loud and clear: if you don't get a good education here, we won't make it up to you, even if you're paying our high prices—but we will tell you where you can pay even more money to get your education elsewhere. Ironically, many American students now use tutors in other countries, through the magic of the Internet;[425] the American higher education system is in such bad shape that many students are only able to get an affordable and helpful education by looking outside the country.

> **Myth: Colleges give their students the support they need in order to graduate.**

Many colleges also have a surprisingly high dropout rate, often because they do not provide enough academic support for their students. As mentioned in Chapter 1, more than one-third of all college students at four-year colleges drop out within six years after they start.[426] In addition, approximately one-third of Americans in their mid-20s are college dropouts.[427] And each year, more than 600,000 students drop out of four-year colleges.[428] Some students even drop out after paying for four years of college expenses but not completing enough credits to obtain a degree.

Although students have some responsibility for dropping out, many colleges don't do enough to help students who are struggling. The worst offenders include about 50 colleges in the United States that graduate less than 20% of their students.[429] Some students even unfairly struggle at colleges due to adverse social factors that their colleges allow to fester. For example, Jose Silva left Princeton University because he grew up in a housing project and couldn't relate to the large number of wealthy students at the school: "I didn't really have a whole lot of friends...my view of what life is like is totally not their...view."[430]

Since colleges require students to complete an application process before being accepted, colleges are somewhat responsible when their students drop out without earning degrees—especially when a particular college's dropout rate is very high. "If you're accepting a [student] into your [college], don't you have [some] responsibility to make sure they graduate?" wonders Melissa Roderick, the co-director of the Consortium on Chicago School Research.[431] Vincent Tinto, a professor of education at Syracuse University, says that too many colleges are unwilling "to commit resources and to align their resources in a systematic way [in order to help students]," and too many colleges don't "understand the importance of [providing] support for student academic success."[432] Finally, Gary Orfield, a Harvard University professor of education, points out that too many colleges get away with their lack of student support because "most colleges aren't held accountable in any way for their graduation rate."

RATING THE SKILLS OF COLLEGE GRADS

Since college services are often deficient, it shouldn't be too surprising that even those students who manage to graduate tend to struggle to be successful. Although some students graduate with good skills, and college degrees tend to give graduates a career advantage, employers aren't very impressed with new grads. For example, employers want to hire employees who have "well-developed abstract thinking skills," "goal setting skills," "interpersonal relationship skills," "writing skills," and "presentation skills"—but employers say that many recent college graduates don't have these basic abilities.[433] Also, the Job Outlook 2004 report from the National Association of Colleges and Employers says, "Unfortunately, the skill employers value most—communication skills—is the skill employers think students most often lack."[434] And, in a 1997 survey conducted by the U.S. Census, only one out of ten employers (10%) said that colleges had done an "outstanding" job in preparing students for jobs.[435]

Even worse, many college graduates have major literacy problems. For example, the U.S. Department of Education has defined five literacy categories, and half of college graduates are <u>not</u> at the top two levels.[436] A more recent government study found that less than one-third of college graduates are "proficient," or skilled, in basic reading and math tasks, and literacy levels declined significantly among college grads from 1992 to 2003.[437] These findings are hard to believe, but they mean that a large number of college graduates don't know how to do basic things like: figure out the main point of a newspaper article, pick the right bus to take from a schedule of several buses, and calculate the correct change from a restaurant purchase. A recent study also found that as many as six out of ten college students (60%) do not have basic technology skills.[438] College graduates' low literacy levels seem to confirm employers' poor opinions of their skills, and this is particularly unfortunate because literacy is one of the main keys to graduates' success. In fact, graduates who have a high level of literacy earn significantly more money than college graduates who have low literacy (about 67% more).[439]

Unfortunately, even many specialized career-related college programs are unhelpful for students, because instructors are often not very interested in specifically preparing students for jobs. For example, David Hemmendinger, professor of computer science at Union College, thinks that employers shouldn't expect that much from computer science graduates, and says that students in other fields also don't learn many job skills while they're in college: "In what fields do brand-new college graduates do production work immediately [after they graduate]? Economics majors don't pick mutual fund portfolios right away. Chemistry majors don't formulate detergents without more work."[440] Kyle Lutes, associate professor at Purdue University, agrees and says, "A common belief among university faculty is that the purpose of a university degree is not to prepare the student to be productive in the workplace the first day after graduation. Training a worker to be effective in an organization is the responsibility of the hiring organization."[441] In addition, many instructors may not even be qualified to teach practical job skills, because they spend their entire careers teaching and/or conducting research within colleges and universities, so they are probably somewhat detached from the "real world" of work.[442]

PUTTING COLLEGES TO THE TEST

Although it can be discouraging to think that colleges aren't providing high-quality services for their students, many students still need degrees in order to pursue their preferred careers, and these students can seek out colleges that offer the best value. Unfortunately, it's almost impossible for students to know which colleges offer the best teaching, because colleges either don't properly test their students' learning, or because colleges hide the test scores. For example, two exams are currently used to measure student learning at different colleges across the country, but many colleges either don't use the tests, or keep the results secret.[443] Specifically, these exams are called the Collegiate Learning Assessment (CLA), and the National Survey of Student Engagement (NSSE). And the accreditation agencies that are supposed to monitor colleges are often surprisingly unwilling to evaluate colleges' educational effectiveness, and to penalize the schools that are educationally deficient.[444]

In September 2005, Margaret Spellings, the U.S. Secretary of Education, gathered 19 education "experts" for a "Commission on the Future of Higher Education," in order to identify current college weaknesses, and develop some potential solutions (the Commission's website is located at: http://www.ed.gov/about/bdscomm/list/hiedfuture/index.html).[445] This committee made several important criticisms, noting that "the quality of student learning at U.S. colleges and universities is inadequate and, in some cases, declining,"[446] and that there is a "woeful lack" of information about colleges' teaching and learning effectiveness, because colleges "make no serious effort to examine their effectiveness on the most important measure of all: how much students learn." The committee also said that "the quality and relevancy of American higher education and its ability to produce informed and skilled citizens... are in question,"[447] adding that colleges have "inadequate transparency and accountability," and that colleges provide "no solid evidence" of their educational performance that people can use to compare the quality of teaching and learning at different schools.

In short, many Commission members and higher education experts (including the U.S. Education Secretary herself) believe that colleges should provide more information about their services and take more steps to improve.[448] For example, Lee Shulman, president of the Carnegie Foundation for the Advancement of Teaching, says, "Higher education cannot drag its feet. It is time for us to do comprehensive, multifaceted assessments [of what students learn at colleges], and make that data public."[449] Robert J. Sternberg, psychologist and dean of arts and sciences at Tufts University, also points out that national college assessment is needed because parents, students, and taxpayers are "paying a lot of money [for higher education] and they ought to know what they're getting."[450] And Shulman agrees, saying, "there ought to be an expectation that every [college] takes on responsibility for demonstrating the 'value added' of their educational programs."[451] Although students still don't have the data they need in order to properly compare the educational effectiveness of different colleges, the rest of this book will present some strategies students can use to try to get the most for their money.

UNIVERSITY RESEARCH: LIFE-SAVING OR SCHOOL-SAVING?

It's clear that part of the reason why students often receive a poor education is that professors (and colleges) are too focused on conducting research—but, ironically, much of this research is of questionable value or quality. For example, a large number of research studies are <u>not</u> cited, or mentioned by other researchers, within five years after they're published, including more than nine out of ten arts and humanities articles, half of social science articles, and two out of ten science articles,[452] and this means that few research studies are truly important. These numbers are actually too generous to researchers, because they include studies that are cited by the original authors themselves. Although many university research studies help to save lives, too many studies may be a waste of educational and financial resources.

Even publication doesn't guarantee that a research study is good. For example, some professors and colleges pay to have their research articles published, with "page charges" often ranging from $50 to $200 per page.[453] And, since research journals receive thousands of dollars by selling journal subscriptions, they have strong incentive to publish articles, even if the articles aren't very important. To try to prove this point, several people have succeeded in having fake reports of meaningless gibberish accepted by conferences and research journals.[454] Amazingly, thousands of different research journals are currently published, again showing that publication does not ensure that a research study is necessarily very special. Of course, many other research studies receive such little respect that they're never published.

Part of the research problem is that researchers have too much independence, and often don't make any effort to coordinate their efforts or establish consistent research procedures, especially in the social sciences. Instead, researchers are surprisingly free to study almost any topic they would like, and use almost any method, no matter how useless. Jeffrey Meldrum, a tenured professor at Idaho State University, provides an extreme example of the current university research system: Meldrum focuses on trying to establish the existence of "Bigfoot," a mythical ape-man creature that has never actually been proven to be real.[455] Although a number of research projects are valuable (and may even save lives), and it's important for researchers to have some independence as they conduct their work, the college research system is somewhat inefficient, and often results in a massive waste of time, effort, and money.

Lackluster university research studies might be less of a concern if students were receiving an excellent education at an affordable price. But, since colleges' research focus often leads to poor instruction and unmanageable student costs, it's reasonable to wonder if the university research system should be overhauled. Economist Richard Vedder even suggests that professors are spending less time than ever on <u>both</u> teaching <u>and</u> research work.[456]

In addition, university research is often marred by misbehavior. For example:

- A large number of professors (including those at prestigious schools) unfairly manipulate their research studies, and sometimes falsify their results;[457]

- Some professors plagiarize other researchers' studies and claim them as their own. Drummond Rennie, adjunct professor of medicine at the University of California, and the West Coast editor of the Journal of the American Medical Association, says: "I've talked to scores and scores of people who allege [research] misconduct, and most of them are entirely right. In some [research] labs, it's routine to steal other people's work;"[458]

- Some professors accept payments in exchange for allowing companies to use their names as authors on promotional articles they didn't actually write (including articles in medical journals that are "ghostwritten" by drug companies that want to promote their products);[459]

- Some universities accept payments from companies who act as "sponsors" of research, but then the schools allow the companies to improperly influence the methods, results, or publication of the results (which can endanger people, especially when the studies are health-related); [460]

- And colleges also sometimes use research projects to improperly obtain extra money from the government (and therefore from all Americans), either overcharging the government or using the funds for things that have nothing to do with research or other educational activities. [461]

THE FUTURE OF COLLEGE EDUCATION

In summary, the current college education system often leads to indifferent college instructors, unprepared graduates, unsatisfied employers, and problematic research—but colleges are not in a hurry to change, so students have to make the most of a bad system. For example, David Ward, the representative for colleges within the Future of Higher Education Commission, recently illustrated colleges' reluctance to change when he was the only committee member who did not agree to sign the Commission's final report.

A close look reveals that most colleges are not actively engaged in making their required coursework significantly more practical and career-oriented. Also, most colleges are not actively pursuing educational improvements to the tenure system, especially since these improvements might require schools to give up more of their profits. Many professors say that they need tenure so that they can have the freedom to express controversial ideas, but tenure hurts education and makes it almost impossible to get rid of some of the worst instructors. By guaranteeing that tenured professors can keep their jobs—even if they are ineffective teachers—the tenure system also often guarantees that students don't receive the education they need (and pay for). On the other hand, some colleges are giving tenure to fewer professors—but these schools are hiring more low-paid part-time instructors, which is also unhelpful for students.

The bottom line is that neither uninterested tenured instructors nor underpaid part-time instructors are good enough for students; students don't need more of either. Instead, students need high-quality passionate instructors who work full-time on teaching at only one school, and who are paid a fair salary and benefits so that they can easily focus on teaching. Since many colleges are rich and charge high prices, they should be able to hire more full-time instructors at a fair wage, but students and taxpayers are not getting their money's worth right now from an educational standpoint. By relying on ineffective instructors, colleges treat education as an afterthought and not a top priority—and this is unacceptable. However, without added pressure from students and government, colleges will probably remain committed only to profit and, by default, poor education.

• • •

So, college services probably won't get much better, or more affordable, over the next few years, and many new graduates are struggling. On the other hand, college degrees can be valuable for students. What's a student to do? The answer is that students should get degrees that will have good value for the cost. The truth about the real costs and benefits of the college investment is revealed in the next chapter.

CHAPTER 5

THE REAL COST AND VALUE OF COLLEGE
Getting the Most for Your Money

College is typically advertised as a must-have investment that can't go wrong, but many students suffer because colleges convince them to spend too much on their degrees. Although college degrees are usually valuable for students, degrees that cost more are often surprisingly not worth more. In addition, college degrees often lead to much lower financial benefits than people expect. Therefore, students need to try to get their degrees while cutting their costs as much as possible. But, before students can cut their college costs, they need to understand them.

EXPENSIVE COLLEGE COSTS THAT ARE OFTEN HIDDEN

Although students often receive financial aid and other discounts, they get into trouble because college usually still costs much more than they expect. Part of the problem is that college costs can be confusing, and colleges usually don't help students understand the true costs. Just like many other businesses (most famously, car dealerships), colleges can get more money from their customers when their real total prices are tough to figure out. But exactly what are students' main college costs? Let's look at a basic estimate.

One of students' largest unexpected college costs is the total cost of their student loans: as mentioned in Chapter 1, college students who use loans to help pay for school graduate

The Real Cost and Value of College 95

with $23,000 in student loan debt, on average. However, these loans actually cost much more for students, because those who use loans must pay expensive interest charges. Since interest charges usually build up over 20 years of loan payments, a $23,000 loan actually costs a total of about $32,400 for students (at an annual interest rate of 5%, after standard tax deductions, not counting inflation or credit debt). Many people mistakenly ignore loan interest costs when they calculate total college costs.

Also, even students who use financial aid must pay for some "immediate costs" while they are in school, including some tuition costs, living expenses, and travel expenses between school and home (such as plane flights). The average student pays about $7,250 in immediate costs for every year that they are in school (after financial aid),[462] for a total of $29,000 over four years of school.

All of these immediate and loan costs include charges for students' housing and food, because many students go to college far away from home, and many schools require students to pay housing and food costs that are much higher than the prices students could pay off-campus.[463] And many families maintain a room for students while they are away at college, so student housing often represents an additional cost for them. In contrast, students who attend college close to home may be able to live at home for free (or for a low cost). Students also pay another college cost by spending time going to class or studying, instead of working for pay. As Ben Franklin said, time is money, and studying has a financial "opportunity cost" for students, because every hour that a student studies or sits in class is an hour that they could be working for a salary. Specifically, full-time college students lose out on about $9,239 in income for every year that they are in school, or $36,956 over 4 years (on average, after taxes). This amount is based on the after-tax difference in salaries between college students ($6,300 per year) and same-aged high school graduates ($15,539 per year), including the fact that about three out of four college students work for pay while they are in college, either during the school year or on breaks.[464] Although many people ignore this college cost, and this cost is not an "out-of-pocket" expense like loans or immediate costs that students must pay, losing out on income is an opportunity cost for students, so it should be considered. After all, $36,956 is almost enough for a down payment on a fairly large house in many areas of the United States.

Of course, college students often lose out on even more money than this, because they would receive valuable employment benefits or perks if they were working full time, such as health insurance and retirement plans. Instead, students often have to pay for their health insurance while they are in school, and postpone saving up for retirement, adding more out-of-pocket expenses or opportunity costs to the price of getting a degree. And college students who have special talents, like computer skills, lose out on more still; these students may have been able to get good jobs straight out of high school without having a college degree. Unfortunately, many researchers and families tend to mistakenly ignore many of these college costs.

THE REAL COST OF
THE COLLEGE INVESTMENT

So, the true total cost of college can be calculated by adding up three key factors. Here's the formula to calculate the pain:

Real College Costs = Loan Costs + Immediate Costs + Lost Income

So the average total college cost is:

Cost of student loans over time:	$32,400
Immediate costs paid while in school:	$29,000
Income lost while in school:	+ $36,956
Total cost of college investment:	**$98,356**

    This includes all tuition, fees, room, board (food), transportation, books, supplies, and personal expenses (after subtracting grants, scholarships, and tax discounts for college expenses).

    This formula is easier to calculate than almost any formula taught in college math classes—but colleges don't teach it. As mentioned above, colleges often profit from their customers' confusion about their true prices. However, students can use this formula to clearly understand how much each school will actually cost them.

    Of course, not all of the $98,356 college cost comes directly from students' pockets, because $36,956 of this cost is due to lost income. However, the average student still pays a total of <u>$61,400</u> in actual out-of-pocket costs ($29,000 for immediate expenses while they go to school, and $32,400 for student loan costs over time).

THE REAL FINANCIAL VALUE OF COLLEGE

With this average college cost in mind, let's take a look at the true college payoff. While college can be more than just a financial investment, because college grads also often enjoy other intellectual, personal, physical, and social benefits, colleges and graduate schools have very high financial costs, so students need to fully understand their expected financial payoffs.

Although college degrees are often worth a lot of money and are usually excellent financial investments over an entire lifetime, college degrees are surprisingly much less financially valuable than people think. Researchers often say that college graduates make about $900,000 more than high school graduates (including all full-time and part-time workers, on average, from age 25 to 64—a full "worklife")[465]—but degrees are actually worth much less than this.

> **Myth: A college degree is worth about $1 million (or more) over a lifetime.**

Here's a basic estimate to show where the calculations often go wrong. First, degrees are worth much less than $900,000 because income taxes have to be subtracted from college graduates' salaries. Income taxes lower people's "take home" salaries by about 30%, so when income taxes are subtracted from both high school graduates' and college graduates' salaries from age 22-64, college graduates "only" make about $688,741 more than high school graduates (on average, over their entire "work-lives," not counting inflation, based on U.S. Census data, including the salaries of 22-24 year old college grads, which should increase the value of the degree).

However, even this value is wrong, because it's distorted by the excessively high salaries of the graduates at the top who are paid the most. For example, researchers tend to use "mean" or "average" salaries in their calculations, but these amounts are skewed too highly by the top earners. Instead, researchers should use "median" salaries that are in the middle and therefore more accurately represent the typical salaries that college graduates earn. When median salaries are analyzed instead of mean salaries, the college advantage drops even further, and college graduates "only" earn $565,352 more than high school graduates (typically, over their entire work-lives).

But college is actually worth even less than this, because college costs must be subtracted from college graduates' earnings. Too many researchers skip this step, but, to understand the actual return on any investment, the original cost of the investment has to be subtracted from the final value. Sure, college graduates receive some financial benefits from their degrees—but they also have to pay high costs for this privilege that non-college students don't. When the typical college investment cost of $98,356 is subtracted from college graduates' median tax-reduced earnings ($565,352), college graduates "only" earn $466,996 more than high school graduates (typically, over their entire lives). While this is still a large amount of money, it's only about half of the $900,000 reward that colleges and researchers usually publicize. Some studies even estimate that the actual value of a college degree is closer to $300,000.[466] It's probably not just a coincidence that many of the studies that over-estimate the financial value of a college degree are sponsored by schools and other organizations that profit when people to go to college.

Unfortunately, degrees are usually worth even less for the many students who pay higher-than-average costs, because these extra costs must be subtracted from the final payoff. For example, the total college payoff can be lower for students who have high student loans, high college credit debt, high immediate college costs, and more than four years of college expenses or lost income. College degrees also obviously have lower financial value for graduates who earn below-average salaries. Therefore, the "real college value" formula is:

Real
Total College = Total Income − College Costs
Value   After College   and Post-College
                                         Income Taxes

STUCK AT THE STARTING GATE

> **Myth: After college, college graduates tend to gain financial advantages over high school graduates very quickly.**

As described above, college degrees tend to be worth much less than people think—and this is especially true during the first 20 years after college. Specifically, the average student who starts college at age 18 does not financially catch up to a high school graduate until they are both about 31 or 32 years old (at least)—and many college graduates take much longer.

In fact, even the College Board admits that typical graduates of <u>public</u> colleges who start college at age 18 and finish in four years do not financially catch up to same-aged high school graduates until the age of 33, and that typical graduates of <u>private</u> colleges who start college at age 18 and finish in four years do not financially catch up to same-aged high school graduates until they are both in their 40s![467] Although college degrees are often valuable over a lifetime, and degrees are required for many jobs and graduate schools, most college graduates are financially stuck at the starting gate.

New college graduates are financially strapped because they have $98,356 in college costs that high school graduates don't have (on average)—and new college graduates' salaries are not that different from the salaries of same-aged high school graduates. For example, after taxes, the average high school graduate earns about $13,917 per year at age 22, but the average college graduate only earns about $18,583 per year at age 22,[468] which is just $5,000 more per year (based on U.S. Census data). And new college graduates usually don't receive large salary raises; in fact, a new study shows that new college graduates can be stuck with low salaries for 10 years.[469]

At this rate, it takes college graduates about 10-12 years after college to earn $98,356 more than high school graduates and catch up to them financially (or a total of 14-18 years, including the 4-6 years of college). And this is true at any age; students who start college after age 18 or finish college after age 21 will take just as many years to catch up.

Even after college graduates financially catch up to high school graduates, it can still take them some time to get far ahead. The calculations in this chapter show that, at the age of 40, more than 20 years after going their separate ways, college graduates are only about $100,000 ahead of high school graduates (on average, after income taxes and college costs are paid). This helps to explain why many college graduates struggle to support themselves and achieve their goals.

Chart 5.1 illustrates the long period of time that it takes for the average college graduate to financially catch up to the average high school graduate. The first column of the chart, "Age," allows for a comparison of same-aged high school graduates and college graduates throughout their lives. The second column, "High School Graduate's Net Salary," includes the median after-tax salary for a high school graduate at each age level. The third column, "College Graduate's Net Salary," includes the median after-tax salary for a college graduate at each age level. And the fourth column, "Net Annual Salary Difference," is the difference between high school graduates' and college graduates' salaries at each individual age level.

Finally, the fifth (and last) chart column, "College Graduate Behind/Ahead By (-/+)...," compares the total lifetime earnings of a college graduate to the total lifetime earnings of a high school graduate, at each age level. Since college graduates start out $98,356 behind high school graduates when they graduate from college (due to all college costs), the first row of the chart has the college graduate behind by $98,356 at age 21. With each passing year, the college graduate gains a little more ground, gradually catching up to the high school graduate, and the college graduate finally passes the high school graduate at age 33. However, as the table shows, a typical college graduate is only ahead of a typical high school graduate by $12,801 at age 34.

In this way, high school graduates are actually in better financial shape than college graduates for many years. It may seem like many college students and new graduates live more expensive lives than high school graduates during this time, but college students and new grads often pay for their living expenses by relying heavily on student loans, credit, other kinds of debt, or financial donations from their families.

Chart 5.1

Age	HS Grad Net Annual Salary	Colllege Grad Net Annual Salary	Net Annual Salary Difference	College Grad Behind/Ahead By (-/+)
21	N/A	N/A	N/A	- 98,356
22	13,917	18,583	4,666	- 93,691
23	13,917	18,583	4,666	- 89,025
24	13,917	18,583	4,666	- 84,360
29	19,399	29,115	9,716	- 35,780
34	19,399	29,115	9,716	+ 12,801
39	22,554	38,362	15,808	+ 91,841
44	22,554	38,362	15,808	+ 170,882
49	24,119	40,151	16,032	+ 251,042
54	24,119	40,151	16,032	+ 331,203
59	22,600	36,179	13,579	+ 399,099
64	12,600	36,179	13,579	+ 466,996

OVEREDUCATED AND UNDERPAID

"When I graduated, you could get a degree in anything and you'd be all right, you'd be fine. [But] the world is different now. It's harder."

—Jill Sanborne,
a financial consultant and career advisor
who graduated from college many years ago[470]

"Our biggest disappointment and upset has been that [our daughter's] college degree has not netted her the salary that

we thought it would. We spent our whole lives telling our children to go to college, and it didn't work out the way they planned."

—Jennifer,
the mother of several recent college graduates[471]

In summary, although college degrees tend to be valuable for students, the average financial payoff is often disappointing—and the reward is even worse for the many students who receive a below-average payoff. In fact, the people who struggle the most are those who have higher-than-average college costs together with lower-than-average payoffs. And the situation is most disappointing when two married or romantic partners both have high educational costs and low financial payoffs. But in what ways do students receive lower-than-average college payoffs?

> **Myth: College leads to an excellent payoff for all students.**

College costs are especially risky for the many students who drop out of college and never complete their degrees. And college dropouts usually have the worst of both worlds: high college costs and debt, coupled with low earning power. For example, after taxes are removed, college graduates of all ages earn $39,000 (median, $50,900 before taxes), and high school graduates of all ages earn $24,900 ($31,500 before taxes), but college dropouts of all ages only earn $29,000 ($37,100 before taxes),[472] which is much closer to the salary of a high school grad than a college grad.

Surprisingly, researchers usually ignore college dropouts in their calculations of the college payoff, but dropouts lower the average value of the degree even further, since dropouts tend to pay many of the college costs but receive few of the payoffs. Dropouts receive a particularly dangerous deal when they pay college costs for 4 years or more and still don't get their degrees.

> **Myth: It's easy for college grads to find high-paying college-level jobs.**

Unfortunately, college is also risky for many students who manage to complete their degrees. For example, by definition, about half of all college graduates earn lower-than-average salaries, especially new grads. In fact, two out of ten college graduates who work full-time (21%) earn lower salaries than an average high school graduate.[473] *The Wall Street Journal* also recently reported that a large number of college graduates have to work two jobs to make ends meet.[474]

> **Myth: It's easy for college grads to find college-level jobs.**

In addition, many college grads can't even get "college-level" jobs. For example, studies have shown that 20-35% of employed recent college graduates took jobs that didn't require college degrees.[475] Also, in 1990, 75,000 college graduates worked as street vendors or door-to-door salespeople, 83,000 college graduates worked as maids, housekeepers, janitors or cleaners, and 166,000 college graduates worked as motor vehicle operators,[476] and many grads work today as waiters, bartenders, retail salespeople[477]— and coffeehouse baristas. Willy Cookson, a recent graduate of the University of New Mexico, and current café server, says: "I don't even know if I'll ever [be able to] use my [college] degree toward a career."[478] And Jenny Russell illustrates her long string of low-level jobs since graduating from a private college in 2004: "I've been a cocktail waitress, a bartender, I worked at a grocery store, I did market research, I sold tickets...and one tragic day I sold vacuum cleaners door to door."[479] Although some college grads want lower-level jobs, most grads take these jobs because they can't find anything else.

> **Myth: It's easy for college grads to get <u>some kind</u> of job.**

Although a college degree can give a significant employment advantage to those who graduate, a number of grads have a surprisingly difficult time getting hired. For example, about 3% of college graduates are usually unemployed.[480] This may not sound like much, but in 2004 it added up to more than one million college graduates in the United States who did not have jobs.[481] Unfortunately, unemployment is sometimes a long-term problem for grads: 19% of people who have been unemployed for a long period of time have a college degree.[482] Although some unemployed college grads may not be looking for work, there are always a number of college graduates who want jobs but can't find them.

And, although college degrees are required for many jobs, many employers have a poor opinion of graduates (as described in Chapter 4). For example, employers think that some grads are "underqualified," because they don't have enough practical real-world job experience or specific career abilities. Some employers also think that new grads lack maturity, and don't know how to act within a professional or corporate environment.[483] On the other hand, some employers won't even hire college grads for lower-level jobs, because they think that grads are "overqualified" for the jobs, and they are afraid that college grads: won't like to follow strict instructions; won't get along well with other people at the company; will want salaries that are too high; or will get bored in the jobs and quit.[484] Mel Levine, author of *Ready or Not, Here Life Comes*, says that many employers believe that new college grads "have trouble starting at the bottom rung of a career ladder and handling the unexciting detail, the grunt work, and the political setbacks they have to bear."[485]

However, a recent survey also shows that it's very difficult for many new college graduates to leave jobs that they don't like. In 2004, only about 6% of new graduates voluntarily left their jobs within one year of starting, and this was the lowest quit rate for new graduates in 12 years.[486] Although today's graduates may be staying in their jobs because they enjoy them, experts say that the quit rate is probably low right now because there aren't enough jobs available, so grads have nowhere else to go.[487]

The college payoff is even disappointing for many students who pursue career fields that have been lucrative in the past. Although some superstars do well, a number of graduates in fields like engineering and science have difficulty finding jobs.[488] Employers verify this story, saying that they reject many college graduates in these fields because they have poor job skills,[489] and some employers reject college grads because they would rather hire lower-paid workers to do the jobs, including workers in other countries (through "outsourcing").

THE FUTURE VALUE OF COLLEGE

Despite providing disappointing payoffs for many graduates, college degrees will probably continue to be more valuable than high school degrees (on average), and also be required for most good jobs—but college graduates may unfortunately face more salary and employment challenges in the near future. For example, college graduates' salaries appear to be shrinking. A recent *BusinessWeek* study analyzed U.S. Census data and found that, after adjusting for inflation, college graduates' earnings have fallen during each of the past four years.[490] In fact, young college grads aged 25 to 34 experienced an 8.5% drop in their earnings from 2000 to 2007 (after adjusting for inflation).[491] Although this decline may be a temporary or small deviation, the net payoff of college degrees will probably continue to drop, especially since college costs and debt are rising much faster than grads' salaries.

Also, employers are requiring college grads to complete more work in their jobs, but employers are also delivering fewer employment benefits. For example, many employers expect their college-level employees to work 50 or more hours per week and be available for work at all days and times, even when they are outside the office, through mobile access devices, like laptop computers, the Internet, or a PDA like a Palm Pilot or Blackberry.[492] At the same time, companies are replacing their high-value "defined benefit" retirement pension plans for their employees with risky or lower-value "401(k)" or "defined contribution" retirement plans.[493] Also, many companies now require their employees to pay much more of their healthcare costs than they have in the past.[494] In addition, college grads are usually not eligible to join unions, or receive overtime pay. And corporate job security is a thing of the past, as companies frequently get rid of their workers through "downsizing," "outsourcing," and "offshoring." One recent U.S. Department of Labor study even predicted that college graduates will outnumber available college-level jobs through the year 2012.[495]

THE COLLEGE OVERSPENDING TRAP

One of the most surprising things about the college investment is that higher spending usually doesn't lead to better payoffs. Some students think they will receive higher payoffs by spending more money on college, but, as described throughout this book, this strategy often backfires. When it comes to achieving college success, overspending is usually not the answer.

> **Myth: Expensive colleges provide better payoffs than other colleges.**

As described in Chapter 2, many people think that more expensive colleges are better than other colleges, and schools take advantage of this, raising their prices specifically to get more applicants—and not because they have improved their services or offer a better payoff for students than other colleges. More than 75 colleges charge total prices of at least $40,000 per year,[496] and there's no way that all of them are worth it. The reality is that expensive colleges usually don't offer a better education than other schools (as explained further in Chapter 8), and students usually don't obtain better careers and salaries by spending more on college. In fact, as mentioned in Chapter 1, high college costs actually prevent many people from achieving their dreams.

> **Myth: Prestigious colleges provide better payoffs than other colleges.**

"A degree from [a prestigious college] is no longer the lifetime guarantee of success it may have been in the past."
—"The Humbling of the Harvard Man," *The New York Times*, March 6, 1994

Surprisingly, it can also be wasteful for students to overspend at the most prestigious colleges, because even these schools usually don't lead to higher salaries, on average. Specifically, research studies have shown that students' success depends mostly on the quality of the students themselves, and not on the price or prestige of their colleges.[497] The most definitive research study on this topic, titled "Estimating the Payoff to Attending a More Selective College," compared one set of students who attended prestigious schools with another set of students who were accepted by prestigious schools but attended other schools, and both sets of students earned the same amount of money after they graduated.[498] This study supports the idea that intelligent and motivated students are special before they enroll in college, so they can earn high salaries and gain admission to top graduate schools, even if they go to less prestigious colleges.

Newsweek recently described this situation in an article called "The Worthless Ivy League?": "Going to [a prestigious college] won't automatically produce a better job and higher pay. Graduates of these schools generally do well. But they do well because they are talented."[499] The results from the definitive study also support the idea that a student's success depends less on the exact school he or she attends, and more on his or her family background (including wealth and career contacts), personal qualities, and specific experiences—for better or worse. In short, prestigious colleges are very good at selecting talented and wealthy students during the admission process, and at convincing these students to enroll (especially through the use of financial aid discounts that Robert Massa, vice president for enrollment management at Dickinson College, calls "bribe money"[500]), but prestigious colleges usually don't offer special educational or career advantages over other colleges.

A recent survey of employers also supports the relative unimportance of college prestige, finding that the actual school that students attend is one of the least-important factors that employers consider.[501] Although many employers require their employees to have college degrees, employers tend to use the degree as just a minimum requirement or screening measure. As long as a student's college is "accredited," or approved by an authorized education committee, employers are usually happy. Instead of focusing on where students went to school, employers care more about students' practical (hands-on, "real world") skills and experience.[502] Warren Buffett, the mega-successful investor and CEO of Berkshire Hathaway, says, "I don't care where someone went to school, and that never caused me to hire anyone or buy [anyone's] business."[503]

Some employers even hesitate to hire graduates of prestigious schools due to grade inflation and other recent suspicious grading practices at these schools.[504] In fact, many graduates of prestigious colleges have trouble finding good jobs; ironically, some Ivy League graduates can only find "freelance, part-time, no-benefits" jobs in which they tutor high school students who want to attend Ivy League colleges.[505] Although prestigious colleges usually don't have special payoffs for many students, it's important to note that these schools may be extremely helpful for low-income, racial minority, and female students, especially by presenting some special career opportunities and helping these students to break through some of the barriers that are put in their way.[506] Therefore, prestigious colleges may be worth some extra costs for these student groups—if the costs are still affordable for them.

MANAGING OTHER
IMPORTANT INVESTMENTS AND EXPENSES

"Dear Mom and Dad: I will never be able to convey how appreciative I am for the huge sacrifices you made in paying

for the majority of the cost of my college education. The only way I can truly thank you is by returning this favor some day to my children."

—Neal W. Bonner,
letter to the Editor, *BusinessWeek*, December 5, 2005

Another important reason for families to not overspend on college is that they probably have many other important financial obligations. Although Mr. Bonner is correct to thank his parents for making sacrifices in order to help him pay for college (see above), he unfortunately plays right into colleges' hands—and so do millions of other people. Many parents have great intentions, wanting to give their children the best of everything, and it breaks parents' hearts to think that college in general, or a particular school, is too expensive for them. But colleges exploit this attitude, using it to get families to spend more. In fact, six out of ten Americans who have children under the age of 18 do not expect their children to attend the college or university that will cost their family the least amount of money.[507] Although it's great for parents to help their kids pay for college, families may benefit by limiting their spending.

Instead of overspending, students and families might be better off spending their money on other important expenses. For example, this money might be better spent on after-college costs, including home purchases, weddings, raising kids, vacations, parents' retirement expenses—or even inheritances. In addition, one-third of young people aged 18 to 34 receive regular cash payments from their parents, often because they receive low salaries after college, so parents may want to save some funds for these costs.[508] After all, college is just an early step for students, and just one of many major life expenses.

Also, families can spend their extra money on valuable

investments. For example, although future profits are impossible to predict, the stock market has given investors a "return," or profit, of about 7% each year, on average, over the past 100-200 years, according to University of Pennsylvania Professor of Finance Jeremy Siegel, and many other experts.[509] And many financial companies offer special investment vehicles, like "stock market index mutual funds," that allow people to easily invest in the stocks that represent the average of the entire stock market. Also, people can invest in safer investments, like bonds or certificates of deposit (CDs) that return about 5% per year. In short, families can greatly increase their profits by spending less on college, and spending more on stocks, bonds, CDs, and other financial investments.

Based on the "rates of return" for these financial investments, it's reasonable to wonder whether students should skip college altogether, and invest in these ways—but this logic is off-target. In some ways, this idea is correct, because a stock market investment could have a financial return that is 2 to 5 times better than the return of a college investment (after subtracting taxes and the original investment).[510] However, this idea misses the main point, because students don't necessarily have to choose between spending all of their money on college, or using all of it for other investments. Instead, students can try to have the best of both worlds, by obtaining a valuable degree at a low-cost or affordable price, and then investing the rest of their money in stocks, bonds, CDs, or other valuable investment vehicles. Since college is valuable in more than just financial ways (and required for many good jobs), a college education should probably not be completely sacrificed just for the purpose of making other investments.

In summary, although some people think that parents do their children a favor by overspending on college, parents might help their children much more by spending a reasonable amount on college, and then using the rest of their money for other major purchases, investments, or gifts. Students and families that are able to resist the pressure to overspend are usually much better off. Mr. Bonner might want to consider this strategy as he plans for his kids' college financing...

MANAGING SOCIETY'S COLLEGE INVESTMENT

The U.S. government spends tens of billions of taxpayer dollars on higher education and financial aid each year, but overspending on college is also not a good idea for the government. Specifically, state and local governments alone spend over $70 billion per year on higher education,[511] and the federal government spends more than $80 billion per year just on financial aid for college students.[512] In fact, contrary to popular belief, government spending on college has recently been increasing at a rate of about 3-6% per year,[513] which has been higher than inflation, but colleges continue to raise their prices.[514] And, as mentioned in Chapter 2, colleges receive many tax discounts, including a discount that allows most public and private colleges to pay no taxes at all. Therefore, since the government's money is actually paid for by all taxpayers, government overspending on college is a waste for everyone (except for the colleges and college employees that get rich from it).

> **Myth: American citizens get good value from all of the government money spent on college.**

In particular, a new research study conducted by Richard Vedder, a Distinguished Professor of Economics at Ohio University, shows that economic productivity does not go up when the government spends more on higher education. Specifically, American states that spend more money on college do not make more money.[515] In fact, state and local productivity seem to go down when the government spends more on higher education. And states that spend more on college do not tend to have more college grads. Part of the problem may be that some of this spending is wasted on the many students who drop out without finishing their degrees.

In addition, research studies show that extra government spending on college and financial aid often leads to higher college costs for students![516] Vedder explains this paradox by pointing out that as the government spends more on financial aid, colleges often exploit this aid and raise their prices to deviously get students to spend more. A specific example of this underhanded process was recently seen in Georgia: after Georgia increased its state aid for college students, Georgia's 4-year colleges both increased their prices and reduced the amount of aid that they provided.[517] Also, student loan use skyrocketed after the U.S. government increased the availability of government-sponsored loans in the early 1990s.[518] Therefore, instead of wasting funds by overspending on college and financial aid, it might be better for the government to adjust its spending strategies. Although it's essential for the government to spend a certain amount on higher education in order to maintain a level of quality and allow talented students from all income groups to attend, a tipping point has been reached where too much government spending is often detrimental.

EVALUATING THE COLLEGE INVESTMENT LIKE A FINANCIAL PRO

Even with government intervention, college costs will

probably continue to rise, but students can get good deals right now by pursuing valuable and affordable degrees. Specifically, students can decrease their risk and achieve college success by striving for three primary goals:

1) Pursue a degree that will have adequate value;

2) Enroll at a school where the costs and debt are affordable; and

3) Reduce college expenses as much as possible (especially debt).

In fact, these ideas reflect the basic strategies that financial professionals (like Warren Buffett[519]) use to manage their own investments. Unfortunately, too many students get into trouble because they are encouraged to do the opposite.

• • •

Everything in the book up to this point has revealed common college traps, and the rising costs and risks of what is essentially a high-stakes gamble. Students who are discouraged by this situation may benefit from a special "Appendix for the Adventurous" at the end of this book, which describes some strategies people can use to obtain knowledge and success without going to college. Some students may also benefit from taking a year off between high school and college, to earn income and/or think about what direction they want to pursue (for example, see *The Gap-Year Advantage*, by Haigler and Nelson), but time off may have costs and risks of its own.

On the other hand, since college degrees can provide many benefits and advantages (especially for racial minorities and women), the second half of this book focuses on information that students can use to: minimize the danger of the Great

College Rip-off, steer clear of bad college outcomes, and successfully obtain a valuable degree at a more affordable price. The practical tips continue in the next two chapters, which focus on crucial college cost-cutting techniques that are often underutilized by students.

CHAPTER 6

ATTENTION SHOPPERS!
The Hidden Costs of "Financial Aid"
and How to Make the Discounts Work for You

One of the best ways for students to cut their college costs is to make excellent use of the college financial aid system—but some kinds of financial aid can actually add to students' costs. Although financial aid may make students feel like colleges are doing them a favor, much aid is designed to get students to pay more. In fact, the amount of discounts students receive is irrelevant. Instead, as with any other purchase, the amount of money spent is more important than the amount of money saved. And, even with financial aid, too many students are spending too much.

Therefore, to help students get the best college deals, this chapter explains: the true costs and benefits of different kinds of aid, how schools figure out how much each student should pay, how students can evaluate schools' financial aid offers, and how students can negotiate better deals that will allow them to get large amounts of "good" aid, and avoid "risky" aid.

FREE COLLEGE CLASSES

Of course, the best kind of college discount is one that lets students take college classes for free. And one of the best ways for students to take college classes for free, or get free college credit, is to take college classes at no cost while in high school.

There are a few ways for high school students to take

free college classes. For example, many high schools offer "Advanced Placement" (AP) classes, and students who do well in AP classes can save money by getting "college credit" that counts toward their college degrees. Many students take advantage of this opportunity: more than one million high school students took AP classes in 2004.[520]

Also, some high schools allow students to take classes at local colleges for free. And the Bill and Melinda Gates Foundation spent over $100 million from 2001-2004 to create over 40 "hybrid," "dual enrollment," or "early college" schools that allow students to earn an Associate's degree, or 2 years of a bachelor's degree, for free while they are in high school.[521]

Since some colleges now charge about $3,000 or $4,000 for a single class, free college credits are often worth thousands of dollars. And high school students who do well in advanced classes can prove that they are ready for college-level work, impressing college admissions departments, and improving their chances of getting accepted to the colleges of their choice.[522] Also, students who don't go to college may earn higher salaries if they take college classes while in high school.

To find out if their schools offer any classes that may count toward college credit later, high school students can check with their schools, or with the College Board (http://apcentral.collegeboard.com). In fact, the College Board's website includes a list of the AP classes that are accepted by each college (www.collegeboard.com/ap/creditpolicy). On the other hand, students who take difficult college classes in high school may feel overwhelmed, perform poorly, and hurt their academic record, so high school students may want to limit their participation in college classes,

THE MOST COMMON KINDS OF FINANCIAL AID

Free college classes are great—when they're available. But students often can't take many—or any—college classes for free. Luckily for students, the good news is that they can use "financial aid" money and discounts to help them pay for their college or graduate education and expenses. For example, the following kinds of "good" financial aid are available for students:

- "Scholarships," or aid that does not have to be paid back. Students can receive scholarships from many different sources, including high schools, colleges, the government, and other organizations. Scholarships are usually given to students as a "merit aid" reward for academic achievements, or some other important personal characteristic (including having excellent school grades or high test scores).

- "Grants," that also don't have to be paid back, are also available from many sources. Grants are often a form of "need-based aid," for less-wealthy students, and the most common government grant for college is called the "Pell Grant."

- "Tuition waivers," or "tuition remission," can make it possible for college students to take classes for free (or at a big discount). These discounts are sometimes available from colleges for some of their students who work on-campus, so students can ask their colleges' financial aid offices about the availability of this aid.

- "Tuition reimbursement" discounts, which can cover all or most of students' tuition expenses, are often given by employers to their employees who take classes while they work part-time or full-time. Some employers pay for all, or most, of their employees' tuition expenses. Students can ask their employers about this type of discount; and

- "Tax benefits" lead to discounts when students spend money on their education costs. These benefits often reduce the amount of taxes that students pay, so these discounts come from the government.

On the other hand, students should watch out for "risky" financial aid, like:

- "Loans," that students borrow and then must pay back at a later time; and

- "Work-study jobs," which are usually part-time jobs on college campuses that allow students to earn income. The specific dangers of loans and work-study jobs will be discussed later in this chapter.

APPLYING FOR FINANCIAL AID

In order to get <u>any</u> kind of financial aid, students are usually required to apply, and every student should apply Studies show that millions of eligible students leave money on the table by not applying for aid,[523] but almost everyone can receive financial aid, regardless of how much money they have, what their gender or race or religion is, or how good a student they are. Specifically, students can receive "need aid," based on their finances, and "merit aid," based on their grades, test scores, and other achievements or aptitudes. And offers of "financial aid" usually aren't binding, so students are allowed to reject any aid that is offered to them, if they choose to do so. Therefore, applying for aid isn't a waste of time, and it doesn't put students in any danger. Students have absolutely nothing to lose by applying, and everything to gain. In fact, many students receive both "merit aid" and "need-based aid," even if they are wealthy.

The most common financial aid application used by almost all colleges is the FAFSA (Free Application for Federal Student Aid). As it says in the name, the FAFSA is <u>free</u>, so any student can apply for financial aid at no cost, and students should not pay anyone for this application. The FAFSA application is available at the website www.fafsa.ed.gov, or by calling 1-800-4-FED-AID (1-800-433-3243) or 1-319-337-5665 (or 1-800-730-8913 TTY for the hearing-impaired). This application is also often available at high schools, colleges, universities, and some libraries and government offices.

On the other hand, some colleges require students to fill out a <u>CSS/PROFILE aid application</u>. This application is available at www.collegeboard.com/?student, as well as at some schools, libraries and government offices. The application is also available by calling 1-305-829-9793 (or 1-800-915-9990 for the hearing-impaired). Unfortunately, this application is not free; students must pay a fee for it. However, some low-income students can apply through their high schools to receive a "fee waiver," so that they don't have to pay the fee.

Students who want financial aid must complete a new application every year, starting in the first year that they go to college. The earliest that someone can apply for financial aid is January 1st during the year that they expect to take college classes. And it's a good idea for students to fill out financial aid applications as early in the year as they can, because students who apply early may get more "good" aid, before these discounts are given away to other students. Since every college can have a different financial aid application deadline, students must check with their schools to find out when the applications are due. Some colleges also have their own special financial aid applications that students need to complete.

Applying for financial aid is sometimes a little tricky, but anyone can receive <u>free</u> financial aid information and advice at websites like www.studentaid.ed.gov or www.fafsa.ed.gov, or by calling 1-800-4-FED-AID (1-800-433-3243) or 1-319-337-5665 (or 1-800-730-8913 TTY for the hearing-impaired). A very valuable "Student Guide to Financial Aid" is also available at these locations, or www.studentaid.ed.gov/pubs and http://studentaid.ed.gov/students/publications/student_guide/index.html. And free aid information is often also available at many high schools, colleges, universities, and some libraries and government offices.

After students apply for financial aid, they receive a report of results, called the "Student Aid Report" (SAR), and they receive financial aid offers from each college that accepts them.

Some other financial aid websites that may be helpful include:

- **FinAid** (www.finaid.com);
- **PIRGs' Higher Education Project** (www.studentaidaction.com);
- **National Association of Student Financial Aid Administrators** (www.studentaid.org); and
- **Peterson's College Planner** (www.petersons.com).

AVOIDING FINANCIAL AID SCAMS

Unfortunately, students need to protect themselves from private companies that try to take advantage of their desire to obtain financial aid. For example, some companies say that they can help students get scholarships or good financial aid packages, but many of these companies are a rip-off, because they charge thousands of dollars but don't deliver on their promises. Some companies even charge students for applications and services that students could get for free from their high schools, local colleges, libraries, government offices, or websites.

In 2002, about 500 students and their families filed complaints about financial aid companies.[524] And, as part of its "Project ScholarScam" program (www.ftc.gov/bcp/conline/edcams/scholarship/ or www.ftc.gov/scholalrshipscams), the government has sued the following companies for allegedly scamming 175,000 people out of a total of $22 million: Career Assistance Planning (CAP); Collegiate Assistance Services; Deco Consulting Services; National Grant Foundation; National Scholarship Foundation; Higher Education Scholarship Program; Student Assistance Services (formerly known as Student Financial Services); and Student Aid Incorporated.[525] Unfortunately, despite these efforts, many other financial aid frauds still exist.

A number of clues may alert students to the possibility that an aid company is dangerous. For example, an aid company could be a fraud if: it promises to find scholarships or aid information that students can't find on their own; it offers "free seminars," but then tries to get people to pay;[526] it "guarantees" to get scholarships for students; it charges application fees or asks for students' credit card or bank account information; it says it will do all of the work in getting financial aid for the student; or it tells students that they have been selected for aid they never applied for.[527]

Students who really want to work with private aid companies should do their homework. For example, students can ask people they know, including people at high schools and colleges, if they have ever heard of the companies.[528] Students can also contact the Better Business Bureau, at (800) 6-THE BBB or www.bbb.org, to see if anyone has complained about the aid companies. Finally, students can try to find information about the aid companies on the Internet, including at www.finaid.com/scholarships/scams.phtml.

Financial aid is similar to most aspects of life in that there are no guarantees, so offers of aid that sound too good to be true are probably scams (especially when the offers come from unfamiliar organizations). Therefore, students (and their families) should probably avoid suspicious companies, and they should never give their bank account or credit card information to a person or company that they do not know well or trust.

HOW COLLEGES DECIDE THE PRICE EACH STUDENT SHOULD PAY

Due to financial aid, each student can pay a different price for college, even within the same school. Colleges decide the price each student should pay by looking at the results of students' financial aid applications. Aid applications require students to report most of their (and their families') money, including income, cash, bank accounts, stocks, bonds, real estate, trust funds, and "529" savings plans.[529] Colleges then use this information to decide what students' costs should be, and how much aid they should receive.

Specifically, colleges often use students' wealth information to calculate students' "Expected Family Contribution," or

"EFC." The EFC is the minimum amount of money that schools usually ask students (and their families) to pay, each year, while the students are enrolled. Since the EFC is a portion of students' total wealth, families that have more money are usually required to pay more.

Colleges also use the EFC to decide how much financial aid to offer to students, by subtracting students' EFCs from the schools' advertised "sticker prices." For example, if a college's sticker price, or advertised full price, is $40,000 per year, and a student's EFC is $10,000 per year, then the college may offer the student $30,000 in financial aid ($40,000-$10,000 = $30,000; see formula below). And colleges typically fill this gap with grants, scholarships, loans, or work-study jobs. If a student's EFC is higher than a college's sticker price, then the student will probably not receive any "need-based" financial aid at that school.

Financial Aid = College's Sticker Price − Student's EFC

Unfortunately, students don't find out how much financial aid they will truly be offered until after they submit their applications to colleges, but it's possible for students to estimate their aid before they receive formal offers from schools, so that they know what kinds of college costs to expect. First, students can estimate their EFCs by looking at the "Student Aid Report" they receive after completing their financial aid applications. In addition, students can estimate their EFCs at any time (even before applying to colleges) by entering their families' wealth information into the free EFC calculators available at websites like these:

- **College Parents of America** (www.collegeparents.org/cpa/

family-contribution-calculator.html);
- **Federal Student Aid Guide** (www.studentaid.ed.gov/pubs; click on "EFC");
- **FinAid** (http://finaid.com/calculators/finaidestimate.phtml);
- **Peterson's College Planner** (http://petersons.com/finaid/efcsimplecalc.asp?sponsor=1&path=ug.pfs.federal); and
- **The Official FAFSA site** (www.fafsa.ed.gov).

Then, students can use their EFC estimates to also estimate how much aid each college will offer to them, by subtracting their EFC from each school's sticker price (as described in the formula above). In addition, as described in Chapter 2, "merit aid" scholarships can lower students' EFC costs, but it's almost impossible for students to predict how much merit aid they will receive. Therefore, to be safe, students should expect that colleges will require them to pay their entire estimated EFC costs. Although students will probably also have other college costs, including loans, they can use their estimated EFC to predict many of their immediate college costs.

In fact, students may be able to obtain a financial aid estimate from colleges before they apply for admission or aid. To do so, students can usually just send their families' most-recent tax return forms (along with their request for an aid estimate) to the college's financial aid office. Students can then use these aid estimates to calculate their potential costs at each school. And, since most students receive financial aid for college, it's more important for them to focus on their actual potential costs rather than on colleges' published tuition sticker prices. Due to financial aid, students may even pay lower costs at colleges that have higher tuition sticker prices.

HOW SAVING UP FOR COLLEGE CAN CREATE EXTRA COSTS FOR STUDENTS

"Saving money is the best way to prepare for meeting the costs of college."
—excerpt from "Paying for College: It Pays to Save," published by the U.S. Government's Initiative on Educational Excellence for Hispanic Americans[530]

As this quote shows, it's often said that students (and their families) should save up money for college—but saving up can actually <u>increase</u> students' college costs. Since colleges offer financial aid to students based on how much money students have, students who have more money saved up for college will receive lower grants and higher costs. On the other hand, students who have less money saved up are usually rewarded with more scholarships and grants, and lower college costs.

In fact, several recent articles report that some financial experts now suggest that parents and students should <u>not</u> save up money to pay for college, including "Why Not to Save for Your Kids' College Years," by the American Association of Retired Persons (AARP).[531] Financial planner Sean Sebold admits that, when he suggested to parents that they not save up for their children's college expenses, the parents "looked at me as if I was crazy at first."[532] But this unconventional advice is based on solid facts and research; for example, Harvard University researcher Susan Dynarski closely studied the financial aid system and she concluded that, "Under current tax and financial aid policies, saving for their children's college education can make parents worse off than if they never saved at all."[533] Tom Muldowney, a financial planner, adds, "people who save aggressively for their kids' education often do not have enough money for themselves at retirement."[534]

It's sometimes said that students who don't save up enough money for college will either not be able to afford college, or will have to borrow a large amount of loans to pay for school—but these fears are not necessarily true. For example, students who don't save up for college should be able to use scholarships and grants to pay for school, including government aid like Pell grants. And plenty of lower-cost colleges are available for students, including public schools. In contrast, schools often require students who save for college to both: a) pay high EFCs, <u>and</u> b) borrow large amounts of money.

Therefore, students should be especially careful before using any college "savings plans," including "pre-paid tuition plans," "529 savings plans," "Coverdell plans," "IRAs," "Upromise," and "BabyMint" (even though some of these plans are supported by the government). All of these kinds of plans could reduce the amount of grants and scholarships that students are offered. These plans also have additional dangers, such as:

- The plans often charge a "penalty fee," if the money is not used for education costs (e.g., if the student decides not to go to college);
- The plans don't guarantee a specific financial payoff, because they're usually tied to the stock or bond markets (so they can lose money or increase more slowly than expected);
- The plans probably won't cover all of the costs of college, because college prices are rising too fast; and
- The plans can cost students a large amount of money in extra fees.

In addition, private savings plans like Upromise and BabyMint provide rebates based on credit card spending (and they often encourage students to buy their investment products), so they can be harmful if they encourage people to spend more than they normally would, build up too much credit card debt, or buy investments that aren't right for them.[535] Upromise and BabyMint also track their members' purchases, and sometimes share their members' personal information with other companies.[536] Therefore, the costs of these "rebate savings plans" may outweigh the typically small benefits. Above all, students need to remember that many college savings plans are products sold by corporations that profit from them. For example, Upromise was recently bought by Sallie Mae,[537] the largest and most profitable student loan lender, and BabyMint was recently bought by Collegiate Funding Services, another major college loan lender.[538] So, before students and their families register for (or invest in) any college savings plans, they should weigh the plans' limitations and dangers, and not depend on the plans to solve all of their college payment challenges.

On the other hand, students and their families should probably save up a basic amount of money for college, because it's always good to have a "safety net" in case of emergency. And wealthy students should probably save up as much as they can, because they likely won't receive any college grants (although they may be eligible for merit aid, even if they save up for college). But any student or family that saves up for college should usually not save the money in the student's name, because schools often try to take a total of 60-75% of students' money over 4-6 years, while taking a lower percentage of parents' money (about 5% per year, or a total of 20-30% during 4-6 years).[539] In addition, people who want to use formal college savings plans should focus on the "savings plans" instead of the "pre-paid tuition plans," because the savings plans usually have much lower costs for students and families, and will allow them to receive more financial aid.[540] Families can find out more about college savings plans sponsored by each state at the "Saving for College" website (www.savingforcollege.com).

And there are some techniques that families can use to safely save up money for other expenses, without being penalized by schools. For example, the formula that some colleges use to calculate students' EFCs does not count the following kinds of savings: retirement accounts (e.g., IRAs, 401(k)s, 403(b)s, Keoghs), "home equity" for primary residences, annuities, and cash value life insurance policies.[541]

It makes sense for families to try to save up money in these ways for other expenses, because, although financial aid discounts are available for college, there's no financial aid for buying a home or paying for retirement, so families need as much money as possible for these kinds of expenses. Warren McIntyre, a financial planner, agrees: "There are many ways to pay for college. However, with retirement, you get just one chance. If you have neglected retirement funding, you could be out of luck in the future."[542] And researcher Susan Dynarski takes a similar view: "Probably the best way to save [money] is by paying down your mortgage, [since] home equity does not count at all in the [schools'] aid formula."[543]

In fact, families are allowed to withdraw money from their homes or retirement accounts, if they need it to pay for college or other expenses! FinAid.com has more information about the benefits and limitations of these withdrawals at http://www.finaid.com/savings/retirementplans.phtml.

On the other hand, it's important to note that some colleges penalize families who own homes or have money in their retirement accounts. Every college has different financial aid rules, and many colleges try to increase their income by using their own aid formulas (instead of relying on the formula recommended by the government), so students should check with individual schools to confirm which kinds of assets will count against their financial need.

"FINANCIAL AID"...OR "COSTS IN DISGUISE"?

After evaluating students' wealth, colleges then offer them financial aid packages, but many of the most common kinds of financial "aid" can (ironically) actually increase students' college costs. Like so many other aspects of higher education, aid is often designed to assist the college first, and the student second. So, to get the best deals, students need to minimize their use of the following "risky" kinds of aid.

Outside scholarships and grants

Although scholarships and grants are the best kinds of financial aid, colleges usually don't allow students to benefit from scholarships and grants that they obtain from sources outside the colleges, using this aid to replace scholarships and grants the colleges were going to provide anyway (as described in Chapter 2). Therefore, it's often a waste for students to even look for outside scholarships and grants (although wealthy students may benefit from outside scholarships, because they probably won't receive any grants from colleges anyway).

Loans

Many colleges also try to create a nice warm feeling of trust by saying that they will meet "all of a student's financial needs," but this is not really true; colleges usually fulfill this misleading promise by socking students with loans they can't afford (as mentioned earlier). Although loans can help students pay for college, loans often have high costs that require students to pay dearly for this "privilege." Therefore, the next chapter will present some important strategies that students can use to avoid borrowing too much.

Work-study jobs

Work-study jobs can also help students pay for college and prepare for careers, but these jobs often have some drawbacks. For example, working for pay can reduce students' study time, especially since many college students work long hours. A recent study supported this idea by finding that working for pay harmed class grades for four out of ten working high school students,[544] and many college graduates say that jobs affected their study time, grades, and ability to participate in internships and other extracurricular activities while in college.[545] Alexis Wolff, a Yale University senior, spent a total of 1,680 hours laboring in work-study jobs during her 4-year college career, and says: "My more affluent Yale classmates had at least 1,680 more hours to dedicate to their classes, reading *The Wall Street Journal,* or writing poetry. No matter how great my innate poetry skills, whom would you predict to be the better poet—me, or the kid with 1,680 more hours of practice?"[546] Working in any job can also increase the possibility that students will drop out of school altogether.

Another problem with work-study jobs is that they usually offer very low salaries, close to "minimum wage"[547]—or about $5.15 per hour in most areas of the country. For example, in 2004, work-study students from at least 15 Massachusetts colleges earned only $6-10 an hour, including students at Babson College, Boston University, Brandeis College, Emerson College, Harvard University, Northeastern University, Smith College, the University of Massachusetts, and Wellesley College.[548] Also, students who have work-study jobs usually don't receive any employment benefits (such as health insurance), and student workers aren't allowed to unionize, or join together, to try to obtain better compensation.[549] Work-study programs benefit colleges by providing them with inexpensive workers and money from the government, but students who take these jobs often receive much lower salaries than they could get at other jobs, especially since a number of regular (non-work-study) jobs off-campus pay more than $10 an hour for students (and some of these jobs offer benefits).

Although work-study jobs offer some important opportunities, students might be better off using their time to study, or work in higher-paying jobs off-campus, instead of participating in college work-study programs.

Tax benefits

Education tax benefits, such as tax deductions and tax credits (e.g., the "Hope Scholarship Credit" and the "Lifetime Learning Credit"), can help students by reducing their income tax costs.[550] However, these discounts are often not that valuable, and they can encourage students to spend too much. First, students have to spend a large amount of money on school before they can receive a tax benefit. For example, students must spend $4,000 on their education expenses in one year to save only $1,200 from a tax deduction (the maximum amount). And students must spend $10,000 on their education expenses in one year to save only $2,000 from a tax credit (the maximum amount). Many students can't afford to spend this much on their education, especially not during every year that they are in school. In addition, students can only receive up to $750 per year from loan interest tax deductions—and they must pay $2,500 in interest charges in one year to get this full 'benefit.'

Also, there are strict limits about which kinds of students can take advantage of tax benefits. For example, students aren't eligible for some or all education tax benefits if they and their families earn more than $41,000-$65,000 in gross salary each year (or $130,000 for couples filing jointly). On the other hand, students who earn very low salaries may not have to pay much money in taxes anyway, so tax discounts won't really help them much either. Therefore, tax benefits are often a misleading paradox, because they're only available for people who don't earn much, but the only way that people save money from the discounts is by spending a lot on college costs—something low-income folks usually can't afford to do.

Although it's usually not a good idea for students to spend or borrow <u>extra</u> money for education just so they can receive a tax benefit, people should use any tax benefits they're already eligible for, while also keeping their costs at an affordable level. In particular, tax credits tend to be more valuable than tax deductions. Students can find out more about education tax benefits at http://www.finaid.com/otheraid/tax.phtml or by contacting the U.S. Internal Revenue Service at www.irs.gov or 800-829-1040.

EVALUATING FINANCIAL AID OFFERS

Since some kinds of financial aid are expensive for students, how can students figure out which college is least expensive for them? The answer is that, after students receive financial aid offers from all schools that accept them, students can calculate their potential costs for each school, compare offers, and figure out which schools will have the lowest costs for them. In this way, "financial aid offers" are really "college cost offers."

As mentioned above, when students calculate their potential costs at each college, they can surprisingly ignore both colleges' sticker prices and the overall amount of financial aid offered by each school. Instead, the key for students is to focus on their expected "out-of-pocket costs," or what it will actually cost them to attend each school they are considering. Students can use their financial aid offers to calculate their potential out-of-pocket costs for each school by adding up their expected immediate and future costs like:

- EFCs;
- Loans (including future interest charges);
- Work-study packages; and
- Any other costs that are not covered by financial aid, including housing, food, transportation/travel, and books.

Students can use the calculator at www.finaid.com/calculators/awardletter.phtml to help them figure out which colleges will be most expensive and least expensive for them. This calculator may underestimate some college costs, but it is useful for comparing the relative costs of different schools.

A handful of colleges now offer excellent financial aid packages to low-income students, reducing these students' immediate out-of-pocket costs and/or loan amounts to almost zero. For example, private colleges like Harvard University[551] and Princeton University are trying these kinds of programs, and so are public colleges like the University of Virginia, the University of North Carolina, Michigan State University, Miami University in Ohio, and Rice University. Unfortunately, many of the schools that offer these deals ironically don't accept many low-income students.[552] However, eligible students can look for these kinds of programs, especially if they have excellent credentials and they can afford the schools' application fees. A list of colleges that offer these programs is available at: http://www.finaid.com/questions/noloansforlowincome.phtml

MANAGING THE COLLEGE PRICING "BAIT AND SWITCH" TRAP

Even when students carefully evaluate each college offer they receive, they can't perfectly predict their total college costs, especially because colleges often use a "bait and switch" technique to change students' financial aid packages and raise their costs every year (as mentioned in Chapter 2). Specifically, colleges raise students' costs when students' income or wealth increases. Colleges also often take away students' scholarships if the students do not maintain a "B" average (or higher) in their classes. And, worst of all, colleges usually increase students' loans each year; for example, colleges often raise students' "subsidized" Stafford loans from $3,500 in the first year, to $4,500 in the second year, to $5,500 for every year after the second year, which is an increase of 22-29% each year. In this way, students' college costs and risks get significantly higher each year. So, students should try to cut their first-year costs as much as possible, to establish a lower starting point.

Some colleges have developed "fixed tuition" plans, which are also called "fixed rate," "levelized," "tuition lock," or "tuition guarantee" plans, that allow students to pay stable costs each year—but these plans are expensively misleading. For example, George Washington University offers a "fixed tuition plan" that allows students to receive the same financial aid package and pay the same tuition rate, each year, for all four or five years that they are at the school.[553] A number of colleges within Colorado and Georgia offer similar plans.[554] However, these plans usually don't lower students' overall costs. Instead, the plans simply add up the estimated costs for four or five years of college, take the average of these costs, and then spread these costs out evenly during each year.

Therefore, although these students pay the same price each year, they pay more than the market rate during at least their first one or two years. This is especially dangerous for students who drop out after one or two years, because the plan requires them to pay more during these years than they would without the plan. Although "fixed tuition plans" make college costs more predictable for students, these plans don't make college more affordable, especially since a number of students who use these plans pay higher total costs than students who don't use the plans. Students should consider these factors before enrolling in any of these plans.

NEGOTIATING BETTER COLLEGE DEALS

The good news for students is that financial aid packages are often open to negotiation, just like buying a car or house. In fact, students can often obtain better financial aid packages, and lower costs, just by writing to colleges and asking for these improvements.[555]

It's stunning that such a simple technique can help students save thousands of dollars, but this strategy often works. Four out of ten four-year private colleges, and three out of ten four-year public colleges, say that they will change their financial aid offers for students, especially when they receive new information about students' financial situation.[556] During this process, students should try to get colleges to give them more "good" aid, and remove more "risky" aid from their deals. In particular, students should try to get colleges to reduce their loan burden.

When students write a letter in response to a college's financial aid offer, there are a number of powerful things they can say to explain why they should receive a better offer. For example:

- If a student's family has experienced any major negative financial changes, the student should mention these changes;
- Students can also explain that they need their costs reduced because they intend to pursue low-paying careers (if this is true); and
- Students who have received better offers from other colleges can mention this in a general way in their letters, without sharing any specific details; it may even be helpful to ask a school why its offer is not as generous as another's. Colleges may try to attract students by matching, or beating, other schools' aid offers. Some first-year, second-year, and third-year college students even apply to transfer to other schools, just so they can obtain competing aid offers they can then use to bargain with their own school.

Although students spend much of the admissions process trying to convince schools to accept them, the balance of power can shift slightly toward students during the aid negotiation process, as they work to try to solidify a good college fit by getting their costs reduced to an amount they can afford. Students are in a particularly good position at this point in the process because colleges have already accepted them and would like them to enroll.

The financial aid negotiation process is serious business, but it should be as friendly and non-confrontational as possible. After all, angry or rude behavior by students (or their families) probably won't encourage colleges to provide better offers.

THE FUTURE OF COLLEGE COSTS

There are many actions that the government can take to make college more affordable for students. For example, the government can: encourage colleges to keep students' total out-of-pocket costs affordable (including loans); encourage colleges, loan lenders, and credit card companies to set affordable student debt limits and/or payments based on students' current or future salaries; encourage student loan lenders and credit card companies to lower their interest rates and fees; encourage loan lenders to receive much lower guaranteed government loan subsidies (and then use some of the savings for student grants); encourage colleges to offer a better selection of less-expensive loans (e.g., Direct Loans) for students who must use loans; encourage colleges to accept and provide aid for a larger number of talented low-income students; and possibly require all colleges to pay taxes (especially private colleges), or at least implement an "endowment, sports, and research luxury tax" for very wealthy colleges, and then use this tax money to pay for "Robin Hood" student grants at less wealthy colleges.

It's important to note that these kinds of changes may be much more essential than simply controlling college tuition prices. For example, if colleges are only required to limit their tuition prices, they will still be able to encourage students to incur high debt, and college will remain unaffordable. Instead, it's time to revisit past debt limits: as mentioned in the next chapter, the government used to have much tighter restrictions on consumer debt until it dangerously "deregulated" debt in 1978. It just doesn't make sense to hamper our best and brightest college students with excessive costs and debt that prevent them from making positive contributions to the country.

Therefore, to get better deals, students, their families, and taxpayers can use their influence to encourage politicians to create new laws that make college more affordable. For example, people can contact their specific government representatives, or they can contact members of the United States Committee on Education and the Workforce Committee. A full list of current Republican and Democratic members of this Committee is available at: http://edworkforce.house.gov/members/109th/memfc.htm. Also, people can learn more about the government's financial aid strategies by looking at the Committee's website (http://edworkforce.house.gov, and http://edworkforce.house.gov/issues/issues.htm, and http://edworkforce.house.gov/democrats/). A large amount of this information is often politically biased, but each of these sites tends to portray one particular point-of-view, so people can obtain a more balanced perspective by reading all of these sites.

• • •

Although the government has the power to make some positive changes for students, colleges and government currently continue to strongly encourage students to borrow too much, so students must take steps to protect themselves from excessive debt. Therefore, the next chapter describes some critical tips that students can use to figure out how much debt they can afford, as well as strategies they can use to lower their debt costs.

CHAPTER 7

AVOIDING THE COLLEGE DEBT TRAP

"I wish they would give you more information [about debt when you start college]...but then you would realize that you can't afford [college]."
—Kim Wilson, recent college graduate[557]

Angel Fox, the first person in her family to go to college, lived very frugally and saved up money for her education, even renting a room in a funeral home at one point, and hoped to become a public defender. She says: "I wanted to help people who don't have the means to help themselves." However, after graduating from law school in Ohio, Angel realized that she would have a very high monthly student loan bill, so she sacrificed her dreams and took a higher-paying job at an insurance company.[558]

Justin Anderson, a student at Johns Hopkins University, dreamed of becoming a teacher, until he figured out how much it would cost him to repay his $101,000 in student loans. He says: "I realized it would take forever to pay down this debt with a teacher's salary." Therefore, Justin took a high-paying job as an investment banker instead.[559]

Trevor Montgomery, a senior majoring in political science at the University of Illinois in Chicago, says, "I'm starting the job search process thinking about the $20,000 [in student loans I owe], thinking about how much that's going to cost, and it's playing a huge part [in my job search]. Some of the jobs I want the most are paying salaries [that will barely allow me to afford to pay my loan bills]. It stinks [that my job search will be affected by] those things."[560]

Unfortunately, Angel, Justin, and Trevor learned an ironic, but common, lesson: although colleges and graduate schools are supposed to provide students with more opportunities for success, high education costs can actually prevent people from achieving their educational, personal, financial, and career dreams. While debt can open some doors, making it possible for students to go to college, debt can also close doors and stifle graduates' options. Max Steir, the president and chief executive officer of the Partnership for Public Service, says, "The effect [of debt] on young people is enormous. The kinds of choices they might have had a generation ago are not available to young people today because of [their] enormous debt."[561]

As illustrated throughout this book, the problem is that colleges often actively encourage students to borrow much more money than they can afford. Specifically, colleges include too much loan debt in students' financial aid packages, and actively expose students to the aggressive marketing of credit cards. Everett Orr, head of a financial planning firm, says, "I'm alarmed by the [amount of] debt people take. They think everyone's doing it. [Parents and students] think it's normal...[but] it's not."[562] Since both loans and credit cards can be dangerous if they aren't used properly, students need to minimize their debt, and borrow as little money as possible. In particular, students need to figure out how much debt they can afford, and then avoid schools that require them to borrow more than they can handle. But exactly how much debt can students afford?

GENERATION DEBT

Average loan debt for a college graduate: **$23,000**
Average credit card debt for a college graduate: **$3,000**
A lifetime of crippling debt: **Priceless!**

The question is, priceless for whom—the student, or the college that makes money on the debt? As described in Chapter 1, many college students and graduates struggle with a number of problems due to their educational debt, including bankruptcy, depression, and unfulfilled dreams.

Indeed, debt is widespread among college students and graduates. About seven out of ten college students in both private and public schools use loans to help them pay for college,[563]—and student loan use is escalating. Each year, about 7 million students (and their families) use federal loans (supported by the government) to help pay for college,[564] and 20% of student borrowing comes from expensive non-government "private loans" (up from 4% in 1995 and 12% in 2000).[565] And student loan debt is rising quickly: even after considering inflation, average loan debt has increased by more than 50% during just the past decade.[566]

Also, about eight out of ten college students have credit cards, and the average student has four cards.[567] And students are using their credit cards for essential expenses, not luxury purchases: more than seven out of ten college students use credit cards to pay for school supplies (74%), textbooks (71%), or food (71%), and one-quarter of students use their cards to pay for tuition (24%).[568]

In addition, many college students and graduates have above-average debt. For example, one out of four graduates leave college with more than $25,000 in loan debt, and one out of ten have more than $33,000 in loan debt.[569] Also, more than one in ten college students owe $7,000 or more to credit card companies.[570] In 2004, all U.S. college students together owed a total of $2 billion in credit card debt.[571] And this doesn't even include graduate school debt!

TAKING AN INTEREST: HOW "INTEREST CHARGES" MAKE COLLEGES AND BANKS RICH AT STUDENTS' EXPENSE

In some ways, students' debt levels may not seem that high, because many people borrow even larger amounts to buy things like cars and homes. However, students' educational debt costs are often much higher than people expect.

First, debt is extremely dangerous because it includes interest charges that can add thousands of dollars to a borrower's costs. These charges are added from the day the money is borrowed until the day it's all paid back. So, someone who takes 20 years to pay back a debt will usually pay 20 years of interest charges. One thing that makes debt so expensive is that interest charges can "compound," or build on each other.

Interest charges are based on the "interest rate," which is a percentage of the total amount of money that still has to be paid back. Therefore, higher interest rates have higher costs. For example, in 2004, some student loan interest rates were at the lowest level they had ever been, about 3%, but student loan rates can be as high as 20%. Credit card rates are usually even higher, averaging 15%[572] (and going up to as much as 29%).[573] The interest rate actually represents the total amount of interest charges for an entire year, but lenders use this rate to calculate interest charges that are added to the debt every day.

In short, students' total debt costs are based on three

factors: 1) the "interest rate;" 2) the principal balance (amount of money that still needs to be paid back); and 3) the "repayment period," or the amount of time that it will take to pay back all of the money. Borrowers pay higher costs when they have high interest rates, high balances, and/or long repayment periods.

STUDENTS' ACTUAL DEBT COSTS

Therefore, although the calculations in Chapter 5 conservatively estimated that student loans cost a total of $32,400 (on average, including interest charges), a $23,000 student loan debt can easily cost a total of about $45,000-$55,000, including a total of about $22,000-$32,000 in interest charges (over 30 years, assuming interest charges at a 5%-8% interest rate, and not counting possible tax deductions that can reduce costs).[574] Also, since credit card interest rates are much higher, credit interest charges can easily add up to hundreds or thousands of dollars each year, even for debts of only $3,000.

In addition, loan lenders and credit card companies also often charge many expensive extra fees. These include "loan origination fees" that are added to students' bills every semester, and interest rate increases when students are late in paying their credit card bills by as little as one minute.[575] In fact, many students see their original loan balances double, triple, or quadruple, just because of lenders' excessive extra fees, and penalties.[576] Former student Alan Collinge, creator of StudentLoanJustice.org, graduated with $45,000 of student debt in 1999, and this debt ballooned to $103,000 in 2006 due to extra charges.[577] In this way, students can pay for their college expenses, including textbooks and pizza, for many years after they graduate.

These charges and fees help to explain why college

graduates use up a large chunk of their net (after-tax) salaries on their debt, especially when they have low salaries. For example, graduates who earn gross salaries of $31,000 per year ($1,808 per month, after taxes) and spend "just" $300 a month on loans and credit costs are using about 17% of their net salaries for these costs. This percentage is a very high "debt-to-income" ratio.

In fact, as mentioned in Chapter 1, about four out of ten student loan borrowers graduate with "unmanageable loan debt," which is defined by experts as 8% or more of their gross income.[578] This may not seem like a large amount, but 8% of gross income can be 11% of net income for new grads—and many people spend an even higher percentage of their salaries on their loan debt (especially if they also have credit debt). For example, one-third of borrowers spend 12% or more of their gross salaries on their loans (potentially 17% of their net salaries, or more), and one out of ten borrowers use more than 20% of their gross salaries (potentially 30% of net salaries, or more).[579] This helps to explain why four out of ten recent college graduates think that their student loans were not worth it.[580]

It's easy to see that many college grads have very little money left over after paying for their debt, housing, food, taxes, transportation, and utilities. Paige Nichols, a recent graduate who has an average amount of debt and earns a higher-than-average salary, says: "[My total amount of debt] isn't even that much, but it feels hefty."[581]

Many graduates who struggle with unmanageable student debt have added their stories to the Student Loan Justice Testimonial Website (http://www.studentloanjustice.org/victims.htm).

LENDERS GONE WILD

While college graduates struggle to manage their hefty debt loads, many lenders and credit card companies take advantage of students and taxpayers to obtain massive wealth. For example, Sallie Mae is the largest student loan lender by far, and it's also the second most profitable company in the United States,[582] receiving several billion dollars in profit in 2006.[583] In addition, student credit card company MBNA has been one of the most profitable firms in the country, racking up over $2 billion in profits just in 2003 alone.[584] And, in 2003, credit card companies received $24 billion just from the penalty fees that they charged their customers.[585] Investment companies also often cash in, with both the companies and their employees making millions by selling bonds based on students' debt.[586] Even the College Board has profited from student loans by encouraging students to use expensive private loans (and getting kickbacks when they do), even though the Board is well aware that private loans are very dangerous for students.[587]

As described in Chapter 2, loan and credit companies are especially dangerous because they tend to aggressively target students and encourage them to use more debt than they can afford (exploiting the fact that many students don't understand debt). It's been estimated that college students represent a full 25% of the people that credit card companies target.[588] Travis Plunkett, legislative director for the Consumer Federation of America, points out that, "The [credit card] companies…are dumping credit-card applications all over campuses without doing the basic tests to determine whether a student is ready to handle a credit card."[589]

Lenders also use a wide variety of other marketing strategies to attract college students. For example, consolidation lender

Collegiate Funding Services recently bought Youth Media and Marketing Networks, a company that specifically targets students and alumni,[590] while student loan lender Nelnet recently bought Peterson's, a company that offers education information to students, including information about financial aid,[591] and Sallie Mae owns Noel-Levitz, an enrollment management company that helps colleges develop their financial aid and loan packages.[592] In addition, some lenders even complete research studies in order to target students and get them to sign up, including Collegiate Funding Services, Sallie Mae, Nellie Mae, and Citibank.[593] Nina Prikazsky, Nellie Mae's vice president of operations, admits that "[lenders have] discovered that students have become their [most profitable] customers."[594] And Elizabeth Warren, Harvard Law professor, says that credit card companies try to "seduce [students] into borrowing more than they can possibly repay. These… companies want to get their hooks into people when they are young and keep them paying…forever."[595]

As mentioned in Chapter 2, lenders also aggressively reward colleges that provide them with student customers. Specifically, credit card companies sign lucrative deals with colleges, and loan lenders also often pay kickbacks and commission payments to schools, which can help them to become "preferred" lenders, and obtain more customers. And lenders have even been caught conducting improper searches within a government database that contains personal information from 60 million students.[596]

Many debt companies also take advantage of the government (and all taxpayers) to increase their profits. For example, it's been estimated that student loan companies have obtained about $6 billion from the government by taking advantage of a legal loophole that improperly allowed them to receive excessively high interest rate payments of 9.5% from the government.[597] Barmak Nassirian, associate executive director of the American Association of College Registrars and Admissions Officers, says, "In American history, this is the most outrageous giveaway ever extended by the federal government to private lenders."[598] In addition, the government allows student loan lenders to charge very high interest rates and fees, and it guarantees to pay the lenders if student borrowers default on their loans.[599]

Credit card companies have also convinced the government to "deregulate" the credit industry, leading to much higher costs for borrowers. Specifically, before 1978, most states had strict limits on credit card interest rates and fees.[600] However, the government deregulated credit interest rates in 1978, and fees in 1996.[601] Now, companies can charge pretty much whatever they want, and can quickly increase their rates at any time with little notice for their customers.[602] Deregulation has also allowed banks to remove other past protections, such as the requirement that applicants needed to have their parents' permission and/or a sufficient income (or any job at all) in order to get a credit card.[603] Companies have capitalized on this change to flood people with credit card offers, regardless of whether they can afford it. And credit card companies have been given permission to allow borrowers to have higher credit limits, and more credit cards, then ever before. These changes have made it easier for people to borrow much more than they can handle.

To get these kinds of favorable deals, debt companies make large lobbying payments to the government through organizations like the Student Loan Servicing Alliance, and the National Council of Higher Education Loan Programs. For example, the top five student loan corporations paid more than $60 million to politicians from 1998 to 2002, and lending executives contributed more than $1 million of their own money to politicians during this time, including the chairmen of the U.S. Congressional Committee on Education and the Workforce, such as John Boehner.[604] These donations may help to explain why Boehner recently told lenders that he would protect them with new government legislation, specifically stating "I have all of you in my two trusted hands."[605] In fact, at least seven former Sallie Mae employees now work in top jobs for the U.S. Department of Education,[606] including Terri Shaw, head of the government's Office of Federal Student Aid.[607] In addition, credit card companies recently spent more than $100 million to successfully lobby the government[608] into passing the most punishing bankruptcy laws ever enforced on consumers, even though it's the companies who are often responsible for using predatory business practices and encouraging unaffordable debt (and most personal bankruptcies are caused by illness, job loss, or divorce, not laziness or irresponsibility[609]). And lender lobbying convinced the government to require borrowers to pay for their student loans even when they declare bankruptcy.[610]

Elizabeth Warren says, "Student-loan debt collectors have power that would make a mobster envious,"[611] and "…the protection goes to the lender, [while] the students get served up."[612] In addition, Senator Carl Levin summarizes the predatory behavior of credit card companies by saying: "The credit card industry thrives on the confusion and powerlessness of consumers to both nickel and dime the average cardholder and to commit highway robbery of anyone who slips up even in the slightest."[613] Therefore, although marketing and lobbying often works out well for lenders, it usually translates into excessive costs and burdens for borrowers and taxpayers. James Scurlock, director of the documentary film about struggling borrowers called *Maxed Out* (and author of the book by the same name), is often asked if unmanageable debt is entirely borrowers' responsibility, but he points to the strong role that lenders play in fueling the problem through aggressive marketing and excessive fees, saying, "What about corporate responsibility?"[614]

HOW MUCH MONEY SHOULD STUDENTS BORROW?

Since colleges encourage high student loan debt, and the government often supports lenders over students, what can students do to avoid bad outcomes? The answer is that students can protect themselves by only borrowing loan money they can afford to pay back. And students can figure out what they can afford by considering their <u>expected starting salaries</u>, <u>debt repayment periods</u>, and <u>debt interest rates</u>. Specifically, before taking out a loan, students can estimate the maximum amount of loan money they can afford by following <u>six</u> steps:

Step One: Starting Salaries

Most importantly, students' ability to pay for their loan bills is determined by their salaries. So, students need to figure out how much money they will probably earn when they graduate from college or grad school. When they do this, students need to focus on the median or average "starting" salaries in their expected career fields; these are the salaries they will earn when they first start working and begin paying back their loans. People can find out current salary information for various jobs at sources like the U.S. Bureau of Labor Statistics website (www.bls.gov/oco), or the website for the National Association of Colleges and Employers (www.naceweb.org). However, since it's difficult for students to accurately predict their exact future salaries, they can play it safe by assuming that they will earn a starting salary of $31,000 per year (a common starting salary for college grads).

Step Two: Five Percent Monthly Payment

Although experts say that graduates can afford to spend up to 8% of their gross salaries on their student loan debt, students can be even safer if they limit their spending to a maximum of 5% of their gross income. Therefore, students can calculate 5% of their expected gross annual starting salary by multiplying this salary by 0.05. For example, 5% of a $31,000 gross annual salary is $1,550. So, people who earn $31,000 per year should probably not spend more than $1,550 per year on their student loans after they graduate. This translates to a monthly payment of about $129 ($1,550 divided by 12 months).

Step Three: Repayment Period

Students also need to figure out their "repayment period," or how many years they want to have to pay back their student loans. Students who are willing to pay back student loans for twenty years after they graduate may be able to take out more money than students willing to pay back the loans for only ten years. For example, a student who will earn a gross starting salary of $31,000 may be able to spend up to $15,500 over ten years ($1,550 x 10 years), or up to $31,000 over 20 years ($1,550 x 20 years), or up to $46,500 over 30 years ($1,550 x 30 years).

However, longer repayment periods lead to much higher total costs, especially because of cumulative interest charges. In fact, a 30-year repayment can cost twice as much as a 10-year repayment, for the exact same loan, just because of the longer repayment. So, students who want to be as safe as possible should probably borrow with a 10-year repayment period in mind, instead of expecting to use 20 or 30 years of repayment.

Step Four: Interest Rate

Of course, students must also consider the loan interest rate. Since interest rates often change and are difficult to predict, students can conservatively estimate that they'll be paying 8% interest on their student loans. By estimating that their rate will be 8%, students will play it safe and protect themselves from borrowing more than they can afford. Students who expect to use "private loans" should anticipate even higher rates.

Step Five: Putting It All Together

In summary, students can protect themselves by taking out a loan that will cost 5% (or less) of their gross starting salary to pay back, for the number of years that they are willing to pay it back. However, students also need to account for interest charges. Therefore, to figure out exactly how much money to borrow, students can plug their estimated monthly payment (from Step Two) into the following formula (for loans that will have an 8% interest rate and be paid back over 10 years):[615]

Total Loan Amount = [Monthly Payment x 1.23] ÷ 0.015

According to this formula, students who want to spend $129 per month on their education loans after college (or $1,550 per year, for a total of $15,500 over 10 years), at an 8% interest rate, can borrow up to about $10,600 during their entire education (including all "origination fees"). This is much less than the $17,000-$23,000 loan amounts (or more) that colleges and banks often encourage students to borrow.

There's also a much easier way for students to figure out how much to borrow: they can multiply their expected gross starting salaries by 0.33, or multiply their expected net starting salaries by 0.50.[616] In other words, students can stay safe if they limit their total borrowing to one-third of their gross salaries or one-half of their net after-tax salaries.

However, these calculations assume that students want to limit their loan payments to 5% of their salaries, at an 8% interest rate, over ten years. Students who have different loan specifications may be able to estimate their affordable loan limits by using online "loan calculators," like the ones at www.bankrate.com, www.moneychimp.com, or www.finaid.com/calculators/, even though these calculators are not exactly set up for this purpose. The calculator at www.finaid.com/calculators/loanpayments.phtml may be particularly helpful in allowing students to estimate what kinds of salaries they will need to earn in order to pay back various loan amounts, at various interest rates and repayment periods.

Step Six: Loans Per Year

After students decide how much total loan money they should borrow during their entire college careers, they have to figure out how much to borrow during each year of school. Since college prices tend to go up each year, students who finish college in four years should borrow up to 15% of their total in their first year, 21% of their total in their second year, 32% of their total in their third year, and 32% of their total in their fourth year. Therefore, a student who wants to borrow a total of up to $10,600 throughout college should borrow up to $1,590 in their first year, $2,226 in their second year, $3,392 in their third year, and $3,392 in their fourth year.

Of course, since many students take six years to finish college, students can be safer by borrowing up to 10% of their total in the first year, 14% in the second year, 17% in each of the third and fourth years, and 21% in each of the fifth and sixth years. For a student who wants to borrow a total of up to $10,600, this translates into: up to $1,060 in the first year, $1,484 in the second year, $1,802 in each of the third and fourth years, and $2,226 in each of the fifth and sixth years. Again, colleges often encourage students to borrow much more than this, but students who can stick to their affordable limits will be safer.

These six steps aren't perfect, but they offer a conservative or safe way for students to figure out how much loan money they can afford to borrow during each year of school. And this information can help students decide which schools they can afford to attend. Of course, students should borrow less than these amounts, if they can, because even these amounts can be difficult for students to manage, and many students will receive below-average starting salaries or expensive interest rates. It may also be a good idea for students to restrict their college debt if they plan to borrow additional money for graduate school, or if they plan to leave the workforce at some point to raise children. And parents can be an important part of the "debt decision" process, helping students to limit their borrowing to an appropriate amount.

IGNORING FINANCIAL POSITIVE ILLUSIONS

Most people have a tendency to believe they are better than other people, and that they will continue to be better-than-average in the future—but this outlook is not very realistic because everyone can't be above average. Therefore, this mindset of "unrealistic optimism" has been called "positive illusion" by psychologists and researchers. However, this attitude surprisingly tends to be completely normal, and usually helps people stay hopeful and mentally healthy.[617]

On the other hand, college students tend to have <u>unsafe</u> financial positive illusions. In particular, as mentioned in Chapter 1, college students tend to dangerously underestimate their student debt costs, and they tend to dangerously expect much higher salaries than they will actually receive when they graduate.[618]

Therefore, to stay as safe as possible, students can try to ignore their financial positive illusions. Specifically, when students decide how much money to borrow for college, they can try to borrow as little as possible, and they can assume they will receive <u>average</u> starting salaries in their career fields. After all, most graduates will receive average or below average salaries, just by definition, so students who expect to be average should benefit by limiting their debt to a manageable level. Of course, in the best-case scenario, students may be able to keep their debt low and then succeed in achieving above-average salaries.

THE BEST AND WORST LOANS

Students who need to use loans to pay for college have many options to choose from, but some loans are much better than others. The best and least-expensive loans for students are usually "Federal loans," or loans supported by the government, such as Stafford loans, Perkins loans, and PLUS loans (Parent Loans for Undergraduate Students). Stafford loans come in two varieties: the "subsidized" version, which is less expensive for students because the government pays all interest charges while students are in school,[619] and the "unsubsidized" version, which requires students to pay all interest charges (but is still less expensive than most other loans). Also, all government loans allow students to postpone payment if they go to graduate school or experience a drop in income.

There are actually <u>two</u> ways for students to obtain government loans for college: 1) the Direct Loan program, and 2) the Federal Family Education Loan program (FFEL; also known as the Guaranteed Loan program). The Direct Loan program offers some important advantages for students over the FFEL program, such as income-based repayment (debt bills start low and rise as borrowers' income rises), and the opportunity to completely wipe away any remaining loan debt after 25 years.[620] In addition, research studies show that the Direct Loan program is <u>fourteen times</u> less expensive for the government and taxpayers than the FFEL program.[621] So, the government could easily save billions of dollars each year if more students would use the Direct program (and this savings could then be used for other college aid, like grants).[622] Although the Direct Loan program offers many benefits for students and taxpayers, lenders have used college kickbacks and government lobbying to try to make it less likely for students to use Direct Loans,[623] because lenders receive much higher profits when students use the FFEL program. But students who want to use government loans should probably try to use Direct Loans as their first option, and then use Guaranteed Loans as an acceptable alternative.

Students who can't get all of the government loans they need may want to consider "private loans," but private loans can be dangerously expensive. Although private loans can offer some benefits for students, such as flexible borrowing and repayment terms, private loans can also cost thousands of extra dollars. For example, private loans can require interest rates of 15-18%, and many private lenders fail to clearly reveal these high costs.[624] Therefore, before using any private loans, students should probably use any federal loans that they are eligible for. One out of five private loan borrowers don't take advantage of all of the federal loans they are eligible for.[625]

Students are also often able to choose between a "fixed" or "variable" loan interest rate, and each of these rates can be better at different times. For example, since fixed interest rates stay the same for the life of the loan, it's better for students to choose a fixed rate when rates are low (e.g., less than 5%). On the other hand, it may be better to choose a variable rate when rates are high, because variable rates can go down. However, variable rates can dangerously rise quickly, leading to unexpected extra monthly costs for grads. Therefore, students should choose their loan type carefully.

In addition, since unsubsidized loans often have more expensive interest charges than subsidized loans, students who use unsubsidized loans may want to borrow less money. The formula presented earlier is meant for subsidized loans, so students who use unsubsidized loans should probably multiply their final result in "Step Five" by 0.85.

More information about different kinds of student loans is available at: http://finaid.com/loans/studentloan.phtml.

CHOOSING A STUDENT LOAN LENDER

When students decide which loans are best for them, they then have many lenders to choose from. In order to save money, students can shop around for the lender that offers the best interest rates and terms.

Lenders' current interest rates are usually available on the Internet (including lenders' websites, or financial aid websites, such as www.finaid.com). Students may also be able to compare the costs of various loans by comparing each loan's "APR," or "Annual Percentage Rate," which includes all of a loan's costs.

Although students may be able to obtain lender recommendations directly from their colleges, colleges can guide students to overly expensive lenders. Some colleges even discourage students from using lenders that are not directly profitable for them, but it's against the law for colleges to prevent students from using certain lenders.[626] Therefore, students can consider colleges' recommendations, and also look beyond schools' "preferred lender lists," asking their schools to allow them to use the lenders of their choice.

A list of the most common student loan lenders is included at the FinAid.com website (http://www.finaid.com/loans/biglenders.phtml). Also, students can investigate the services of a new student loan lender, "My Rich Uncle," which appears to offer the lowest interest rates for federal loans, and competitive rates for private loans (www.myrichuncle.com). Many lenders offer both federal and private loans, and students who plan to use both kinds of loans should usually try to use the same lender for both, because using different lenders may increase students' costs.

BRIGHTEN THE FUTURE
BY AVOIDING THE CREDIT DEBT TRAP

"My number one message is that when parents worry about the safety of their children, they usually think that means drinking, driving, and other physical safety issues. But credit cards are among the most dangerous products their children will encounter while in college."
—Elizabeth Warren, Harvard Law professor[627]

As described earlier, credit cards are often even more

problematic than student loans, especially since credit interest rates are often high and variable. In fact, many credit cards offer low interest rates at first, sometimes at a 0% rate, but the rates then suddenly skyrocket, quickly and often unexpectedly hitting people with large extra costs. Also, while many student loans are required to be fully paid back within twenty or thirty years or less, credit cards do not have a similar limit, and extra repayment years create extra credit costs.

The surprising fact is that a credit debt does not have to be very large to take an entire lifetime to repay: someone who has a credit card debt of only $8,000, but only pays the minimum required bill each month, can take over 50 years to fully pay off the debt, and it can cost them over $30,000 (including over $20,000 in interest fees).[628] Even a credit card debt of only $3,000 can take anywhere from 15 to 30 years to repay, and cost a total of $5,000-$10,000 in interest fees, depending on the interest rate and typical monthly payment. Some banks now require borrowers to pay 1% of their total remaining principal balance each month, but borrowers who only pay this amount will probably still pay expensive costs and take many years to pay off their bills, especially since borrowers can continue to make new purchases and have interest charges added to their debt.

Credit cards have several additional disadvantages. For example, although student loans may have some tax benefits, or discounts, credit cards have none. And although the government pays all interest charges for subsidized loans while students are in school, credit cards don't offer this benefit. Also, some loan payments can be deferred while students are in school, or even completely wiped away if students pursue certain careers—another benefit that credit cards don't match. Credit card debt can also be more damaging than student loan debt to someone's credit or financial rating, because a student loan is considered an asset or investment, but credit card debt is considered a liability or problem.[629]

Although students should avoid using credit cards whenever they can, it can be helpful for students to have one credit card, so that they build up a positive credit history. In that case, students who want to use credit cards can stay safe by following one basic rule: they should only use the cards for items they can completely pay off each month. When people pay their credit card bills in-full and on-time each month, they can avoid expensive interest charges and fees. Specifically, students should try to limit their total monthly credit card purchases to less than 5-10% of their gross monthly salaries (at most), keeping their debt as low as possible. This means that someone who earns a gross salary of $31,000 per year ($2,583 per month) can stay safest by charging only $129-$258 per month (5-10% of $2,583), and then paying off his or her entire balance each month. Students who have no income should obviously try to avoid all credit debt, and only use cards to buy items they can afford, or items their parents have agreed to pay for.

Students who want credit cards can try to sign up for cards that have the lowest interest rates, and they can check some rates by using the website www.bankrate.com. In addition, students can block most unwanted credit card offers by registering for the free blocking service at www.optoutprescreen.com, or www.privacyrightsnow.com/, or 1-888-5-OPTOUT (1-888-567-8688). Also, Consumers for Responsible Credit Solutions (CRCS), a national group, offers a free online program to help families discuss the safe use of credit cards (www.responsiblecredit.com).

Other helpful websites for credit and debt information include:

- **Coalition for Consumer Bankruptcy Debtor Education** (www.debtoreducation.org);
- **Consumer Credit Counseling Service of New York** (www.cccscny.org);
- **National Council on Economic Education** (www.ncee.net);
- **Jump$tart Coalition for Personal Financial Literacy** (www.jumpstart.org);
- **Anya Kamenetz's blog, Generation Debt** (www.anyakamenetz.blogspot.com);
- **Credit Abuse Resistance Education Program** (www.careprogram.us/chronicles.php);
- **The Institute for College Access and Success** (www.ticas.org);
- **Generation Debt** (www.generationdebt.org);
- **Credit Card Nation** (www.creditcardnation.com);
- **Young Money** (www.youngmoney.com);
- **Project on Student Debt** (www.projectonstudentdebt.org);
- **Student Loan Justice** (www.studentloanjustice.org);
- **Student Loan Watch/Higher Ed Watch** (www.studentloanwatch.org or www.higheredwatch.org both addresses go to the same site);
- **Student Debt Alert** (www.studentdebtalert.org);
- **The Truth About Credit** (www.truthaboutcredit.org); and
- **Student Loan Advocates and Volunteer Exchange** (http://www.studentloanslave.org).

In addition, an excellent calculator that people can use to figure out what they need to do to pay off all of their credit debt is available at: http://www.youngmoney.com/calculators/credit_card_and_debt_management_calculators/credit_card_payoff

And students can obtain more financial advice by hiring a professional "financial planner," or "financial adviser." Directories of Certified Financial Advisors are located at sites like www.cfp.com, www.feeonly.org, and www.garrettplanningnetwork.com.

• • •

Once again, it's important to note that the loan and credit estimates in this chapter are presented as maximums, so students should borrow even less for school if they can. Although students may not be able to attend college without borrowing some money, they should keep their debt as low as possible. After all, students who keep their costs and debt low can brighten their futures considerably, having fewer restrictions and more flexibility as they try to fulfill their dreams.

The key for students is to find schools that will be affordable <u>and</u> provide them with the financially and educationally valuable training they want and need. The next chapter explores students' college options, and shares some strategies that students can use to identify and enroll in appropriate schools.

CHAPTER 8

GOT VALUE?
Choosing an Appropriate College

Of course, before students can get financial aid or borrow money for college, they have to decide which schools to apply to. Students who understand all of their college options are best able to find affordable schools that will provide them with a valuable education.

LOOKING BEYOND THE MYTH OF PRESTIGE IN THE SEARCH FOR QUALITY AND VALUE

As described in Chapter 5, prestigious colleges usually don't offer better payoffs for students than other colleges—and, as described below, prestigious colleges also surprisingly tend to offer few academic advantages over other colleges. Therefore, prestigious schools are sometimes not the best option for students, even when students can afford them.

> **Myth: Prestigious colleges provide a better education than other colleges.**

Specifically, research studies show that there's little connection between the prestige of a college and the quality of teaching that its students receive.[630] Also, a recent survey found that the students who were least satisfied with their instruction were those at many of the largest and most well-known colleges.[631] And, although the odds of finishing college within four years rise dramatically when students attend prestigious schools, these schools present no guarantees; for example, two out of ten students <u>do not</u> graduate within four years at respected schools like Stanford University, Cornell University, Columbia University, Brown University, and Northwestern University.[632]

It's hard to believe that prestigious colleges don't usually offer special benefits, but this makes some sense. After all, as described in Chapter 4, professors at prestigious schools tend to spend more time doing research than teaching, and they often teach large classes when they're in the classroom, so students usually don't have much personal contact with them. And, as described in Chapter 2, many colleges raise their prices just to increase their income, keep pace with their competitors, and get more applicants—and not because they offer better educational value. Besides, most of the world's knowledge is widely available, especially through the power of the Internet, so it's not as if students at prestigious colleges have access to special or secret books and information that other students don't. A recent *Wall Street Journal* op-ed article exposed the prestige myth in an innovative way by claiming that Ivy League colleges have maintained their generally strong reputations just because they have graduated many prominent journalists and reporters who tend to write flattering articles about them.[633]

In addition, most colleges tend to have different strengths and weaknesses, including prestigious and expensive ones, so they are stronger in some subject areas, and weaker in others. For example, MIT is highly respected for its engineering program, NYU has a highly respected Film Studies program, and Berklee College is known for its music programs, but Harvard University doesn't have a Film Studies program at all, and Emory University doesn't have its own engineering program. So it's often a waste for students to attend prestigious colleges that don't offer strong programs in their areas of interest. Student Gabriel Slavitt illustrated this idea by turning down an acceptance from Brown University because he wanted to attend a lesser-known school that offered a better arts program.[634]

Also, prestigious colleges can be academically punishing for students. For example, some students at prestigious schools receive lower grades than they deserve because these schools sometimes "grade on a curve," or base students' test grades on how everyone else in their class scored. This system unfairly harms students by restricting the number of high grades that can be awarded, in a type of "grade deflation." In fact, some prestigious schools have recently increased their curve grading, giving out fewer top grades, to try to fight the perception that they unfairly inflate their students' grades.[635] However, curve grading is especially problematic for students at prestigious schools, because they are graded in comparison to students who are among the best test-takers in the world. David Freeman, a recent graduate of the University of California's Marshall School of Business, says that he was passed over by 12 employers because of his school's system of curve grading: "Without the curve, my [grades] would have been high enough to qualify for these interviews."[636] For this reason, curve grading can lead to extreme stress and competition among students, and student Greg Smith says that he looked for a less prestigious college to attend specifically because he wanted to avoid "all [the] hypercompetitiveness."[637] Unfortunately, most top colleges tend to use problematic grading policies, but schools such as Sarah Lawrence College and Hampshire College have moved away from test scores, instead focusing on measuring student progress through projects, research papers, and essays.[638]

And, just like other schools, prestigious colleges often

deliver poor career preparation for students. For example, many prestigious colleges tend to focus on general classes, instead of more practical, career-oriented classes. In addition, although some prestigious colleges allow their students to have access to special career connections among top employers, few students really benefit from this supposed advantage. In contrast, students can have an advantage in obtaining internships and jobs when they attend colleges that are located in big cities, near the headquarters for many major companies and organizations, whether their colleges are prestigious or not.[639] Author and counselor Loren Pope points out that, in general, "[colleges' career] connections won't do a whole hell of a lot of good. It's your own specific gravity, not the name of a school, that matters."[640]

In addition, the prestige of a college is often even less important for students who go to graduate school. In fact, graduate schools tend to admit students based on college grades, standardized test scores, recommendation letters, and practical experience, while the exact college they attended is relatively unimportant. Also, graduate school alumni are usually judged on the prestige of their graduate school, while the prestige of their college is ignored. For example, a graduate of an average college who attends Harvard Law School will probably obtain an excellent law job, while a Harvard University college graduate who attends a low-quality law school will probably have more difficulty in their law career.

In many ways, "prestige" is just a marketing trick that colleges use to get more money by falsely convincing people that they are better than they really are. Even the "Ivy League" is not necessarily as exceptional as people think, because this group of eight schools was formed in 1954 as a sports division, and not as a special academic division.[641] Given that young people tend to prefer new developments over old trends, it's actually somewhat surprising that the Ivy League remains as popular as it is, especially since these schools are the country's <u>oldest</u> colleges (and not necessarily the country's <u>best</u> colleges), and the other nickname for these schools is "The Ancient Eight."[642]

However, as described in Chapter 5, it's important to note that prestigious colleges may offer special benefits for low-income students, racial minorities, and women. On the other hand, prestigious colleges are often a poor value for many other students, especially those who borrow large loans, pay high tuition prices, or pay high costs for travel, food, and housing to attend these schools. Therefore, although some students want to attend prestigious colleges so that they can impress their friends and families, these colleges may not be best for them.

THE "MAJOR" COLLEGE PAYOFF FACTOR

An interesting quirk of college pricing is that every "major" (area of academic concentration) within a school usually costs the same price (even after financial aid is considered)—but different majors lead to very different salaries. For example, a student who majors in accounting will earn an average starting salary of $46,000 per year, but a student who majors in psychology will earn only an average starting salary of $30,000 per year,[643] even though both majors cost the same price. Other examples of the wide range of average starting salaries for college graduates include: English $30,906; sociology $30,944; communications $31,876; political science and government $32,665; history $32,697; business management $42,048; geology sciences $44,191; economics/finance $45,112; civil engineering $46,023; information systems $48,593; and chemical engineering $56,335.[644]

In fact, students' choice of major has more of an impact on their salaries than where they go to college, and this has been supported in various research studies.[645] For example, psychology grads tend to earn low salaries, even when they attend prestigious colleges. A recent survey of employers confirmed this idea, finding that "academic major" is one of the top 3 criteria that employers look at when they evaluate job candidates (along with practical experience and interview skills), while "specific college attended" is much lower on the list.[646] Bill Krueger, president of CollegeGrad.com (an employment website), acknowledges the importance of college majors, saying, "It's more important [for students] to have taken the right major and classes for [their] career at a local [public college] than to have majored in [a less helpful major] at an Ivy League school."[647] Therefore, when students decide which college to attend, they should think carefully about which subject they want to "major" in.

> **Myth: Students should study the subjects they enjoy most, regardless of the costs.**

Since some majors lead to higher average salaries, students may be better off studying the more lucrative subjects. This is a great way for students to try to get their money's worth from their college education. Although future salaries cannot be guaranteed, students have a better chance of earning a higher salary (and better college payoff) when they pursue higher-paying careers. And students should be able to find lucrative majors that tap into their natural interests; for example, students who are interested in math can study economics, accounting, or finance; students who are interested in psychology can study marketing or management; students who are interested in teaching can study human resources and corporate training; students who are interested in political science can study management; and students who are interested in English or journalism can study marketing and public relations.

On the other hand, many students want to study academic majors that happen to <u>not</u> lead to high-paying jobs, just because students enjoy these subjects. For example, one out of every four college students "majors" in a subject that tends to lead to low-paying jobs, such as literature, fine arts, performing arts, liberal arts, general studies, or social science.[648] In fact, many of the most popular majors[649] offer low salaries, including psychology, education, nursing, English, and communications. And it's important for students to have the opportunity to pursue these majors, because society needs skilled people in these fields.

Although students who study low-paying majors are at greater risk for poor college payoffs, the good news is that they can safely study these majors by following one basic rule: pursue degrees within colleges that will have lower costs for them. As described earlier, students can make good college choices by adjusting their school costs according to their expected salaries. For example, students who expect to earn starting salaries of $30,000 per year would be wise to keep their immediate college costs and total college debt very low. Students can study the college subjects that they enjoy, but they need to pay the right price for what they study. Some students may not expect or want to be rich, but they also do not expect or want to be poor. It's especially important for students to keep their college costs low because: many of them don't know what kind of major or career they will pursue; many of them switch from high-paying to low-paying majors while they are in college; and they can't perfectly predict their later salaries.

Of course, some students have their hearts set on attending particular colleges that will just happen to cost them a large amount of money. These students may be able to cost-effectively attend these schools by picking majors that will help them earn higher salaries when they graduate. Or, these students can have a "double major" (or second major), or a "minor," studying one subject that they enjoy, and one subject that usually leads to high-paying jobs (e.g., business). Colleges often allow students to have a "double major" at no extra cost, which basically allows students to get two degrees for the price of one (and all within 4 years)! These options can allow students to obtain better value at more expensive schools—especially if these students keep their costs and debt at affordable levels.

As students think about which majors they want to pursue, there are many sources they can use to learn more about their options. One book that offers more information about the financial return for different majors is the *College Majors Handbook with Real Career Paths and Payoffs*, by Neeta Fogg, Paul Harrington, and Thomas Harrington. Other popular career books for students include: *What Color is Your Parachute?* and *What Color is Your Parachute for Teens*, both by Richard Nelson Bolles; *How to Choose a College Major*, by Linda Landis Andrews; *The Everything College Major Test Book*, by Burton Nadler; *The Princeton Review Guide to College Majors*; and *The College Board Book of Majors*. In addition, Monster.com offers a free online "Career Converter" tool that students can use to easily match types of college majors with specific job titles and job listings, at http://content.monstertrak.monster.com/tools/careerconverter.

Students may also benefit from taking personal career assessment tests, such as the "Self-Directed Search," or the "Strong Interest Inventory," which are offered by many high schools, colleges, libraries, private counselors, and psychologists.

Finally, it's important to note that some colleges (including the University of Kansas, the University of Illinois, Arizona State University, the University of Wisconsin, and Iowa State University) have recently started charging higher prices for some majors (including low-paying majors like education, fine arts, and journalism).[650] Therefore, students should confirm the costs of their preferred majors, and then decide if any extra costs are worth paying, or if it might be better to choose a less expensive major or school.

EXPLORING COLLEGE OPTIONS

Eventually, students need to decide which colleges they want to apply to for admission. And, although some colleges are not a good fit for students due to their high prices, very selective admissions processes, significant academic limitations, or disappointing payoffs, the good news is that students have plenty of other college options to choose from. But what are the strengths and weaknesses of these options?

Private colleges vs. Public colleges

Almost half of parents want their child to attend a private college, instead of a public college, and almost half of parents think that private colleges offer a better education than public colleges[651]—but public colleges are often as good (or better) for students than private colleges. However, this shouldn't be too surprising, since many public colleges have more of a focus on teaching, and have more dedicated teachers.[652] Also, many public colleges offer "honors classes" for their most talented and motivated students.[653] And many public colleges have better resources than private colleges; for example, in

November 2005, Miami-Dade College (a public school) broke ground on a brand-new, state-of-the-art $25 million science facility. Also, in September 2005, the public Georgia State University pledged to build a new humanities center of classrooms and labs, at a cost of $77.5 million.[654] Georgia State also offered brand-new housing to its students in 1996, 2002, and 2007.[655] Finally, many graduates of public colleges achieve prestigious careers in medicine, law, and business; even the 2006 CEOs of Wal-Mart, Intel, Costco, Bank of America, Hershey, Ford, and Berkshire Hathaway attended public colleges.[656] One family that has benefited from public education is the McGinnis family, who were able to pay for each of their three children to attend state colleges in Virginia, without accumulating any debt. Tom McGinnis, a retired army captain, says, "Why would I have spent $45,000 a year to send them somewhere else?"[657]

On the other hand, some private colleges can be surprisingly less expensive for students, because these colleges often have more money than other schools for discounts, grants, and scholarships that help lower students' costs. In addition, public colleges can be more expensive than people realize, because they usually only make their low prices available for students who live in the same states where the schools are located, charging much higher prices for out-of-state students. In fact, out-of-state students can be charged triple what they would have paid if they lived in the same state where the school is located, similar to the price of a private school. For example, during the 2007-2008 school year, the University of Maryland charged $7,968 for in-state tuition and fees, but $22,206 for out-of-state students (not including room and board).[658] To get better deals, students can ask public colleges outside their home states to allow them to pay in-state rates (some public schools give these discounts),[659] but there's no guarantee that these requests will be granted.

Non-profit schools vs. For-profit schools

Most public and private colleges are considered "non-profit," and it's often assumed that "non-profit" colleges are best for students—but "for-profit" schools are sometimes actually better. Richard Ruch, a former administrator at the University of Michigan, Harvard University, and DeVry University, points out that "for-profit" schools, like DeVry University and University of Phoenix, are sometimes more effective and efficient than non-profit schools—even though for-profit schools are usually less famous and prestigious than other schools.

For example, for-profit schools can offer some benefits to students, including a lower price than private non-profits, instructors that are focused on teaching instead of conducting research projects, flexible class schedules (including classes that are offered online, at night, and during the summer), strong customer service, a focus on teaching practical information and skills, degrees that can be completed in a shorter amount of time, and focused job placement services.[660] And, according to the Career College Association, 65% of students at for-profit schools graduate within 6 years,[661] which is similar to the graduation rate at non-profit schools. This may help explain why "for-profit" schools are very popular these days; it's been estimated that over 700,000 students take classes at for-profit schools each year.[662]

The effectiveness of for-profit schools is supported by the fact that many non-profit schools even run their own for-profit schools "on the side!" For example, for-profit programs are managed on the side by both private and public non-profit schools like the University of Miami, Emory University, the

University of Maryland, and Washington University, and these programs are often called "continuing education" or "extension" programs.[663] Even Ivy League schools like Harvard University and Columbia University host very profitable continuing education programs on the side, including Harvard's "Extension School."[664] In fact, Harvard instructors say that their Extension classes are exactly the same as their on-campus classes, but extension students save thousands of dollars by paying only $550 per class, while on-campus students pay about $4,000 per class.[665] In addition, the Harvard Extension degrees seem to be as valuable as the regular degrees; some graduates of the program even go on to medical and law schools, including Harvard's.[666] And non-profit colleges tend to make lots of money from their for-profit programs; the University of Massachusetts obtained $11 million in 2003 from its online programs, and 90% of this was profit.[667] By running less expensive, high-quality, profitable for-profit programs of their own, non-profit schools implicitly acknowledge that these programs have merit for both them and their students.

On the other hand, it's important to note that a large number of for-profit programs are treacherous scams, offering high costs and debt, false promises of career success, and horrible payoffs[668]—but the misbehavior of these particular schools does not condemn every for-profit school. In fact, for-profit schools are often criticized unfairly. For example, it's sometimes said that for-profit schools engage in questionable behaviors, such as: aggressive marketing; accepting students that are not ready for college-level work; misleading students about the amount of time it will take to complete their degrees; having low graduation rates; employing part-time instructors; offering low-quality instruction; and trying to influence politicians.[669] However, as described earlier, non-profit schools are often guilty in exactly the same ways. In addition, it's unfair to criticize for-profit schools for their profitability, because non-profit schools also often receive more money than they spend. And for-profit schools give back to society by paying taxes on their income, while non-profit schools pay no taxes and hoard their profits.[670]

Of course, for-profit schools are not right for every student. For example, for-profit schools are usually much more expensive than public colleges, and they don't offer every major. And many for-profit schools don't offer supplementary features that some students may want, such as gyms, libraries, or student housing (although the lack of these features allows schools to charge lower prices). Also, students at for-profit schools tend to be older than typical college students, and tend to go to school part-time; while some students may benefit from these students' focus, motivation and practical experience, others may not enjoy this arrangement. In addition, many non-profit schools refuse to accept class credits when students transfer to them from for-profit schools;[671] this policy helps non-profit schools increase their income, but often unfairly punishes students who have completed adequate classes at for-profit schools. Finally, some for-profit students may suffer because their preferred employers are not familiar with their schools, or don't respect the schools.

However, some employers have greater respect for for-profit schools than they do for non-profit schools, especially since for-profit graduates often have excellent skills. Therefore, for-profit schools can be a good choice for students who are able to pick affordable and valuable for-profit degrees that allow them to succeed. Before students enroll in a for-profit program, they can protect themselves by verifying the typical employment rates and average salaries of graduates at each school they are considering, as well as checking with employers in their preferred career fields to ensure that their degrees will have value. A large list of for-profit colleges and universities is available at: http://en.wikipedia.org/wiki/List_of_for-profit_colleges_and_universities

Online programs vs. Traditional programs

Many colleges also offer classes and degrees over the Internet, including public colleges like the University of Massachusetts, the University of Maryland, Troy University in Alabama, Pennsylvania State University, Washington State University, and the University of Illinois.[672] These online programs are often helpful for students (and profitable for schools), because the programs are less expensive than on-campus programs, the class schedules are somewhat flexible, and the programs often use the exact same instructors and learning materials as the on-campus programs. In fact, student Joel Gragg believes that online class discussions are better than those in classrooms, because more students have a chance to participate: "There's young people, there's old people, there's moms, professional people. You really learn a lot more."[673] A new study even illustrates that online students are just as engaged as students in classrooms, and online students often have more contact with their instructors.[674] This helps to explain why online programs are becoming much more popular; for example, from just 2002 to 2003, 34% more students enrolled in the University of Massachusetts' online program.[675] A Sloan Consortium study found that more than 3 million students took at least one online class in fall 2005 (at both public and private colleges).[676]

Also, many employers respect online degree programs: a recent Vault survey found that 45% of employers believe that traditional and online degrees are equal in quality, and 86% of employers would be willing to consider an online grad for employment.[677] One employer says that graduates of online programs particularly deserve respect because "it takes a lot of discipline to complete an online degree."[678] Another employer who hired an online grad says: "The person was tested in all aspects of their field of study with respect to the position and won the position. Great hire it turned out to be!"[679]

On the other hand, some employers have a negative view of online degrees. For example, 54% of employers tend to favor traditional degrees over online degrees, and 14% of employers wouldn't be willing to hire an online grad.[680] Therefore, students should check with employers in their preferred career fields before they enroll in an online program. In particular, employers tend to favor some online degrees over others; in a 2000 Vault survey, 77% of hiring managers said that online degrees earned from well-known traditional schools were more valuable than online degrees from online-only schools.[681]

Students who want to learn about specific online programs can take a look at the book "Peterson's Guide to Online Learning." Reviews of some online programs are also available at www.geteducated.com, or www.OnlineDegreeReviews.org, or www.oedb.org/rankings. Students can also find out if an online program is adequately accredited by submitting the name of the program to "http://geteducated.com/services/diplomamillpolice.asp". Although online degree programs aren't right for everyone, these programs can be an excellent educational and financial choice for many. A number of schools also offer programs that combine on-campus classes with online classes.

Division I sports schools vs. Other schools

College sports can be fun, but schools that focus on sports may not be a good fit for students—especially if these schools are too expensive or offer a poor education.

Students who want to attend colleges that are less focused on sports may want to avoid "Division I" schools, which are most focused on sports, or "Division II" schools, which are also sports-focused. Instead, students can explore "Division III" schools, where sports are even less of a priority. Some examples of <u>Division I</u> schools include: Duke University, University of Miami (Florida), University of Maryland, Michigan State University and University of California-Los Angeles (UCLA). Examples of <u>Division II</u> schools are: Adelphi University, University of Bridgeport, University of California-San Diego, Kutztown University of Pennsylvania, San Francisco State University, University of Tampa, Valdosta State University, and Virginia Union University. And <u>Division III</u> includes schools like: Emory University, New York University, Bryn Mawr College, Brandeis University, Carnegie Mellon University, City College of New York, University of Chicago, Franklin and Marshall College, and University of California-Santa Cruz.

The website www.ncaa.org/conferences/ offers a directory listing of all Division I, II, and III schools, and students can use this website to figure out which schools are in which Divisions. In addition, some schools are not affiliated with <u>any</u> NCAA divisions, and these schools usually have an even smaller focus on sports.

A MATTER OF DEGREE

As students decide where to apply for college admission, they also need to consider the kinds of degrees they want to obtain. Many students think that the "bachelor's degree" (a 4-year degree) is best, but other degree options can be a better fit for some students. For example, Associate's degrees from community colleges or junior colleges tend to offer lower cost ($2,361 for one year of tuition and fees in 2007-08, on average[682]), and these programs usually only require two years of classes instead of four.

In addition, Associate's programs often provide personalized attention for students, small classes, and a focus on teaching instead of research.[683] In fact, instructors at public community colleges spend more time teaching than instructors at other kinds of schools.[684] And Raymond Slinski, a recent graduate of Northampton Community College in Pennsylvania, says, "The classes are just as hard as anywhere else. A lot of our professors [have] taught at [four-year colleges like] Lehigh and Lafayette."[685] And one recent study found that students who attend two-year schools are more satisfied with their education than those who attend four-year schools.[686]

Also, several studies predict that there will be more new jobs for associate's grads than bachelor's grads during the next few years.[687] Associate's degree graduates are particularly "in demand" because associate's programs are often more practical and "hands-on" than bachelor's degree programs, and employers like hiring graduates who have this extra experience. Although bachelor's graduates tend to earn more money than associate's graduates (on average), unemployed bachelor's degree graduates don't earn anything, so the employment strengths of an associate's degree are very important.

In fact, many associate's grads go on to complete another two years of classes at an advanced school to earn a bachelor's degree. And the transition from an associate's program to a bachelor's program is usually smooth, because associate's grads tend to be just as knowledgeable as students who have finished the first two years of a bachelor's program.[688] In addition, research studies show that students who transfer to a 4-year school after going to a 2-year school have the same chance of getting a bachelor's degree as students who go to a bachelor's program directly after high school.[689] And students can protect themselves by attending associate's programs instead of going directly into bachelor's programs, because associate's grads usually earn more money than bachelor's program dropouts.[690] Some public 4-year colleges (like the University of Wisconsin and the University of Virginia) even guarantee admission to their schools for community college graduates who meet certain guidelines.[691]

The McGoff family of Maryland represents one community college success story: they saved $26,000 by sending their daughter to Montgomery College (a 2-year school) before she will finish her degree at a more expensive four-year school. Chris McGoff says that he's very happy with the value his family received: "I admit I had a stigma about community college. Not anymore."[692] Douglas McDevitt, a recent student at Metropolitan Community College in Nebraska, agrees: "You're wasting your money by going anywhere but community college. It's almost a scam going to a four-year program for your first two years because you can pay three times less [in an associate's program] for the same classes."[693] Students who want to attend a bachelor's program after an associate's program can get the best value by taking associate's classes that will then transfer to their bachelor's program. Students can accomplish this by checking with their preferred bachelor's program before enrolling in the associate's classes.

On the other hand, many associate's grads are successful without completing a bachelor's degree, especially because the associate's degree can qualify them for a variety of jobs, such as: registered nurse, dental hygienist, medical laboratory technician, computer technician, commercial artist, hotel/restaurant manager, administrative assistant, and auto mechanic.[694] Of course, associate's programs are not perfect, but they often offer an excellent and valuable education at a more affordable price, so the associate's degree may be the degree of the future. One guide to associate degree programs is *Two-Year Colleges,* published by Peterson's. It's important to note that associate's programs offered by public schools are usually <u>much</u> less expensive for students than associate's programs offered by private schools.

It's also important to note that students who pursue either associate's degrees or bachelor's degrees often get better value by obtaining degrees in "Science" as opposed to degrees in "Arts." Confusingly, both kinds of degrees are often offered for every single major; for example, students can either get a "Bachelor's of <u>Arts</u> in psychology," or a "Bachelor's of <u>Science</u> in psychology." However, the Science degrees are usually more valuable because they tend to include classes that are more practical, or they require students to complete some kind of internship, research project, or other "hands-on" work. While students probably shouldn't ignore a school just because it doesn't offer a "Science" degree in their preferred major, students who have a choice between the two kinds of degrees can usually get the best value for their money by pursuing the "Science" degree (as long as this degree does not require too much extra money or time to complete).

In addition, some students can benefit from pursuing "Technical" or vocational degrees, instead of bachelor's or associate's degrees. Technical degree programs offer the opportunity for students to learn special, practical skills that help them get jobs in fields like business, technology, graphic arts, remodeling and repair, nursing, law, fashion design, or "culinary arts" (cooking). However, technical degrees are usually only valuable and useful in the subject areas in which they are earned, and technical degree grads usually can't go on to graduate school. For example, a technical student who studies auto repair is usually only able to use his or her education for a job in the auto repair field, but a student who earns an associate's or bachelor's degree in biology can get a job in a field that isn't related to biology. Also, associate's and bachelor's grads can go to graduate school to study a totally different field, like law, for example. In this way, technical grads can have limited career flexibility, and may not be able to switch career fields as easily as other kinds of grads.

On the other hand, a large number of college graduates are now enrolling in technical schools, because they can't find good jobs with just a college degree, and technical programs can provide good career training.[695] These students may have been able to save a lot of time and money if they had simply enrolled in technical school in the first place, before ever attending a two-year or four-year college. Students who want to learn more about technical programs can take a look at Peterson's guide to *Vocational and Technical Schools,* which includes descriptions and advice for thousands of accredited programs across the country. Once again, students should check with potential employers and graduate schools to verify that the degrees they plan to pursue will have adequate educational and financial value. Some career fields even offer on-the-job training, and therefore don't require a technical degree.

Finally, some students benefit from combined undergraduate-graduate "joint degree" programs. For example, some schools offer a five-year combined college/MBA program, or a six-year combined college/MD or college/JD program. These programs can reduce the number of years that students must spend in school (and therefore reduce students' overall costs). Students who are interested in these programs can look for the specific schools that offer them. However, students should also watch out for pitfalls, such as the possibility that they may change their career plans while they are in college (and then may have to switch schools).

DECIDING WHERE TO APPLY

Some students know what kind of college and degree they are looking for, but they are afraid that no college will accept them. However, the truth is that almost any student can go to college, if they want to. It's only the most prestigious schools that are very difficult to gain acceptance to, and many of them may not be worth the effort. In fact, 83% of the 857 largest non-profit four-year colleges accept more than half of the students who apply.[696] In addition, four-year colleges tend to accept 70% of the students who apply, on average,[697] and 70% of college applicants gain admission to their first-choice school.[698] Finally, students who are not accepted at a four-year school can often get accepted at a two-year (or associate's degree) school, where admission rates are often even higher.

However, most students don't want to spend too much time and money on pointless college applications. One way to avoid this is to apply to schools that best fit their interests. To narrow their list of options, students can start by considering their general preferences, such as where a school is located, the number of students at a school, or the types of classes, majors, and extracurricular activities that a school offers (including which classes are required, which classes are off-limits, and whether the school will require them to complete any summer school). Then, when students have a small list of college options, they can focus on more important factors, like which schools offer the best quality and value. And students can estimate each school's affordability by calculating their potential out-of-pocket costs at each one, remembering that colleges with high sticker prices may actually have lower costs for them, depending on their financial situation and merit aid eligibility. As mentioned in Chapter 6, students may even be able to obtain financial aid estimates from colleges before they submit any formal applications.

Students should also check that their preferred colleges are properly accredited. Many students have recently been getting degrees from schools that are not accredited, but these degrees often have low value. To find out if a school is properly accredited, people can look at the website for the Council on Higher Education Accreditation, www.chea.org. The most-respected college accrediting organizations are the six "regional" organizations, which include: the Middle States Association of Colleges and Schools; the New England Association of Schools and Colleges; the North Central Association of Colleges and Schools; the Northwest Commission on Colleges and Universities; the Southern Association of Colleges and Schools; and the Western Association of Schools and Colleges. Colleges that are not accredited by these agencies may be wasteful for students to attend, because employers and graduate schools may not value their classes or degrees. Students should also make sure that any school they are considering has a phone number and mailing address, and has a website address that ends in "edu."[699] Many of the most famous colleges are accredited, but it may be helpful for students to ask each school's admissions office about the school's accreditation organization, and whether the school is on "accreditation probation" (which might signal a serious problem). Students can also check with each accrediting organization, to make sure that the schools are telling the truth about their accreditation status.

In addition, although students often enjoy easy classes, they may benefit by looking for the schools that will provide the best instruction and personal attention in their preferred majors (rather than the schools that will simply encourage them to memorize information they will easily forget, require them to write many useless term papers, or provide them with poor instructors). Students can review ratings for some college teachers at websites such as www.ratemyprofessors.com, and www.reviewum.com. Some colleges even publish pamphlets containing student ratings of their professors. Also, students can consult general college guides and directories, accreditation or certification agencies, graduate schools, employers, friends, teachers, and guidance counselors. And students can talk to people who have actually spent time at the colleges, including current students, instructors or administrators, and recent graduates.

As described previously, non-profit 4-year colleges that focus on research (including many prestigious schools) are sometimes <u>not</u> the best place to find good college-level teaching, so students may want to consider a wide variety of schools. In particular, Loren Pope believes that small, private "liberal arts" colleges offer strong student communities, and professors who are dedicated to teaching,[700] and Pope has written a book that describes some of these schools, titled *Colleges That Change Lives* (www.ctcl.com). Another website that highlights approximately 200 promising schools is called "Colleges of Distinction" (www.CollegesOfDistinction.com).

Surprisingly, some of the least-famous schools are also the ones that provide the best education and the best value for students. As Marilee Jones, admissions dean at MIT, points out: "Just because [students] haven't heard of a college doesn't mean it's no good."[701] Maria Furtado, admissions director at Clark University, adds: "[It's good for students] to be brave and bold and explore [colleges they] haven't heard of before."[702] However, students should also make sure that the school they choose will be affordable and provide adequate career preparation.

Students can also check the graduation rates at each of their preferred schools; schools that have unusually low graduation rates may have serious problems, and should probably be avoided. The College Results website (http://www.collegeresults.org/) includes the graduation rates, by student demographic group, for all colleges, and another helpful website is located at http://nces.ed.gov/globallocator. In addition, the U.S. Department of Education manages one of the best college databases, College Navigator, which is free for students to use and features a wealth of data on almost every college, including accreditation status, degrees offered, admissions data, most-popular majors, and graduation rates (http://nces.ed.gov/collegenavigator/).

Also, students probably don't want to waste time and application costs on schools that won't accept them. Therefore, students can estimate their acceptance chances by comparing their own academic grades and scores to the average grades and scores of the students that each school usually accepts. For example, students can find lists of schools' recent average admissions data in books and websites, such as the *Ultimate College Guide,* by *U.S. News and World Report,* or *The Best Colleges,* by The Princeton Review. Some good news for students is that there are now over 700 schools that <u>do not</u> require or place much emphasis on students' SAT or ACT scores when making admissions decisions, and a list of these schools is available at: www.fairtest.org/univ/optional.htm.

When students develop a list of their preferred schools, they can then classify all of these schools into one of three categories:[703] "Safety" (the applicant's scores are much better than average scores at the school), "Reach" (the applicant's scores are a little lower than average scores at the school), and "Good Match" (the applicant's scores are about equal to the average scores at the school). Then, students can apply to an equal number of each of these three kinds of schools.[704] So, since experts often suggest that students should apply to at least 9 schools, students can apply to at least 3 'safety' schools, 3 'reach' schools, and 3 'match' schools. It's also probably a good idea for students to apply to at least one or two schools with low sticker prices, such as public 4-year and 2-year colleges within their home states.

WINNING THE COLEGE ADMISSIONS GAME

When students decide on a list of about 9-15 schools that might be a good fit for them, they then have to apply to the schools. Although colleges usually require students to complete a costly and complicated application process, there are some things students can do to successfully survive this ordeal.

For example, students who take admissions tests may be able to reduce their costs by applying for SAT "fee waivers" at http://www.collegeboard.com/student/testing/sat/calenfees/feewaivers.html, or ACT "fee waivers" at http://www.actstudent.org/faq/answers/feewaiver.html. Students may also be able to avoid paying expensive college application fees by writing a letter to schools that describes their difficult financial situation and requests "an application fee waiver." In addition, students may be able to use the application fee waiver form at: "www.nacac.com/downloads/form_feewaiver.pdf", or create a similar one for their own personal use.

Some students, and their families, hire professional counselors to help them gain admission to their preferred colleges, but professional admission counseling can be an expensive waste. The problem is that these counselors often charge students and their families hundreds or thousands of dollars for services that are unhelpful, or unnecessary. For example, some professional admission counselors will only work with students who already have good grades, so these students probably don't really need any special help to get accepted by the schools of their choice.[705] Students who still want to use a professional counselor should first evaluate the counselor by getting opinions from other people who have already used his or her services. Since offers that sound too good to be true are usually scams, students should be suspicious of counselors that guarantee student acceptances to any particular college.

Although students should probably not use any "early admissions" or "early decision" college application plans, they often have the best chance of getting accepted to a school when they send in their regular application to the school as early as possible. For example, many schools accept regular applications up to a year before enrollment, using a "rolling admissions" process, and filling their student spots as they receive the applications, in a non-binding way that does not force students to attend the schools if they are accepted. When students submit regular applications as early as these schools allow, there are more open admissions spots available for them. In fact, students can gain an advantage at almost any school by submitting their regular applications early, so students should try to send in their regular applications as early as schools will accept them (this date can be different for each school). In addition, students can safely use schools' "early action" or "early option" admissions plans, because these plans give students much more power and choice, and are therefore not as problematic as schools' other binding early admissions plans.

It's also important to note that, although schools sometimes use students' enthusiasm against them, by offering them less valuable financial aid packages, students should still express as much enthusiasm and interest as they can during the admissions process. The reason for this is that many schools won't accept students unless they express clear enthusiasm, so students can gain a significant admissions advantage by conveying their excitement. Then, once accepted, students can use the aid tips and negotiation strategies described in Chapter 6 to try to get the best financial deals from the schools.

Finally, students can often obtain free information and assistance regarding the college admissions process within places like high schools, colleges, libraries, counseling centers, and the Internet (at sites like http://www.collegenet.com/about/index_html, www.collegeview.com, http://colleges.com/admissions/collegesearch/index.html, www.xap .com, and www.collegeconfidential.com).

RESPONDING TO REJECTION

Although students work very hard on their college applications, the reality is that many students get rejected from at least one school that they apply to. If a student believes that he or she has been unfairly denied admission to a school, the student can write a letter to the school about the situation. In their letter, students can politely express their desire to attend the school, and try to encourage the school to reconsider them for admission by once again highlighting their skills, aptitudes, interests, and strengths (including any new achievements that they did not include on their original applications).

It can be very disappointing for students when a preferred school denies them from being admitted, but the good news is that there are usually many other excellent college options for them to choose from. For better or worse, there's no such thing as a "perfect college." And students who don't receive any acceptances from 4-year schools can consider applying to public 2-year schools, which often accept students at all times of the year.

DECIDING WHICH COLLEGE TO ATTEND

After students consider different kinds of college options, apply to schools, and receive offers of acceptance and financial aid, it's then time for them to make a decision about which school to attend. Students can make this decision by carefully comparing the potential educational, financial, and emotional costs and benefits for each school that accepts them. And students should probably try to avoid getting too distracted by less important college factors, such as: how close a school is to a boyfriend or girlfriend; the number of social events at a school; the quality of a school's Greek system (fraternities and sororities); or the quality of a school's sports teams and sporting events.

It's especially important for students to pick colleges that will have long-term affordability for them, so that they will be able to pay for all of the costs for the 2-6 years or so that they will need to get their degrees. Many students who can't afford the long-term costs at a particular college are forced to drop out,[706] and this often delays (or prevents) their graduation date and increases their overall costs. Justin R. Erickson, a freshman at Grinnell College, is not sure he can continue to afford the school, and he illustrates a dangerous college affordability attitude: "It will be interesting to see what happens down the road."[707] Unfortunately, students who don't enroll at affordable schools may experience former student Debbie Alford's common problem: "I was paying for college myself. I hardly ever spent money on going out or having fun. But I still managed to get into a hole just from living expenses, to the point where I felt like the only way I could get out of debt was if I left school."[708]

In summary, since every student has different goals, and every school has different advantages and drawbacks, and college prestige is usually meaningless, students just need to pick an affordable school that is a "good enough" fit for them. Students who follow the strategies in this book should be able to pick a school that fits this description. A.G. Lafley, Proctor & Gamble's CEO, reminds students to not get too crazy about the college search, or overspend for college, because, as long as students seek out some basic standards, "Any college will do."[709] And Thomas Neff, chairman of employment firm Spencer Stuart, points out that when it comes to long-term career success, "It's what you've accomplished [after college] that matters."[710] For some additional assistance in picking an appropriate college, readers can review the second Appendix at the end of this book, "Putting Colleges to the Test," which collects some key questions about the education investment that students (and their families) can ask and answer before enrolling in any school.

Many students worry about their college choice, and they should; after all, their time, money, hopes and dreams are riding on it. However, students are not necessarily stuck with their college decision forever. After spending some time at a college, students may decide that the school is a bad educational, financial, or emotional fit for them. Although students have to pay the costs for any time that they spend at a college, they always have the option of transferring to a different one.

• • •

In addition to picking an appropriate school, and getting a good financial aid deal, there are many other things that students can do to save money on their college investment. The next chapter highlights some additional money-saving tips that students can use once they actually enroll.

CHAPTER 9

GETTING MORE FOR LESS
Saving Money While Enrolled

Even after students pick affordable and valuable schools and enroll, there are a few more things they can do to save money, get better value, and lower their college risk.

TUITION TIPS

First, students can use several additional tuition strategies to get a good education for less.

TIP #1: Take classes during traditional school-year breaks
Colleges often charge lower prices for the classes they offer during their break periods, including summer breaks, fall breaks, winter breaks, and spring breaks. Students are even sometimes able to take an entire course during one two-week break. And students who take classes during breaks may also be able to save money by graduating earlier and getting into the workplace faster.

TIP #2: Transfer credits from one school to another
Students can sometimes take one or more classes at an inexpensive school (such as a 2-year or 4-year public college), and then "transfer" these credits to a more expensive (but still affordable) school (such as a private college). It's even possible for students to take these less expensive classes during their regular school's breaks. In addition, many students now save

money by attending a less expensive school for one or two years, and then transferring over to a more expensive school to complete their degrees. Some students even transfer from community colleges to Ivy League schools like the University of Pennsylvania and Columbia University.[711] In this way, students can cut their costs but still receive a degree from a more expensive school.

Unfortunately, some students may not be able to transfer all of their credits to a new school. For example, to increase their income, many schools restrict the number of credits that students can transfer from other schools. To try to avoid this problem, students should ask potential schools if they would accept transfer credits (and then enroll in the classes that will be accepted). It's often easier for students to transfer class credits that are granted by regionally-accredited schools. Although transferring from one school to another can require some re-adjustment, it's often worth it if a student can cut their costs or switch to a school that's a better fit.

TIP #3: Take extra classes each semester at no extra cost

Most colleges tend to charge one set tuition price for one entire semester, no matter how many classes or credits students take during the semester, so students can use this pricing system to take extra classes for free. For example, although many full-time students take a total of 4 classes per semester, students may also be allowed to take one extra class, for a total of 5 classes per semester, at no extra charge. In this way, students can get more for their money, and possibly graduate earlier than usual, saving thousands of dollars.

TIP #4: Take fewer classes during the senior year

Students who have completed almost all of the credits they need in order to graduate can sometimes take fewer classes than usual during their senior, or final, year. For example, if a student only needs 2 more classes in order to graduate, then he or she may be able to save money by only taking 2 classes in the final semester, instead of the usual 4 classes.

A WORD OF CAUTION

Although many students use these kinds of tuition strategies to save thousands of dollars, these strategies do <u>not</u> make sense for every student. For example, students who receive scholarships or grants may not be able to save any money by using the strategies above, since these students already receive a discount on their tuition costs. Also, students may have to pay extra costs in order to take classes during school breaks. In addition, it doesn't make sense for students to take extra classes during a semester if their school charges extra for these classes, or if they can't handle the extra work. And many students have to work for pay, so they don't have the time to take extra classes during the regular school year, or on breaks. Finally, some health insurance plans and loan programs require students to take a certain number of classes during every semester, so students could lose their health insurance coverage or loan funding unless they check with these companies before taking fewer classes. Therefore, since tuition strategies can be harmful if not properly used, students should talk with the "registrar" (registration office), or other advisor, counselor, or staff member at their schools before using any of these techniques.

EXPLORING HOUSING OPTIONS

To avoid schools' over-priced or unhelpful on-campus housing, students should consider and compare the costs of both on-campus and off-campus housing near their schools, realizing that off-campus housing may be their least expensive option (if their schools allow them to live off-campus). Students who live off-campus may have to pay extra for furniture and utilities, but off-campus housing may still be a less expensive option, even with these expenses. In addition, students can sometimes find low-cost housing within their schools' fraternity or sorority houses (or other "theme" houses), but these organizations may have their own costs and drawbacks. And, although many students don't want to live at home with their parents while they go to college, this is probably their least expensive option, helping them (and their families) save thousands of dollars.

Students who plan to live on-campus can consult the guides published by The Princeton Review (*The Best Colleges,* and *The Complete Book of Colleges*), which feature fire safety ratings and general quality-of-life ratings for many schools.

FRUGAL FOOD STRATEGIES

Since many schools offer unhealthy, unenjoyable, or overpriced food choices, students may be able to find schools that <u>do not</u> require them to purchase meal plans. However, since most schools require meal plans, students can often reduce their total costs by choosing the plans that offer the lowest number of meals, such as picking a 5-meals-per-week plan instead of a 10-meal plan (even though 5-meal plans feature a higher price per meal).

The best college meal plans are usually "flex," or "debit," plans that allow students to have flexibility by only charging them for the food that they eat (and offering refunds for any food they don't eat). These kinds of meal plans are offered by a number of schools, including: Iona College in New York, Loyola College in Maryland, North Idaho College in Idaho, and Rochester Institute of Technology in New York. In addition, some student organizations, such as fraternities and sororities, offer low-priced meal plans for their members (but, once again, these groups may have their own costs and drawbacks).

AVOIDING EXTRA FEES

Some students may also be able to save money on the many expensive extra fees that schools charge. For example, students who can avoid paying their school bills on their credit cards will protect themselves from debt and avoid schools' extra credit card fees. In addition, students who don't want to participate in athletics or campus activities can ask their schools to waive their "athletic" and "activity" fees. And, to avoid paying extra fees for dropping or adding classes, students can sign up for the classes that they are fairly confident they will complete over the full semester.

AVOIDING INTERNSHIP FEES

Since practical experience is so essential for students' career success, many students obtain real-world training experiences while they are in college. For example, millions of students complete internship, co-op, volunteer and other practical career experiences every year. Specifically, more than six out of ten college students have at least one internship experience.[712] The problem is that many schools charge their students thousands of dollars for the internship experiences, especially when the internships are required for graduation—even though about half of all interns are unpaid[713] (or low-paid), and schools often have little involvement in the internships.

To avoid schools' expensive internship fees, students can try to obtain internships or volunteer positions without college involvement, especially positions that do not require college credit. To find these kinds of positions, students can consult books and websites like *The Internship Bible,* by The Princeton Review, www.monstertrak.com, and www.internships.com.

However, many students can't work in volunteer jobs or internships because they either can't afford schools' fees, or they need to work for pay. The good news is that students can get paid practical experience, without paying their schools, by getting regular part-time or full-time jobs in their preferred career fields. In fact, students may be able to earn high salaries by directly submitting their resumés to any companies they admire (through companies' Human Resources, or HR, departments). Students may also be able to obtain high-paying short- and long-term jobs through staffing agencies in their cities and towns, such as Office Team (www.officeteam.com), Kelly Services (www.kellyservices.com), Manpower, Inc. (www.manpower.com), The Creative Group (www.creativegroup.com), or Robert Half International (www.rhmr.com). And some websites are devoted to listings of temporary and permanent jobs, such as www.monstertrak.com, www.net-temps.com, www.craigslist.org, www.hotjobs.com, and www.monster.com.

It's important to note that many paid jobs are located within corporate or administrative environments, which can provide good salaries but may require basic computer skills (including Microsoft Office software) that can be self-taught from books.

Students can also gain some excellent practical experience by working in on-campus jobs or positions at their schools. To find these jobs, students can check with offices at their schools, such as the financial aid office, career services office, student services office, or a student organization office, to see if any of these positions are available. Unfortunately, on-campus work-study jobs usually offer low salaries, or no salaries, but some lucky students can receive tuition discounts by holding high-level jobs at their schools while they also attend classes full-time. Students may also be able to gain unpaid practical experience by participating in "extracurricular activities," or student clubs, at their schools, including music clubs, newspapers, magazines, radio stations, yearbook committees, volunteer organizations, political groups, and the Greek system (fraternities and sororities).

THE NEED FOR SPEED

Another way for students to cut their college costs, including their living expenses, is by finishing their degrees on-time (in four years or less). Therefore, students may want to finish college as quickly as possible, while also keeping costs low and affordable. In order to accomplish this, students can try to avoid actions like changing majors, failing classes, and dropping classes—especially when the costs of doing so will not justify the benefits.

Some students think that they should "drop" classes in the middle of the semester if they are getting bad grades, so that the classes won't hurt their total "grade point averages"—but dropping classes can increase students' costs. Specifically, students are usually required to pay for the classes they drop, and then they also must spend more time and money to make up the classes during a later semester. Therefore, students should probably not drop a class unless they are definitely on-track to fail the class, or if a bad grade in the class will adversely affect their ability to keep a scholarship, transfer to another college, get into graduate school, or get hired by an employer. In addition, it can be helpful for students to talk to an academic advisor before completing a drop, to ensure they are making a correct decision.

Finally, many students wonder if they should either go to college on a part-time basis or a full-time basis, and they can make this decision by weighing the costs and benefits of each option. For example, it can be helpful for a student to go to college full-time if they will earn a high salary when they graduate: the sooner they can obtain this salary the better. On the other hand, if a student's employer will pay for all or most of their college expenses, it can make sense for them to work full-time and complete college part-time. In addition, it can be better for students to attend college on a part-time basis if they need to work for pay and can't afford to attend college full-time.

CUSTOMER SERVICE SOURCES

Although many colleges deliver poor customer service, students can use a number of strategies to try to resolve their concerns and complaints, and get the services they pay for. For example, students can contact the specific administrative department associated with their concern, such as the admissions department, Registrar, bursar, office of student services, housing or financial aid office. And students who have a concern regarding a specific academic department can ask for help within the specific department, be it the psychology department, business department, English department, or music department, for example.

Specifically, most academic departments have a "chairperson" or "dean" that students can try to contact. Students can also contact the main administrators at their schools, like the vice presidents, deans, provosts, trustees—or the school presidents. Administrators who receive enough complaints about an issue may try to take action to solve a student's problem or improve the school.

Finally, many schools have an "ombudsperson" that students can contact for assistance. The ombudsperson is someone who helps settle disagreements between different people at the school, including students, professors, and administrators. The ombuds is usually a safe person to talk to, because ombuds conversations are confidential, or private. Although the ombudsperson isn't the most powerful person in the school, and offers no guarantees, the ombuds has a significant amount of influence and can help students resolve many kinds of problems. Students can contact the ombuds through email, phone, or even in their offices.

SIDESTEPPING THE OTHER SHARKS

Of course, schools are not the only organizations that want students' money. Therefore, students also need to protect themselves from the marketing efforts of many other companies and businesses that specifically target them.

Textbook companies

Textbook companies tend to take advantage of students by charging very high prices. For example, book companies raise textbook prices by 6-7% every year, and companies raised prices by 33% from 1998-2004[714]—which is much faster than general inflation. In fact, publishers often raise book prices by "bundling," or combining, the books with extra features that students don't need, like CD-ROMs. At least half of all textbooks come with bundled materials[715]—but more than six out of ten professors say that they rarely or never use the extra materials.[716]

Publishers also release "new" editions of textbooks every year, even though three out of four professors say that they don't need them and can use the older editions instead.[717] However, new editions allow publishers to increase their profits, because once a new edition is released, students are required to buy it, and six out of ten students say that it's difficult or impossible for them to find (less expensive) used versions of the books they need.[718] This strategy also allows publishers to increase their income by making older editions worthless.

In addition, some textbook companies pay thousands of dollars to professors and entire college departments, who then require their students to buy the companies' expensive books.[719] A textbook salesperson recently admitted these kickbacks to the *Chronicle of Higher Education*, saying: "To be blunt, you have to find a way to buy off the professor." And Paul Heilker, director of an English program at Virginia Tech, admits that his department specifically chose textbooks that would lead to publisher payments because the department was "looking for external revenues," and realized that this kind of deal "could really help out [the department] financially."

College textbook publishers leverage these kinds of strategies to increase their income, while students foot the bill for the extra costs. For example, the average college student pays $900 per year for textbooks (and graduate students often pay even more), generating over $7 billion per year for textbook publishers, distributors, and stores.[720] Specifically, publishers get $4 billon per year,[721] and college bookstores get about 23% of the money spent on textbooks.[722]

A number of public interest groups have criticized textbook publishers' policies,[723] and some students have signed a petition to encourage publishers to lower their prices.[724] Even the federal government has launched its own investigation into textbooks, confirming the problems,[725] but not forcing any changes yet. On the other hand, some individual states are taking action, and a legal bill has been introduced in California to try to get publishers to lower their prices.[726] To fight for lower textbook prices, several groups have banded together to form a campaign called "Make Textbooks Affordable" (www.MakeTextbooksAffordable.com).

Although publishers continue to raise textbook prices, students can use several strategies to try to save money. For example, students may be able to: borrow their textbooks for free from a library; share the purchase with other students; rent the book from a textbook rental service; or buy less-expensive electronic versions of the books. In fact, several schools and states are planning new textbook rental services for students, including California.[727] Students may also be able to legally buy the books they need at lower prices by looking in other countries, such as Mexico,[728] sometimes saving as much as $50 on the price of each book.[729]

In addition, students may be able to save money on their textbooks by buying them from discount websites like: www.bookfinder.com; www.campusbookswap.com; www.half.com; www.walmart.com; www.textbookx.com; www.amazon.com; www.ebay.com; www.bigwords.com; www.barnesandnoble.com; www.booksoncampus.com; www.bookdonkey.com; www.scseller.com; www.calpirgstudents.org; www.bookcentral.com; www.cheapbooks.com; or www.craigslist.org. And students may be able to obtain free textbooks from websites like: Freeload Press (www.freeloadpress.com); Textbook Revolution (www.textbookrevolution.org); Gutenberg (www.gutenberg.org and www.gutenberg.org/browse/scores/top); and Google (http://books.google.com).

Finally, students can sometimes get some money back by

selling the books they have already used. However, bookstores will only pay about half the price that they paid to the publisher (which can end up being only 25% of what the student first paid),[730] and there are many used books that stores won't buy back (especially if a new version is already available). Therefore, students may get more money by selling their used books directly to other students (either in-person or online), if they are lucky to have a book that is still in use.

Honor societies

Students may also want to avoid costly "honor society" memberships; in some ways, many honor societies are looking for the smartest suckers they can find. Students sometimes join "honor societies," like Phi Beta Kappa, because they believe that membership will allow them to gain prestige or respect. But honor societies often just take students' money, without delivering any true value.

In 2002, over 300,000 college and university students joined honor societies within the Association of College Honor Societies, and these students spent a total of $10 million on membership fees[731]—but this only includes about 70 organizations, or only about half of all honor societies, so many more students joined across the country. These fees are a jackpot for the societies, allowing their executives to receive hundreds of thousands of dollars each year.[732] For example, Golden Key has paid its founder and chairman $300,000 per year, and three top aides received $100,000 each. In addition, both the Phi Beta Kappa and Phi Kappa Phi chiefs receive over $100,000 per year.[733]

Each honor society can cost $50 for students to join, which isn't very expensive—but students usually don't receive any helpful services by joining. In fact, the only thing that students usually receive from their honor societies is a paper membership certificate. And few employers or graduate programs care whether students have honor society memberships.[734]

In addition, many honor societies use suspicious membership practices. For example, some honor societies ask their current members to pick their new members, but this system is suspect because it has more to do with popularity than with good academic performance. Also, some societies lower their academic standards so that they can accept more students and continue to receive a large amount of money every year.[735] Therefore, although honor societies offer some social and charitable benefits, honor society costs are often a waste of money for students.

Other targeted marketing

An entire industry has been created that focuses on marketing to college students, shamelessly and profitably pitching products to this valuable group. For example, companies like Alloy Inc., 360 Youth, and Amp Agency specifically target college and graduate students through publications, advertising, product sample distribution, marketing events, market research, regular mail, and email. Alloy explicitly brags about its ability to "engage transient and elusive college students," using an aggressive marketing network that "targets college students, in their places, on their terms, 24/7," to get students to buy products, and allow companies to benefit from college students' "$200 billion in spending power per year."[736] Although these marketing efforts can help students find new products they might like, these efforts can also encourage students to spend more than they can afford, so students should realize they are being targeted, and manage their money very carefully.

• • •

Students can use the kinds of strategies discussed in this

chapter to save thousands of dollars while they're in school, but students usually also have to pay expensive college costs after they leave school—especially if they have loans or credit charges to pay off. Therefore, the next chapter includes an overview of money-saving strategies students can use after their college education is over.

CHAPTER 10

TIL DEBT DO US PART
Managing Debt After Leaving School

The joy of graduation can be reduced by the reality that expensive educational debt from loans and credit cards must now be paid back. However, there are a number of strategies that people can use to make this payment process easier.

LOAN FORGIVENESS

First, some lucky graduates can have a portion of their student loan debt "forgiven," or cancelled, by working in certain public service jobs for several years, such as teaching, social work, health care, or public interest law. Specific information about student loan forgiveness is available at http://www.finaid.com/loans/forgiveness.phtml. In addition, some employers pay for some or all of their employees' student debt. But loan forgiveness only solves debt problems for a small number of students, so it's important for students to understand their other options.

THE BENEFITS AND DANGERS OF THE "LOAN GRACE PERIOD"

Students are often allowed to use a "loan grace period," but this feature has both benefits and drawbacks. For example, the grace period allows students to not pay any loan bills for the first six to nine months after they leave school, which can be especially helpful for those who have low salaries—or no job at all.

However, the drawback of the grace period is that expensive interest charges can build up during this time. For example, a six-month grace period can easily lead to an extra $2,500 in loan interest costs for the average student (over 30 years of loan payments).[737] While this may only add an extra 4%, or $7, to students' monthly expenses, the costs may outweigh the benefits over many years of bills; $2,500 is a lot to pay for just a 6-month delay in payments. In addition, some lenders may increase students' interest rates during the grace period, leading to even higher costs.

Therefore, students need to decide if they either want to use the grace period, or want to start paying back their loans as soon as they leave school. It's usually a good idea for students who have subsidized loans to use all or part of their loan grace period, especially because the government pays for their loan interest costs during this time. On the other hand, unsubsidized loans build up interest charges during the grace period, so students who have these loans may want to decline the grace period and start paying the loans back right away, if they can afford it.

LOAN CONSOLIDATION BENEFITS AND DANGERS

In addition, students are sometimes allowed to "consolidate" their loans, but student loan consolidation also offers some important benefits and drawbacks. For example, since students often have one loan for every semester they've completed, consolidation makes repayment easier for them by combining all of their loans into one monthly payment. Consolidation also sometimes allows students to lock in a fixed interest rate, which can help students save thousands of dollars if the interest rate is low. Students can even sometimes get an interest rate discount if they consolidate their loans during their grace period. And many consolidation lenders promise to reduce the cost of students' monthly loan bills.

However, these benefits aren't exactly free. Since consolidation often extends students' loan repayment period from 10 years to 30 years, a consolidated loan can cost thousands more in interest charges than a regular loan—but lenders don't warn students about this extra cost. For example, a $23,000 loan that's paid off in 10 years can cost a total of $33,000 (at 8% annual interest), but the same loan can cost $60,000 when paid off over 30 years!

On the other hand, most students should use loan consolidation, because lower interest rates and reduced monthly bills are helpful for new grads, who often struggle to make ends meet on low salaries. In addition, consolidation doesn't force students to use all of the repayment years that are available to them, so students can always save thousands of dollars in interest charges by repaying their loans early, or "prepaying" their loans, if they choose to. For example, a student who has a 30-year loan is allowed to repay the loan in 10 years, if they want to, and if they can afford it. Therefore, it's usually good for borrowers to get the longest possible debt repayment period for any of their loans, so that the extra repayment time will be there if they need to use it.

Although loan consolidation is usually a good idea, students should make this decision carefully; once students "consolidate" their loans, they cannot usually reverse this adjustment (their loans must stay consolidated), and they cannot usually switch lenders. In addition, it's important to note that students can best protect themselves by borrowing a loan amount that they will be able to pay back over 10 years, and then extending the affordable 10-year debt to 20 or 30 years of repayment.

PICKING A CONSOLIDATION LENDER

College students and grads are often flooded with many aggressive consolidation offers from loan companies, and it's common for each graduate to receive several contacts from consolidation companies each week.

The most dangerous aspect of consolidation companies' marketing is that many of their advertisements and offers are misleading, or don't give students all of the information that they need to make a good decision. For example, many consolidation companies "bait and switch" students by advertising lower interest rates than students can really obtain. Some loan consolidation companies also charge very expensive fees. And companies usually don't warn students about the much higher costs they may pay by extending their repayment periods.

However, there are a few things students can do to protect themselves and figure out which consolidation offers will be least-expensive for them. For example, before consolidating their loans, students can figure out how much each consolidation company will charge them per month (including interest charges and extra fees). One possible way to do this is to compare each company's "APR" (see Chapter 7).

Students can also keep their costs low for the life of their loan by selecting consolidation lenders that offer low fixed interest rates and low fees. In addition, loan interest rates often change every July 1st, so students need to figure out if they will save money by consolidating before or after July 1st. And, although students should consider many different lenders because they can now use any lender to consolidate their loans, students' best bet is often to consolidate their loans with the original lender who gave them their loans in the first place. Also, it can be helpful for students to use lenders that do not charge extra fees for "prepayment." Finally, to get the best deals, students should usually consolidate their federal and private loans separately.

The consolidation process can be confusing, but students can ask for advice and assistance from people at their schools, including financial aid officers (although students should also use other sources, such as www.finaid.com, to confirm the accuracy and helpfulness of any loan advice they're given). Since some consolidation companies are much more expensive than others, students should be careful and not sign any contracts or papers about loan consolidation until they're sure they're getting a good deal.

Information about consolidation for Direct Loans through the U.S. Department of Education is available at 800-557-7392 or http://loanconsolidation.ed.gov/borrower/borrower.shtml. Lists of other potential consolidation lenders and their costs are available at: http://www.finaid.com/loans/biglenders.phtml, http://www.finaid.com/loans/privateconsolidation.phtml, and www.consolidationcomparison.com.

STUDENT LOAN REPAYMENT STRATEGY

> **Myth: Borrowers should pay back their student loans as quickly as possible.**

After graduation, some student loan borrowers may have extra money, and may think about paying off their loans as quickly as possible. However, although borrowers should pay their required monthly loan bills, it may be unhelpful for them to completely "prepay" their student loans (or pay them back quicker than originally scheduled).

There are several reasons why borrowers can benefit by just paying the required loan bill amount each month, without paying any extra. For example, tax discounts are not available for loans that are already paid off, so prepayment can reduce students' tax discounts. More importantly, students often have other debt that has higher interest rates than their student loan debt, and it's usually better for people to pay down the debt that has the highest interest rate. Specifically, it's usually best for borrowers to use their extra money to pay for current and expected credit debt, instead of using it to pay for student loans. And it's usually better for borrowers to use their extra money to pay for their home mortgages, if the mortgages have a higher interest rate than their student loans. Loan borrowers may even want to use their extra money for a home down-payment, especially if home ownership will be less expensive for them than renting their housing. Borrowers may also benefit from investing their extra money, instead of using it to pay down their loan debt; this is especially true when the investment return is higher than the debt interest rate, and when this investment return is guaranteed in "safe" investments like government bonds and CDs. Finally, it may be better for borrowers to save their extra money in case of emergency, rather than use it to prepay their student loans.

FIXING DEBT PROBLEMS

On the other hand, as described throughout this book, many student borrowers have the opposite problem: they can't afford to pay their required monthly debt bills because they were encouraged to borrow too much in loans and credit. However, the good news is that there are many ways for borrowers to get on the right track, and it's never too late to start this process.

Borrowers who are struggling should explore their debt payment options as soon as possible, because debt doesn't just disappear, and late payments usually increase borrowers' costs and reduce their repayment options. For example, borrowers who don't pay their bills will get charged for extra interest and late fees, and they can also be declared "delinquent," or "in default," possibly making it more difficult or expensive for them to buy other things in the future, obtain housing, or even get hired by an employer. The following strategies can help borrowers meet their payment obligations, even if they are already delinquent or in default:

- **Contact the financial aid office at school.** The financial aid office may have some good ideas and suggestions, making it easier for people to manage their debt.
- **Contact the lender or credit card company.** Lenders and credit card companies want to get paid, so they are usually willing to work out solutions with people who can't afford to pay their bills. For example, borrowers may be able to get a new payment plan, or new payment terms, including a lower interest rate, if they just ask directly. People should make these requests as soon as possible, because they may have more bargaining power while their credit rating is still solid.
- **Extended repayment.** Some lenders allow borrowers to extend the number of years that they have to repay their loans, and this can reduce their monthly bills. Of course, extended repayment can increase borrowers' costs over time, but this can be a great option for those who are struggling. Lenders that do not charge prepayment fees for these loans may be best, especially if they also offer

low interest rates.
- **Graduated repayment.** Only one out of ten college students are aware of this helpful program,[738] but this option allows people to have their debt bills lowered when they first graduate, and then steadily increased later, when it will (hopefully) be easier for them to afford the bills. "Income-contingent repayment" is a kind of graduated repayment in which people's debt bills are directly tied to their income, rising and falling along with changes in their salaries. Graduated repayment can cost extra money in interest charges over the long-term, but this program can make things easier for people who are struggling. Lenders that do not charge prepayment fees for these loans may be best, especially if they also offer low interest rates.
- **Deferment.** Only one out of three college students are aware of debt deferment or forbearance programs, but these options are also important.[739] Deferment allows borrowers to have their debt payments postponed for a few months or a few years. Of course, deferment can increase students' interest costs, but students won't be required to pay for the bills, or the interest fees, until their deferment period is over. People can contact their lenders to see if their debt payments can be deferred, but there's a limit to the number of times or number of months that borrowers can defer their debt. So borrowers should only use this option if they go back to school or have major trouble paying their bills.
- **Forbearance.** Forbearance is similar to deferment, because it allows borrowers to postpone, or lower, their debt payments, for a few months or years (often with extra interest costs). And forbearance can also only be used for a limited number of times. But forbearance is worse for borrowers than deferment, because forbearance can have

a negative impact on a borrower's credit rating, as well as more expensive interest fees. However, borrowers who have trouble paying their bills and who are not able to use deferment can contact their lenders to see if they are eligible for forbearance.
- **Refinancing.** It may be possible for borrowers to "refinance" their debt, and possibly obtain a lower interest rate. Refinancing may be available from the original lender, or by switching the debt to a different lender. Before refinancing, students should be careful to avoid extra charges and fees from the switch that could increase their overall debt costs.
- **Contact the Federal Student Aid Ombudsman.** Students who have trouble repaying a federal student loan can contact the FSA Ombudsman at the U.S. Department of Education, and the Ombuds may try to develop solutions between students and lenders. This Ombudsman can be contacted at: www.ombudsman.ed.gov; email: fsaombudsmanoffice@ed.gov; phone: 1-877-557-2575 or 1-202-377-3800; fax: 202-275-0549, or regular mail: U.S. Department of Education, FSA Ombudsman, 830 First Street, NE, Fourth Floor, Washington, DC 20202-5144.
- **Contact a lawyer or other legal counselor.** Lawyers can help borrowers work out new payment plans with their loan and credit companies. Current and former students may be able to consult with free legal counselors at their schools or other locations. In addition, borrowers can hire their own private lawyers.
- **Bankruptcy.** When someone files for bankruptcy, they may be able to have some or all of their debts erased, allowing them to make a new start. However, bankruptcy filings go on peoples' permanent credit records, possibly making it more difficult or expensive for people to buy other things

in the future, obtain housing, or get hired by employers. Also, in 2005, the U.S. government passed some new laws that make bankruptcy less helpful for borrowers (and more expensive),[740] and bankruptcy <u>never</u> erases borrowers' student loans. In addition, it's difficult or impossible for borrowers to file for bankruptcy more than once, so it's important to hold on to this option as long as possible. Therefore, borrowers should avoid bankruptcy and only use it as a final option, after they have exhausted all of their other reasonable options and have no other ways to pay off their debt.

Borrowers can learn much more about debt management strategies by reading books devoted to the topic, such as *The ABC's of Getting Out of Debt*, by Garrett Sutton, *The Money Book for the Young, Fabulous & Broke*, by Suze Orman, and *Generation Debt: Take Control of Your Money*, by Carmen Wong Ulrich. Borrowers can also look for debt management information on the Internet, at websites like http://ftc.gov/bcp/conline/edcams/credit/coninfo.htm.

AVOIDING THE DEBT COUNSELING SCAM

Some "debt counseling" or "credit counseling" companies can help people figure out effective ways to pay off their debts, but many of these companies are dangerous frauds. Too many of these companies charge high fees and provide poor service, doing more harm than good. For example, in March 2005, the government announced a legal settlement with four debt counseling companies that swindled customers out of a total of more than $100 million (the companies were: the National Consumer Council, Debt Management Foundation Services Inc., Better Budget Financial Services Inc., and AmeriDebt

Inc.).[741] Lydia Parnes, head of the U.S. Federal Trade Commission's consumer protection division, said "[These] companies lied about who they were, what they could do for consumers, and how much they charged."[742]

Unfortunately, many fraudulent companies still exist, so, before using the services of a debt counseling or credit counseling company, borrowers should be very careful and do their homework. For example, borrowers can ask around to see if anyone they know has heard of the company. Borrowers can also contact the Better Business Bureau to ask if any complaints have been reported. In addition, *BusinessWeek* suggests that borrowers should be suspicious of any companies that: charge more than $25-50 in monthly fees, offer a debt management plan within the first 20 minutes of the first meeting, or quickly ask about their credit card debt.[743] And the U.S. Federal Trade Commission recommends that people should avoid any debt counseling companies that "guarantee" to completely get rid of their debt.[744]

Although many debt counseling services are scams, people may be able to find affordable and approved debt counselors by calling the National Foundation for Credit Counseling at 1-301-589-5600, or going to www.nfcc.org, or http://www.debtadvice.org/takethefirststep/locator.html. In addition, a list of approved debt counselors is available at the website for the Association of Independent Consumer Credit Counseling Agencies, at www.aiccca.org, or http://aiccca.org/find.cfm. Finally, as described in Chapter 7, people who want help managing their finances can also consult a "certified financial adviser," and people can block companies from sending future debt offers by registering for a free blocking service.

THE MOST IMPORTANT RESOURCE OF ALL?

Sometimes, the toughest aspect of debt management involves dealing with frustration: people who have debt often feel overwhelmed, helpless, sad, embarrassed, ashamed, guilty, angry, desperate—or all of the above. However, borrowers are not alone in their situation, so anyone who feels upset about debt bills or financial problems should tap into their most important resource: the people they know. For example, borrowers can talk about their stressful situation with other people who can be helpful, like friends, family, co-workers, and teachers. Stress can make it difficult to think clearly and rationally, so worried borrowers can always benefit from the opinions, guidance, and assistance of others.

In addition, when someone has bad feelings or bad thoughts that don't go away, it's essential for them to consider obtaining mental health counseling. Counseling is usually affordable for anyone, because counselors, like psychologists, social workers, and therapists, often use "sliding scale fees," that allow lower-income clients to pay lower prices. In addition, many colleges and grad schools have counseling centers that are free for current and former students, and some schools and counseling training programs have centers that are open to the local community as well. People can also talk on the phone with a professional counselor for free, at any time and on any day, by calling 1-800-273-TALK (8255), OR 1-800-784-2433. General counseling information is also available on many websites, including http://www.campusblues.com/college_list.asp or the site managed by Psychology Today at http://www.psychologytoday.com/topics/, and http://therapists.psychologytoday.com/. And people who have trouble lowering their debt may also improve their situation by going to meetings for "Debtors

Anonymous," www.debtorsanonymous.org, or (781) 453-2743.

• • •

Once again, no matter how much debt someone has, it's never too late to start fixing debt problems. Sometimes, people just need some help to figure out the solutions—and many kinds of help and solutions are available. So, people should seek out the help they need to solve their debt burden and feel better.

Unfortunately, high education costs are also a major problem for graduate students. Therefore, the next (and final) chapter exposes the "Graduate School Rip-off," offering some strategies to help students get valuable graduate degrees at more affordable prices, and also offering some concluding advice for all readers.

CHAPTER 11

GREEDY GRAD SCHOOLS
Avoiding More Bad Deals

After college, many people want or need to go to graduate school in order to pursue master's degrees (like MBAs), doctoral degrees (like PhDs), or professional degrees (like MDs and JDs) that will allow them to fulfill their career dreams or obtain better salaries. Some people also go to graduate school because they can't find good jobs; Amy Wohlert, interim dean of graduate studies at the University of New Mexico, says, "it's a well-known truism that when the economy goes down, grad enrollment goes up."[745] Specifically, a total of about one out of five college graduates go to graduate school.[746]

Although many graduate students finish their degrees and achieve their goals, the graduate school investment is often more risky and dangerous than the college investment. To an even greater extent than colleges, graduate schools often encourage students to pay expensive prices and borrow too much, even if the degrees have little financial payoff. In fact, too many graduate school alumni have low salaries—or no jobs at all. Due to these high costs and frequently poor payoffs, many graduate school alumni are crushed under the weight of their educational expenses (monthly debt bills of $1,000 are common), and some postpone or cancel their career, personal, or financial goals.[747] One new lawyer says: "Having over $100,000 in student loan debt is not fun. Do I regret going [to law school]? No, but it certainly didn't pan out the way I thought it would. I am working like a fiend, not getting paid what most people think lawyers make, and struggling daily with money and budgeting. There are hundreds [of people], from my [graduating] class alone, who are in the same boat."[748] How can students get the benefits of graduate degrees while minimizing the common costs and risks?

GRADUATE SCHOOL PITFALLS

First, students need to understand the graduate school dangers. Since students need graduate degrees to pursue many careers, graduate schools can get away with charging even higher prices than colleges. Gary W. Reichard, the executive vice chancellor and chief academic officer for the California University system, says "because MBAs can offer tremendous salary boosts down the road, we can charge higher tuitions to students."[749] Grad schools also increase their profits by: raising their tuition prices; benefiting from their students' debt; accepting too many students (e.g., PsyD, law programs) or too few students (e.g., medical programs); aggressively soliciting donations; and offering low-quality or expensive food and housing. Many grad schools also benefit from cheap labor by accepting extra students who teach the schools' college classes and conduct research studies for them.

And, just like colleges, grad schools often provide poor instruction and customer service to their students. Specifically, non-English speaking instructors are often a problem, especially in particular programs like mathematics. Also, grad students often receive lectures from instructors who are more devoted to research than teaching. In addition, graduate programs often provide little career guidance for their students, neglecting to fully explain all of their career options and how to obtain them. And few graduate schools teach business skills to students in fields like medicine, law, accountancy, architecture,[750] or psychology, even though entrepreneurial skills are often critical for success in these careers.

Many graduate students even think that their classes are a waste of time. For example, many medical students believe they should be seeing patients instead of sitting in classrooms.[751] And many law school students believe that their schools waste the third year of law school by offering very little practical information they can use in their careers.[752] A recent study by the Carnegie Foundation supports the idea that typical law training has significant weaknesses.[753] Todd Rakoff, a Harvard Law School professor, also points out that most law schools, including Harvard's, haven't changed their teaching methods since "before the [invention of] the telephone,"[754] over one hundred years ago. This may help explain why only 50-60% of "bar exam" test-takers pass the exam in states like California, Delaware, Indiana, Maine, Nevada, New Hampshire, and North Carolina,[755] even though the vast majority of test-takers are law school graduates.

Even graduate business schools are often problematic for students. For example, Richard Schmalensee, dean of the MIT Sloan School of Management, says that business school instructors tend to offer poor practical training, and are too focused on conducting their own research studies.[756] Schmalensee writes: "The academic system's current methods for hiring and rewarding professors don't necessarily attract or encourage the kind of practitioner-oriented faculty we need to make business school research and MBA education much more attuned to meeting today's and tomorrow's management challenges." And business school employment recruiters tend to agree with him: a number of recruiters say that business school grads lack key skills, such as strategic thinking, leadership abilities, adaptability, and communication proficiency.[757]

In addition, many graduate schools have lowered their admissions standards, just to get more students to apply and pay their high prices. For example, a number of graduate business programs have dropped the requirement that students must spend several years working full-time before enrolling, including Washington University in Saint Louis, the University of Texas, Stanford University, Harvard University, and the University of Rochester.[758] While this strategy may allow schools to maintain their financial profits, it also tends to lead to decreased educational quality and a higher number of struggling grads.

As graduate schools strive to increase their financial income, they also often have strong incentive to inflate their students' grades, especially since many programs require their students to maintain "B" averages in order to remain enrolled.[759] Even worse, some of the most respected graduate business schools use "grade non-disclosure," refusing to reveal their students' grades to potential employers, including Chicago, Wharton (Pennsylvania), Stanford, and Harvard.[760] While this policy can be helpful for below-average students, it can also shield students from the kind of real-world competition they're supposed to be preparing for, and it frustrates employment recruiters because it prevents them from knowing which students have the best career preparation.

Finally, many graduate schools also force their students to pay high tuition prices for the opportunity to complete required work assignments that the schools have little to do with, including off-campus "practica" rotations, and internships in fields like psychology, education, business, and health sciences. High graduate expenses are especially unfair because many graduate students receive the bulk of their practical career training while they are not students. For example, medical students spend several years in hospital residency after medical school, business and law students have practical off-campus summer jobs that often lead to full-time employment after graduation, and clinical psychology trainees complete 12-month off-campus internships.

THE GRAD SCHOOL DROPOUT DISASTER

Unfortunately, graduate students also face a significant "dropout danger," because many of them pay high costs but don't finish their degrees. Specifically, graduate students can invest 2-10 years (or more) in graduate school, spending thousands of dollars, and then drop out with nothing to show for their investments. But whose fault is this? Isn't it students' responsibility to make sure they graduate?

Although graduate students' talent, motivation levels, and personalities can play a role in their degree completion, the reality is that graduate schools are largely responsible for their students' completion or attrition (non-completion). In fact, research studies reveal a surprising fact: there are no differences in academic ability between graduate students who drop out and graduate students who complete their degrees.[761] Peter Diffley, an associate dean of the Graduate School at the University of Notre Dame, analyzed 10 years of data and found that dropouts and completers are actually very similar.[762] This means that it's not just the weak students who drop out; instead, very talented students frequently fall by the wayside. It makes sense that many graduate-level dropouts are gifted, because schools often carefully evaluate and screen students before accepting them, putting them through a rigorous admissions process. However, this trend signals a major problem within graduate schools.

But exactly how are graduate schools responsible for their students' lack of effective progress? Unfortunately, grad schools often neglect their students in several ways. First, some graduate programs don't have enough teaching or research "assistantship" positions that often cover tuition costs and include stipend salary payment for students, so some students leave school because they can't afford to stay.

More commonly, graduate schools don't provide enough guidance, help, and direction to their students. In particular, students are usually matched up with individual faculty advisers when they are first admitted, but these relationships can be a poor fit from the start, or develop into a poor fit while the students are in the programs. Chris Golde, a senior scholar at the Carnegie Foundation for the Advancement of Teaching, says that student-advisor relationships are often "like a bad dating situation."[763] And more than three out of ten graduate students feel like they don't have a faculty mentor.[764]

In addition, graduate programs and advisors often don't set strict guidelines or deadlines for their students to finish certain graduation requirements. In contrast, students have a higher completion rate, and finish more quickly, in the rare programs that give them clear guidelines and deadlines.[765] Robert Peters, author of *The Smart Student's Guide to Earning a Master's or PhD*, adds: "One of the most common reasons [graduate] students are slowed down [(or prevented) from finishing their degrees] is that professors sit on [their] manuscripts for long periods without reading them. In my own case, my first adviser took fourteen months to read my thesis proposal, losing three copies before I gave him a fourth and forced him to read it in my presence."[766] Since many schools don't give students the structure and assistance they need, many graduate students never finish their degrees.[767]

But why would graduate programs not make more of an effort to help their students graduate as quickly as possible? In trying to figure this out, it's hard to ignore the fact that schools and professors can make more money by neglecting their students. For example, schools often require students to pay tuition costs during every semester until they graduate, even if a student is not taking any formal classes and is never on-campus! In addition, many schools increase their profits by using grad students as cheap sources of labor, and schools can continue to do so until the students graduate. And many professors profit from this situation as well, benefiting from their students' research work, and focusing on their own research and administrative work, and its rewards, rather than helping their students make reasonable and appropriate progress toward completion of their programs.

Since many talented and motivated grad students are not given enough support and guidance to complete their degrees, graduate attrition takes a huge emotional toll on them (in addition to the steep financial costs). Barbara Lovitts, author of *Leaving the Ivory Tower: The Causes and Consequences of Departure from Doctoral Study,* says that attrition is a "tremendously painful" disappointment for students.[768] Lovitts notes that many graduate school dropouts are the cream of the educational crop, and complete several years of graduate work before they experience "a tremendous opportunity cost," by being prevented from graduating, so "it takes people a lot of years to get over it."[769] Michael S. Teitelbaum, a program director at the Alfred P. Sloan Foundation, adds, "If actual attrition is really [at a high rate for graduate students], then this is a scandal. It's a serious waste of resources and a terrible waste of time and energy on the part of students."[770]

Many graduate school non-completers may feel like they've failed, but it's really the graduate schools that are to blame for students' lack of success. Even Robert Thatch, dean of Washington University's Graduate School of Arts and Sciences, admits that graduate attrition "destroys people's confidence in themselves when they perceive themselves as failures, when the problem should be laid at other doors. We [shouldn't] be in the business of disappointing people."[771] In addition, Lewis Siegel, chairman of the Council of Graduate Schools and dean of the Graduate School at Duke University, calls student attrition "the central issue in doctoral education in the United States today."[772]

To fix the graduate attrition problem, Dr. Lovitts says that schools need to take more action and responsibility: "My personal feeling is that when a university admits a graduate student to a program, they have an implicit contract to get them through. But a lot [of schools] fall down on that score."[773] Daniel Denecke, director of best practices for the Council of Graduate Schools, agrees that graduate programs need to make some important changes: "Probably the single most important thing that programs can do to promote [grad school] completion is truth in advertising. And there's not necessarily a uniform culture for advisers checking in [with students to assess their progress]."[774] However, since graduate schools will probably not change very much in the near future, students can try to protect themselves by enrolling in programs that will deliver the assistance they need.

THE RISKIEST GRAD SCHOOL INVESTMENTS

Graduate school is often a good investment, but some graduate programs are much riskier than others, especially those that require more time and money. For example:

- Many graduate programs have high tuition costs of $30,000 per year (or more), especially business schools, law schools, and medical schools;
- Some graduate programs require students to complete

up to 8 years of work (or more) after college, especially doctoral programs (leading to higher costs and more full-time income possibly sacrificed);
- Many graduate programs require their students to complete low-paying internship and fellowship experiences, including psychology and social work programs;
- Many professions require students to pay thousands of dollars in licensing fees, and students must pay these fees while they are in school, when they finish their degrees, and every few years after graduation for license renewals;[775] and
- The average graduate or professional student leaves school with a grad school loan debt burden ranging from $27,000 to $131,000, or a total loan debt burden ranging from $50,000 to $154,000 (including the average college loan debt of $23,000, but credit debt is extra). Some typical graduate school loan debt burdens are listed in Table 11.1.

In addition, many graduate students are burdened with higher-than-average debt levels. For example, students at 38 medical schools graduate with more than $130,000 average grad school debt (New York Medical College tops the list with $163,000 average grad school debt[777]). It doesn't help that average debt for all medical students has increased by 9% annually during the past 20 years, a total increase of 500%[778] In addition, students at 80 law schools graduate with more than $75,000 average grad school debt (University of Chicago tops the list with $114,000 average grad school debt).[779] And students at 24 graduate business schools leave school with more than $50,000 average grad school debt (Harvard University tops the list with $81,000 average grad school debt).[780]

Table 11.1 [Source (except where noted): 2003-2004 National Postsecondary Student Aid Study (NPSAS), as cited at http://www.finaid.com/loans/]

Grad Program	Percent of Students Borrowing	Approximate Cummulative Grad Debt
All Programs	60	$37,000
Masters	58	$27,000
Doctoral	51	$49,000
Professional	87	$83,000
M.S.W.	77	$27,000
M.B.A.	53	$36,000
Ph.D.	40	$37,000
Ed.D.	53	$49,000
Law (L.L.B or J.D.)	88	$71,000
Medical (M.D.)	95	$131,000[776]

Recent graduates like Kristin Cole and Paul-Henry Zottola represent some of the worst-case grad school debt scenarios.[781] Cole, who graduated from Michigan State University's law school, owes $150,000 in student loans, and has monthly payments of $660 (soon rising to $800). Due to her student loan debt, she says, "I could never buy a house. I can't travel; I can't do anything." Dr. Zottola is a periodontist who owes more than $300,000 in student loans, requiring monthly payments of $1,600, on top of his mortgage and $1,500 monthly bills for an additional loan he used to start his private practice. Zottola says, "It would be very easy to feel crushed by [my debt]. All my income for the next 10 years is spoken for."

It's true that many graduate students receive some

scholarships, grants, stipend payments, tuition remission, and assistantship or work-study positions to make their programs more affordable—but, since many of these students also graduate with very high debt levels, it's clear that these forms of assistance are not enough. Steve Desroches, a recent graduate of Columbia University's Graduate School of Journalism, says: "My student loan debt is my biggest source of stress in my life at the moment. I live paycheck to paycheck. My graduate education was invaluable [to my career], but it wasn't worth...the debt."[782]

> **Myth: Graduate degrees always lead to an excellent payoff for students.**

In addition to high costs, many graduate degrees lead to relatively low average salaries, including degrees in the arts, education, speech therapy, counseling, social work, and psychology. Some specific graduate-level careers that require large investments of time and money, but offer low financial payoffs, include:[783]

- Archaeologist: $38,620 (average annual salary);
- Architect: $34,000 for first-year intern, $68,900 for senior architect (after about 4 years for college, 3 years for a master's degree, and 3 years as an intern);
- Chef: $9.86-$19.13 an hour;
- Clergy: $39,900 (although their congregations may help pay for some living expenses);
- Social worker: (master's level): $40,000-$50,000;[784] and
- Teacher: $41,400-$45,920 (median).[785]

> **Myth: Prestigious jobs that require graduate degrees always pay well.**

In fact, graduate school even leads to some disappointing payoffs within the most prestigious professions, including some medical specialties. Part of the problem is that medical training has such high costs: these students attend medical school for 4 years, and rack up an average debt of more than $131,000 (as described above, plus college debt). Med school grads must then complete hospital "residency" programs (lasting 3-5 years) where they earn a salary of about $45,000 per year, which is lower than the salary of an average college graduate—even though medical residents work about 90 hours per week (making their dollar-per-hour rate quite low). Many students also complete master's degrees before or after medical school, further adding to their costs. And students who want to be "specialists" may need to complete 3-5 more years of "fellowship" program experience after residency, also at low salaries. Physicians must also complete a licensing process, including expensive exams and license applications that often cost thousands of dollars both at the beginning of their careers and every few years thereafter. And, in contrast to law and business school students, medical students can't pursue high-paying summer jobs because they must complete training during the summers.

The other part of the problem for medical graduates is that a number of them earn surprisingly low payoffs even after they finish their residencies, and the pediatrics field is particularly disappointing. Since new pediatricians usually can't afford to start their own practices, they have to find regular salaried positions. While some medical specialists earn hundreds of thousands of dollars per year, it's common for pediatricians to receive starting salaries of about $95,000.[786] Although this may seem like an excellent salary, it's only about $66,500 after taxes, and then only about $54,500 per year after pediatricians pay typical costs of $1,000 per month for their student loan bills. In this way, pediatricians can pay very high "debt-to-income" ratios of about 18% or more (after taxes), which is much more than experts recommend. In addition, although pediatricians' student debt has increased over 37% since 1997, their starting salaries have been <u>decreasing</u> since 1997 (after considering general inflation),[787] and their salaries tend to remain almost exactly the same during their first few years of work,[788] allowing general inflation to weaken their spending power even more. Also, pediatricians who work in private practice often work very long hours, including weekends in the office and hospital, and they must answer patients' phone calls from home, often all night long. Private practice pediatricians also usually receive no health or retirement benefits, and few holidays, sick days, personal days, or vacation. And doctors can't get tax deductions for their student loans, because their gross salaries are higher than the cutoff for this benefit. Since pediatricians often pay high costs, receive disappointing payoffs, and also lose out on many years of income while they train without pay, a pediatrician who completes 11-13 years of training (including college, medical school, residency, and possibly master's program) often won't financially catch up to a high school graduate until they are in their 40s or 50s, and it can take even longer to catch up to a typical college graduate. Ironically, doctors' salaries also usually aren't adjusted for cost-of-living expenses, so those who live in expensive areas get an even worse deal. In fact, physicians tend to receive higher salaries when they work in rural areas, because employers offer higher pay to attract doctors to these less desirable locations.[789] And doctors in big cities face stiff competition and struggle to find good jobs, especially in private practice.

Although the financial payoffs are disappointing for many prestigious graduate degrees, the worst average grad school payoff probably belongs to "doctoral" degrees, like the PhD

("Doctor of Philosophy," meaning "Doctor of Knowledge"), EdD ("Doctor of Education"), and PsyD ("Doctor of Psychology") diplomas. First, doctoral students have high education costs, including an average of 8-10 years <u>after college</u> for classes, thesis, and dissertation.[790] In addition, it's been estimated that as many as 40-50% of all doctoral students drop out of their programs (including two-thirds of doctoral students in the humanities)—a waste of talent at an incredible rate and at an incredible cost.[791] Amazingly, many of these dropouts have even reached the status of "ABD," an unofficial title meaning that they've spent many years and much money completing all of their graduation requirements, but can't obtain their degrees because they haven't received enough assistance with the final requirement, completing their dissertations ("<u>A</u>ll <u>B</u>ut <u>D</u>issertation"). And many doctoral grads receive relatively low salaries, including scientists, non-tenured professors, and psychologists. In addition, a number of doctoral grads have trouble finding employment: according to recent data, U.S. universities graduate about 25% more doctorates in science and engineering than the country has jobs for.[792] And doctoral students who expect to become professors are often disappointed, since many schools now use low-paid part-time instructors instead of hiring full-time tenured professors.

Unfortunately, medical and doctoral grads are not the only ones who struggle with employment challenges. In fact, the employment outlook is bleak for many graduate alumni,[793] especially since many graduate schools don't offer much assistance during the employment search. For example, in 2002, there were at least 11,000 unemployed lawyers in the United States,[794] and several studies indicate that the country may have more lawyers than available jobs for them.[795] In addition, many new business school grads find that their salaries don't adequately cover their grad school costs and debt (including lost income while in school). Specifically, average salaries for graduate business school grads were relatively flat from 2000-2005, while tuition prices at top business schools rose 55% during this same period.[796]

Many graduate alumni get so frustrated with their jobs that they leave their fields entirely: almost half of new teachers leave the profession before the age of 30.[797] However, many graduate alumni also have trouble finding good jobs outside their fields, because employers usually prefer to hire people who already have practical experience in their specific industries. Danielle Biggs, who recently completed graduate school, says: "What's ironic is that when you graduate from college, they tell you [that] you had better go on to graduate school because you won't find a position paying any kind of money with just a bachelor's degree. Now what I'm finding out is that you can't find a position when you have a graduate degree either. It's easier now to find a position that only requires a college degree."[798]

As mentioned above, the professional licensing process also often makes things more difficult for graduate professionals. Although licensing is critically important in order to ensure professional competency and protect the public, the high cost of this process adds to students' and professionals' already-high expenses. In addition, the licensing process restricts new professionals by requiring them to complete "approved" training experiences as interns, residents, and "fellows." The problem with this requirement is that there are a very limited number of approved training sites, so employers are able to pay very low salaries to these professionals, even though these "trainees" have usually already completed many years of preparation, have excellent skills, and perform high-quality work on the job.

PSYCHED OUT:
WHY THE "DOCTOR OF PSYCHOLOGY" DEGREE
MAY BE THE WORST GRAD SCHOOL INVESTMENT

Out of all graduate degrees, and possibly all post-secondary degrees, the "Doctor of Psychology (PsyD)" degree (created in 1973) is probably the most financially risky for students, especially since these degrees often have some of the highest costs and some of the lowest financial payoffs. The problem is that, after completing many years of training, both PsyD and psychology PhD students receive the same relatively low salaries (a median starting salary of only $51,000),[799] but PsyD grads have much higher costs for their graduate tuition and debt. Specifically, psychology PhD grads had median grad school debt of $50,000 in 2003, but PsyD alumni had median grad school debt of $90,000 (up from $53,000 just six years earlier).[800] Therefore, PsyD grads also incur much more debt than law school and business school grads, while also receiving much lower financial payoffs. And, while PsyD student debt is skyrocketing, starting salaries have basically stayed flat, and have even decreased for private practice positions.[801]

Patricia Pike, PhD, dean of the Rosemead School of Psychology in California (and its PsyD program), acknowledges the unmanageable costs of PsyD programs, saying, "the jobs are…often not paying as much as students' loans demand. Salaries aren't going up as fast as tuition's going up. Our alumni from the past four years have twice the loans of students in the previous four years."[802] Tamara Anderson, PhD, Rosemead's director of clinical training, counsels students on managing their debts, and says that PsyD students get worried as they reach Graduation Day: "They realize they'll be paying up to $1,000 in loans [every] month on a [relatively low] salary, and [they] wonder how they'll meet their expenses."[803]

Although students are responsible for enrolling in expensive PsyD programs, the PsyD programs are responsible for the student debt problem, especially since they often encourage students to borrow much more than they can afford. For example, Patty Mullen, vice president of enrollment and marketing for the California School of Professional Psychology, says, "We tell [students] that a manageable loan payment is between 5 and 15% of gross income"[804]—but, as described throughout this book, financial experts actually consider payments over 8% to be unmanageable. And many PsyD graduates have loan payments that take up even more than 15% of their gross income, especially when college debt is included. Heidi Lilienthal, a PsyD graduate of Nova Southeastern University, represents the typical and unfortunate PsyD burden: she has over $100,000 in loan debt, she earns $25,000 in a post-doc fellowship position, she works extra jobs to make enough money to cover her rent bills, and she says that she expects to "be paying off loans well into my 60's."[805] This situation is particularly regretful since many PsyD graduates have excellent professional skills.

In addition, PsyD programs hurt the employment potential of all doctoral psychology alumni, because PsyD programs accept and graduate too many students, leading to increased competition and lower salaries. For example, while PhD programs accept only 5 or 6 students each year, PsyD programs tend to accept 50 or more students each year.[806]

Philip Farber, a Florida Institute of Technology professor and president of the National Council of Schools and Programs of Professional Psychology (NCSPP, an organization that represents PsyD programs), doesn't think that PsyD programs have a responsibility to admit fewer students, saying, "If there's market oversaturation, the word will get out, and fewer students will enter. Marketplace forces will take care of it."[807] However, the truth is that PsyD programs manipulate marketplace forces by appealing to students' career aspirations, and telling them that they can afford the high costs. At the same time, the programs do little or nothing to warn students that their educational debt can become the main obstacle to the rewards they seek. Lilienthal, the PsyD graduate, says: "I don't think anyone goes into psychology to get rich, at least I didn't. But I did expect to be able to make a living."[808]

It's clear that PsyD programs can be financially punishing for their students—and many students don't fully understand the burden until they leave the programs, receive poor salaries, and get the expensive debt bills. Therefore, it's reasonable to wonder if these programs violate any of the American Psychological Association's five main Ethical Principles:[809] Beneficence and Nonmaleficence; Fidelity and Responsibility; Integrity; Justice; and Respect for People's Rights and Dignity. In fact, perhaps PsyD programs should be required to have their students sign educational "informed consent" documents; after all, psychologists' ethical code already requires them to do this with their clinical clients and research participants. A program's educational consent document could include full information about its students' and graduates' total costs, total debt, monthly debt payments, employment rate within the psychology field, starting salaries, number of years to degree completion, dropout rates, and actual job titles upon graduating.

WINNING THE GRAD SCHOOL GAMBLE

Since many graduate degrees have high price tags and/or poor financial payoffs, students can get the best deals by carefully analyzing their potential graduate school costs and benefits, comparing options, and picking a good one that minimizes their expenses and maximizes the value. This is especially true for students who are interested in very expensive graduate programs, or careers that happen to be low-paying. Students can also make sure that both their college debt and grad school debt will be affordable for them with the starting salaries they will receive after they leave grad school.

Although graduate school alumni earn higher salaries than people with lower degrees (on average), some graduate programs are more valuable, and less risky, than others. For example, some doctoral programs have lower costs and higher payoffs, especially if they lead to jobs in high-level research, math, or finance. And some specialties in law, business, and medicine lead to much better payoffs, often double or triple the salaries earned by others in their fields (and many law and business students also earn high salaries during their summer grad school breaks, as well as tuition reimbursement from their employers). In addition, although salaries have been flat or falling in prestigious fields like medicine (after inflation),[810] earnings have increased steadily in other fields, like business or law. For example, average starting salaries in private practice law rose from $50,000 to $90,000 from just 1991 to 2001.[811] And it's common for graduate business school alumni to receive starting salaries of $100,000 or more.[812]

In addition, many graduate degrees lead to very similar careers, so students can obtain the best value by considering all possibilities. For example, someone who wants to treat medical patients can get a master's degree in physician's assistant studies, a physical therapy degree, a nursing degree, an optometry degree, a DO degree (Doctor of Osteopathy), or an MD degree; someone who wants to work in the legal field can get a law degree, a certificate in paralegal studies, or a master's in government, legal administration, legal studies, public policy, or criminal justice; someone who wants to be a psychotherapist can get either a master's degree in counseling, a master's degree in social work, a PsyD, or a PhD, or an EdD; someone who wants to teach can get either a master's in education, a master's in the subject they want to teach, a PhD, or an EdD; and someone who wants to be a researcher can get a master's or doctoral degree. In addition, graduate degrees are offered in both traditional and online programs by many kinds of schools, including public, private, non-profit, and for-profit schools. Of course, since different degrees have very different costs and benefits, students should do their homework and analyze the costs and benefits of each program they're considering.

To get the best value, students can evaluate the quality of graduate programs in the same ways that they evaluate colleges. For example, students can check with "recognized accrediting organizations" to see if their preferred schools are accredited (e.g.,http://www.chea.org/pdf/CHEA_USDE_AllAccred.pdf). Proper regional accreditation is especially important for online graduate programs. Students can also check schools' attrition rates, completion rates, average time to degree completion, employment rates, average starting salaries (and typical employers), and average amount of student debt. Students who plan to attend research programs can also try to find academic advisors that will be a "good fit" in terms of personality, professional interests, and commitment to facilitating a timely graduation (although this is difficult to determine in advance). And students can also obtain feedback about graduate programs from the programs' current students or recent graduates, although some people may be afraid to say unflattering things about their programs, especially if they work in a student recruitment role. It can also be helpful for students to ask potential employers if they will value a graduate degree from a specific program; for example, Gloria Odogbili, assistant MBA recruiter for UBS Investment Bank, discourages students from getting online graduate business degrees, saying, "The only way we'd hire [a graduate from an online MBA program] is if their resume is strong and they can explain why they had to get their MBA online."[813]

In addition, students can get good value by attending graduate programs that offer special "hands-on," practical learning opportunities. For example, Rutgers University Business School gives its students the opportunity to work with seven pharmaceutical companies, San Diego State University's business students work on sports management issues with the Padres professional baseball team, and the University of Minnesota's business students spend 20 hours a week for three semesters completing consulting work for some of the world's top companies.[814]

Also, although prestigious colleges are often not worth paying extra costs over more affordable schools, it can be helpful for students to attend prestigious graduate schools since they can lead to much better payoffs compared to other graduate programs. This is especially true within the law and business fields, because "top-tier" law and business schools often have special career connections for students. Specifically, graduates of more prestigious business schools can easily receive an extra $40,000 in salary per year,[815] and much higher bonuses, leading to an advantage of hundreds of thousands of dollars, especially 10 years after graduation.[816]

On the other hand, higher average payoffs for prestigious graduate schools may have nothing to do with the schools themselves. As explained in Chapter 5, better payoffs at prestigious schools may be caused by the fact that students at these schools are more talented than students at other schools. For example, Wharton Business School may appear to have a better payoff than other business schools because Wharton is just better at recruiting talented students, and not because Wharton offers a better education or better career contacts than other schools. Therefore, prestigious grad schools may offer special advantages for many students, but talented students may get an excellent payoff from any grad school.

Also, no graduate school or degree offers any guarantees of success. In fact, a recent *BusinessWeek* article told the stories of two graduate business school alumni—one from Stanford University and one from the University of Pennsylvania—who could only find jobs as a server in an ice-cream shop and an $8-an-hour temporary worker at Pottery Barn, respectively.[817] In addition, it's important to note that graduate school prestige is <u>not</u> very important for some career fields: for example, in the education field, teachers usually don't get higher salaries by going to more expensive graduate schools, and, in the medical field, all of the graduates at the least-prestigious accredited medical school in the country get to call themselves "MDs" (and few patients know or care which medical schools their doctors attended). In short, the value of a school's prestige is just another factor for students to critically evaluate, along with the school's other costs and benefits.

Of course, before enrolling in a graduate program, students should also make sure that they need graduate-level training for their preferred careers; some high-level career fields surprisingly do not require a graduate degree. For example, some states don't require people to have law degrees in order to obtain a license to practice law[818] (although a law degree may still be required for most legal jobs). In addition, graduate degrees are often not required for high-paying jobs at "alternative investment firms," like hedge funds and private equity groups.[819] And graduate degrees are usually not required in order to start a new business or company (although MBA degrees can be helpful for entrepreneurs, especially those who plan to pursue outside funding for their businesses).

As students choose among graduate schools, many books and online directories are available to help them make their decisions, including Peterson's *Graduate Schools in the U.S.,* and websites like www.gradschools.com, www.graduateguides.com, and www.petersons.com/gradchannel. Some resources even focus on "distance learning," including www.GraduateGuideDL.com and www.distance.gradschools.com, while others focus on specific career fields, including business, law, medicine, and psychology.

SUCKERS NO MORE

"Don't let school get in the way of your education."
—Mark Twain

In summary, college and graduate school programs can be financially, academically, and personally rewarding, but schools and banks often take advantage of people who cave in to the pressure to spend too much money on education. Therefore, it's largely up to students and parents to play it smart when they make decisions about their educational investments.

The key for consumers is to independently analyze their educational options and pick the school that's the best fit, rather than just follow the crowd. After all, the most successful people are usually those who have a special ability to examine problems and challenges, and see opportunities and solutions where others do not.

Although schools and banks often aggressively strive to maximize their profits, leaving no sucker—or victim—behind, the cautious and savvy student can overcome this challenge, and thrive.

APPENDIX A

SUCCESS WITHOUT COLLEGE
An Appendix for the Adventurous

Andy Blevins has the kind of life that many Americans dream of. At the young age of 29, Andy works as a buyer of fruits and vegetables for a supermarket company. His job provides him with health benefits, a 401(k) plan, and a salary that allows him to support a wife and son, and own a house in a great location of Virginia. Also, Andy has a short commute to work, enough time outside work to play golf, and he's surrounded in his town by a large number of friends and family members. And Andy has achieved all of this without ever earning a college degree.[820]

On the other hand, Andy has doubts. He spent one year in college, and he regrets not finishing the degree. He worries about losing his job, and wonders if his life would have been better if he had completed college. He says he feels "trapped," adding: "Looking back, I wish I had gotten that degree. Four years seemed like a thousand years then. But I wish I would have just put in my four years."

However, Andy has a more fulfilling life, and more financial stability, than many college grads—and he's not alone. Can skipping college be good for you?

> **Myth: College degrees are required for success.**

In fact, some of the most successful people do not have college degrees, including many wealthy individuals. For example, Bill Gates didn't need a college degree to become one of the richest people in the world. Other successful people who never got college degrees include:

- Peter Jennings (newsperson),
- Steven Spielberg (movie director and producer),
- William Faulkner (author),
- Maya Angelou (poet),
- Michael Dell (founder of Dell Computers, Inc.),
- Jane Austen (author),
- Nina Totenberg (newsperson),
- Walter Cronkite (newsperson),
- Ted Turner (founder of CNN, TBS, and other cable TV stations),
- Quentin Tarantino (director),
- Woody Allen (director),
- Richard Leakey (anthropologist),
- John Glenn (astronaut and senator),
- Ray Kroc (founder of McDonald's),
- Alexander Graham Bell (scientist and inventor),
- Thomas Edison (scientist and inventor),
- Wayne Huizenga (owner of Blockbuster Video, sports teams, and hotels),
- David Sarnoff (head of RCA radio and electronics empire),
- Ernest Hemmingway (author),
- Frank Lloyd Wright (architect),
- Alex Haley (author),
- Steve Jobs (founder of Apple Computer and CEO of Pixar),
- the Wright Brothers (inventors of the modern airplane),[821]
- Richard Branson (chairman of the Virgin Group of businesses),

- Janus Friis (Co-founder of Internet technologies KaZaA and Skype),
- Rachael Ray (author and television host),
- Anna Wintour (philanthropist and editor-in-chief of American Vogue magazine),[822]
- Leonard Riggio (founder and chairman of Barnes and Noble),[823]
- David Geffen (founder of Geffen Records and Dreamworks),[824]
- Sean "Diddy" Combs (musician, producer, and CEO of Bad Boy Records),[825]
- Russell Simmons (founder of Def Jam, and Rush Communications),[826]
- Kanye West (musician and music producer who named his debut album "The College Dropout"),[827] and
- United States president Harry S. Truman.[828]

In addition, one out of three members of the Forbes list of the 400 richest people in the world do <u>not</u> have a college degree (129 members are non-graduates).[829] And a recent survey found that less than half of the people who earn the highest salaries in America have college degrees, and almost 30% never went to college at all.[830] In fact, less than half of business executives (46%) say that their college and graduate degrees are "very closely related" to their careers, and more than eight in ten executives (84%) say that "street smarts" are more important for business success than college or graduate degrees.[831]

Of course, many non-graduates may have been successful because they began their careers many decades ago, when college degrees were not required by employers. However, successful non-graduates show that, while college <u>degrees</u> may be important to many employers, a college <u>education</u> is often not required for exceptional achievement. And, although many successful non-graduates have been white men, other groups may be inspired to "even the score" in the future.

In fact, as described in Chapter 5, several recent studies support the idea that college degrees are not even the main cause of success for graduates. For example, two studies illustrate that college graduates' success has more to do with the special qualities of the graduates themselves than with their schools or their degrees.[832] Another study, conducted by the National Center for Education Statistics in 2000, found that college graduates' salaries and success could be predicted by what they were like before they even went to college.[833] In other words, gifted people have natural talent that can propel them to success, regardless of whether they obtain a college degree. And four full years in college may distract or impede some talented people from achieving their full potential.

Myth: Everyone should go to college.

Although college degrees are usually valuable, the degrees also often have high costs and poor payoffs, so some people enjoy more success by skipping college. In fact, the vast majority of jobs that will be created between 2002 and 2012 will <u>not</u> require a college or graduate degree of any kind, including many of the fastest growing jobs.[834] In addition, data from the U.S. Department of Labor shows that the country will <u>not</u> need a larger number of college graduates between now and 2012, because there will not be enough college-level jobs for them to fill.[835]

Also, when more people graduate from college, there's more competition for college-level jobs, which can lead to lower salaries and higher unemployment for all grads. Randall Collins, a professor at the University of Pennsylvania, points out that a harmful system of "credential inflation"[836] has already been created over the past fifty years, as the financial payoffs and employment advantages of college degrees have dropped. Too many students have been encouraged to get degrees—and this has also led to increasing pressure for students to get graduate degrees, which require additional costs for students but also often lead to disappointing financial payoffs. Of course, as author Linda Lee points out in her book, *Success Without College*, sending too many students to college is also not a good idea because many students are not academically or personally ready for it.

Even Robert Frank, a Cornell University economist, says: "I agree that, from the perspective of society as a whole, it would be better if fewer people went to college."[837] America needs financially stable, skilled workers, not financially crippled incompetent college grads and college dropouts. Therefore, instead of going to college, some people are better off developing the real-world practical work experience and maturity that employers value.

CAREER SUCCESS WITHOUT COLLEGE

The good news for people who don't go to college is that college degrees are not absolutely required for survival, and there are many career options available to them. For example, some high-paying jobs for people who do not have a 4-year college degree include: storage and distribution manager or transportation manager (average salary $66,600); non-retail sales manager ($59,300); fire-fighting and prevention supervisor ($58,902); real estate broker ($58,720); elevator installer and repairer ($58,710); sales representative ($58,580); dental hygienist ($58,350, requires an associate's degree); criminal investigator ($53,990); police detective or records officer ($53,990); and registered nurse ($52,330, requires an associate's degree).[838] The 2006-07 Occupational Outlook Handbook also notes the following median salaries for some additional jobs that do not typically require a 4-year college degree: flight attendant ($43,440); real estate appraiser ($43,390); court reporter ($42,920); and electrician ($40,000). It's important to note that workers in these career fields must usually complete some on-the-job training and several years of experience before earning these salaries.

Other jobs for non-college graduates that are expected to have many new openings from 2002-2012 include: bookkeeping, accounting, auditing clerks (431,000 new openings, median salary = $27,000); executive secretaries and administrative assistants (424,000 new openings, median salary = $33,000); general and operations managers (394,000 new openings, median salary = $68,000); supervisors of retail sales workers (367,000 new openings, median salary = $30,000); sales reps (341,000 new openings, median salary = $43,000); and supervisors of office workers (297,000 new openings, median salary = $39,000).[839] In short, the career fields that will be most promising for people without college degrees include office and administrative support, healthcare, construction, police and protective services, education and childcare, and computers and technology.[840] It's also important to note that some graduate schools accept students who do not have college degrees, including some law schools and master's degree programs.

Although some people may think that these kinds of jobs are not very interesting, there's no evidence that these jobs are any more or less interesting than the jobs currently available to college grads. This is especially true since many college grads have jobs that do not require a college degree. In addition, almost every job in the world has some unfulfilling aspects, including jobs that require a graduate degree, such as doctor, lawyer, accountant, and engineer. And, although some college- or graduate-level jobs offer "status" or "prestige," many of these jobs lack the opportunity for creativity—a distinction many graduates don't fully understand until they experience their mid-life crises, approximately 29 or so years into their careers. The *New York Times* recently reported that nearly 60% of doctors have considered leaving medicine, and 44% of lawyers would not recommend their profession to young people. [841]

A MAP FOR THE NON-COLLEGE PATH

One of the best ways for non-college graduates to achieve success is to start their own businesses. As mentioned above, many of the richest and most successful people in the world are business leaders or business owners—and people don't need a college degree to start a business. In fact, many colleges and graduate schools don't even teach their students how to start and run their own businesses, or how to be successful entrepreneurs. Therefore, instead of going to college, people can complete a <u>free</u> Small Business Administration training program (see www.sba.gov).

In addition, many people can receive free on-the-job training from their employers. Plus, some sales jobs require no prior experience, and a number of "apprenticeships," or similar career training positions, are also available.[842] Information about these kinds of opportunities can be found at "http://www.careervoyages.gov" or "http://www.doleta.gov/atels_bat/fndprgm.cfm". Some government jobs also do not require a college degree.

**Myth: People have to go to college
to get a "college education."**

Some more good news is that people don't have to go to college in order to learn new things; colleges have a monopoly on degrees, but they do not have a monopoly on knowledge.

For example, there are many training programs that are less expensive than college. Specifically, many organizations and community centers offer low-cost "continuing education" classes to the public, such as The Learning Annex (www.learningannex.com), or local YMCA's, YMHA's, high schools, and junior high schools. Actually, many regular colleges also offer these kinds of low-cost "extension" classes. And students can take individual classes, without obtaining a degree, at many colleges and universities, and websites like http://training.cyberu.com.

In addition, many prestigious colleges now offer college classes for free (or a low price) at sites like: "http://open.yale.edu/courses/index.html," "http://ocw.mit.edu/index.html" (which features free material for 1,500 classes), "http://ocw.nd.edu," "http://ocw.tufts.edu," "http://ocw.uci.edu," "http://www.uocwa.org," "http://webcast.berkeley.edu," "http://video.google.com/ucberkeley.html," and "http://openlearn.open.ac.uk". Users of iTunes can also access "coursecasting," or free video recordings of classes and lectures from schools like the University of California at Berkeley, Stanford University, and Duke University's School of Business, at http://www.apple.com/education/products/ipod/itunes_u.html. Unfortunately, students who use free class materials cannot earn course credit or a degree, but they can obtain significant knowledge, which is supposed to be the main point of education anyway.

People who want a more focused and personalized education than the one that colleges usually provide can use the services of private tutors and vocational centers. Tutors can be found at websites like www.tutor.com and www.craigslist.com.

All of these options allow students to learn the information they need or want, instead of being forced to take a bunch of classes they have no interest in.

There are also a number of sources that people can use to teach themselves. For example, just about any book is available to be borrowed, for free, from a library (and libraries that don't own the books can borrow them from other libraries). In addition, many classic books are available for free online, at websites like www.gutenberg.org, http://www.gutenberg.org/browse/scores/top, and http://books.google.com, and free textbooks are available at websites like www.freeloadpress.com and www.textbookrevolution.org. Books are also obviously available for sale in bookstores and online outlets. And there's nothing to stop "independent learners" from reading the exact same books that colleges use; Amazon.com even offers "Great Books of the Western World," a 60-volume, 37,000-page set of books published by Encyclopedia Britannica that represents over 500 works and covers a large portion of the books that represent a typical liberal arts college education, for only about $1,000. Better yet, a learner could borrow these books from a library.

Also, many free websites offer information about almost any topic. This includes new "wikipedias," or free encyclopedias, such as www.wikipedia.com. Other sites can be found by using Internet search engines like Google.com. Although these kinds of learning sources may not be as respected by employers as a college degree, these are excellent options for people who choose not to pursue a more formal education. The amazing fact is that, although knowledge can be priceless, it can often be obtained for free.

Finally, several books offer additional information for non-college graduates, including:

- *Success Without College,* by Linda Lee;
- *America's Top Jobs for People Without College,* by J. Michael Farr;
- *Gallery of Best Resumes for People Without a Four-Year Degree,* by David F. Noble;
- *300 Best Jobs Without a Four-Year Degree,* by J. Michael Farr, LaVerne Ludden & Laurance Shatkin;
- *202 High Paying Jobs You Can Land Without a College Degree,* by Jason R. Rich;
- *Top 100 Careers Without a Four-Year Degree,* by Michael Farr;
- *America's Top 100 Jobs for People Without a Four-Year Degree,* by Ronald Krannich & Caryl Krannich; and
- *The Independent Scholar's Handbook,* by Ronald Gross

APPENDIX B

PUTTING COLLEGES TO THE TEST
Twenty-Five Questions Before You Enroll

(Note: Relevant chapters are indicated in parentheses for each question.)

First Things First
1. Why do you want to go to college? Write down the answer as specifically and in as much detail as possible.
2. What specific college features are you looking for? Write down the answer as specifically and in as much detail as possible.
3. Have you picked one or more preferred majors? (Chapter 8)
4. Have you determined the average starting salaries for your preferred majors? (Chapters 7, 8)

Picking a Valuable College
5. Have you explored different kinds of educational options and colleges, including public, private, in-state, out-of-state, 2-year, 4-year, small, large, prestigious, less prestigious, non-profit, for-profit, online, on-campus, extension programs, sports schools, and non-sports schools? (Chapter 8)
6. Have you explored several kinds of degree and certificate options, including the bachelor's degree, associate's degree, and technical or vocational degree? (Chapter 8)
7. Have you identified several "Safety," "Reach," and "Good Fit" schools to apply to? (Chapter 8)

8. Have you identified some low-cost 2-year and 4-year programs to apply to, such as public schools within your home state? (Chapter 8)
9. Are your preferred schools accredited, preferably by one of the 6 regional accrediting agencies? (Chapter 8)
10. Have you checked that your preferred schools have reasonable graduation rates? (Chapter 8)
11. Do your preferred schools offer strong instruction in your preferred majors? (Chapter 8)
12. Do graduates of your preferred schools get good jobs, as well as admission to good graduate schools, and earn average or above-average salaries in their fields? (Chapter 8)
13. Have you talked with employers and graduate schools about the potential value of your preferred degree and school? (Chapters 5, 8)

Picking an Affordable College
14. Do you understand all of the common college price scams? (Chapters 1-5)
15. Do you understand all of the common college debt scams? (Chapter 7)
16. Have you maximized your "good" financial aid and minimized your "risky" financial aid? (Chapter 6)
17. Have you sent a financial aid negotiation letter to the schools? (Chapter 6)
18. If you will need to use loans, have you evaluated several kinds of loans and lenders, including lenders that are not on your school's "preferred" list? (Chapter 7)
19. Have you calculated and compared the expected out-of-pocket costs and financial benefits for each school that has accepted you? (Chapters 5, 8)
20. Will you be able to afford all of your immediate

out-of-pocket costs, including housing, food, books, transportation, and travel, during all years that you attend the school? (Chapter 5)
21. Will the school require you to borrow more money than you can afford, including the debt for any graduate training you want to pursue? (Chapter 7)
22. Will you be able to afford cost and debt increases during each year that you attend the school? (Chapters 5-7)
23. Will you be able to afford to attend the school for more than 4 years, if necessary? (Chapters 5-7)
24. Will your total out-of-pocket costs be reasonable and affordable based on your expected starting salary? (Chapters 5-7)

Last But Not Least
25. Have you selected a school to attend that will minimize your financial costs and maximize your educational and financial benefits? (Chapters 5, 8)

APPENDIX C

WINNING THE COLLEGE GAMBLE
Online Resources for Success

This section collects all of the websites mentioned throughout this book.

Chapter 1
None

Chapter 2
- **The United States Student Association:** www.usstudents.org/main.asp
- **College Parents of America:** www.collegeparents.org
- **Public Interest Research Groups:** www.pirg.org and www.studentpirgs.org
- **The Project on Student Debt:** www.projectonstudentdebt.org

Chapter 3
None

Chapter 4
- **The Spellings Commission on the Future of Higher Education:** http://www.ed.gov/about/bdscomm/list/hiedfuture/index.html

Chapter 5
None

Chapter 6
- **AP Central:** http://apcentral.collegeboard.com
- **AP Credit Info for Each College:** www.collegeboard.com/ap/creditpolicy
- **Free Application for Federal Student Aid:** www.fafsa.ed.gov
- **College Board Resources:** www.collegeboard.com/?student
- **Financial Aid Info:** www.studentaid.ed.gov
- **The Best Financial Aid Site on the Internet, FinAid:** www.finaid.com
- **PIRGs' Higher Education Project:** www.studentaidaction.com
- **National Association of Student Financial Aid Administrators:** www.studentaid.org
- **Peterson's College Planner:** www.petersons.com
- **Scholarship Scams to Avoid:** http://www.ftc.gov/bcp/conline/edcams/scholarship/ and http://www.ftc.gov/scholarshipscams
- **Better Business Bureau:** www.bbb.org
- **More About Scholarship Scams to Avoid:** www.finaid.com/scholarships/scams.phtml

Some Free Financial Aid Calculators are Available at:
- **College Parents of America:** www.collegeparents.org/cpa/family-contribution-calculator.html;
- **Federal Student Aid Guide:** www.studentaid.ed.gov/pubs; click on "EFC";
- **FinAid:** http://finaid.com/calculators/finaidestimate.phtml;
- **Peterson's College Planner:** http://petersons.com/finaid/efcsimplecalc.asp?sponsor=1&path=ug.pfs.federal; and

- **The Official FAFSA site:** www.fafsa.ed.gov
- **State-Sponsored College Savings Plans:** www.saving forcollege.com
- **Using Retirement Plans to Pay for College:** http://www.finaid.com/savings/retirementplans.phtml
- **Education Tax Benefits:** http://www.finaid.com/otheraid/tax.phtml and www.irs.gov
- **Calculator to Compare Costs at Different Colleges:** www.finaid.com/calculators/awardletter.phtml
- **Colleges That Waive Costs for Low-Income Students:** http://www.finaid.com/questions/noloansforlowincome.phtml
- **Excellent "Student Guide to Financial Aid":** www.studentaid.ed.gov/pubs and http://studentaid.ed.gov/students/publications/student_guide/index.html
- **U.S. Committee on Education and the Workforce:** http://edworkforce.house.gov and http://edworkforce.house.gov/issues/issues.htm and http://edworkforce.house.gov/democrats/ and http://edworkforce.house.gov/members/109th/mem-fc.htm

Chapter 7
- **Student Loans:** http://www.finaid.com/loans/
- **Testimonials of Struggling Student Loan Borrowers:** http://www.studentloanjustice.org/victims.htm
- **U.S. Bureau of Labor Statistics:** www.bls.gov/oco
- **The National Association of Colleges and Employers:** www.naceweb.org
- **Loan Calculators available at:** www.bankrate.com or www.moneychimp.com or www.finaid.com/calculators/ and www.finaid.com/calculators/loanpayments.phtml

- **Information About Student Loans:**
  http://finaid.com/loans/studentloan.phtml
- **The Most Common (But Not Necessarily Best) Student Loan Lenders:**
  http://www.finaid.com/loans/biglenders.phtml
- **My Rich Uncle:** www.myrichuncle.com
- **Current Credit Card Interest Rates:** www.bankrate.com
- **Opting Out of Debt Offers:** www.optoutprescreen.com or www.privacyrightsnow.com/
- **Consumers for Responsible Credit Solutions (CRCS):** www.responsiblecredit.com
- **Coalition for Consumer Bankruptcy Debtor Education:** www.debtoreducation.org
- **Consumer Credit Counseling Service of New York:** www.cccscny.org
- **National Council on Economic Education:** www.ncee.net
- **Jump$tart Coalition for Personal Financial Literacy:** www.jumpstart.org
- **Anya Kamenetz's blog, Generation Debt:** http://anyakamenetz.blogspot.com
- **Credit Abuse Resistance Education Program:** www.careprogram.us/chronicles.php
- **The Institute for College Access and Success:** www.ticas.org
- **Generation Debt:** www.generationdebt.org
- **Credit Card Nation:** www.creditcardnation.com
- **Young Money:** www.youngmoney.com
- **Project on Student Debt:** www.projectonstudentdebt.org
- **Student Loan Justice:** www.studentloanjustice.org

- **Student Loan Watch/Higher Ed Watch:** www.studentloanwatch.org or www.higheredwatch.org (both addresses go to the same site)
- **Student Debt Alert:** www.studentdebtalert.org
- **The Truth About Credit:** www.truthaboutcredit.org
- **Student Loan Advocates and Volunteer Exchange:** http://www.studentloanslave.org
- **Another Debt Calculator:** http://www.youngmoney.com/calculators/credit_card_and_debt_management_calculators/credit_card_payoff
- **Locating a Certified Financial Advisor:** www.cfp.com and www.feeonly.org and www.garrettplanningnetwork.com

Chapter 8

- **Career Converter Tool, to Match Majors to Careers:** http://content.monstertrak.monster.com/tools/careerconverter
- **Large List of For-Profit Colleges and Universities:** http://en.wikipedia.org/wiki/List_of_for-profit_colleges_and_universities
- **Reviews of Online Degree Programs:** www.geteducated.com and www.OnlineDegreeReviews.org and www.oedb.org/rankings
- **Find Out if An Online Program is Adequately Accredited:** http://geteducated.com/services/diplomamillpolice.asp
- **Sports Divisions for All Colleges:** www.ncaa.org/conferences/
- **List of Accredited Colleges at the Council for Higher Education Accreditation:** www.chea.org
- **Ratings of College Instructors:** www.ratemyprofessors.com and www.reviewum.com
- **Loren Pope's List of "Colleges That Change Lives":** www.ctcl.com

- **Colleges of Distinction:** www.CollegesOfDistinction.com
- **Listings of College Graduation Rates:** http://www.collegeresults.org/ and http://nces.ed.gov/globallocator
- **College Navigator:** http://nces.ed.gov/collegenavigator/
- **List of Schools That Do Not Require Admissions Tests:** www.fairtest.org/univ/optional.htm
- **SAT Fee Waivers:** http://www.collegeboard.com/student/testing/sat/calenfees/feewaivers.html
- **ACT Fee Waivers:** http://www.actstudent.org/faq/answers/feewaiver.html
- **College Application Fee Waiver:** www.nacac.com/downloads/form_feewaiver.pdf
- **More Free College Information:** http://www.collegenet.com/about/index_html and www.collegeview.com and http://colleges.com/admissions/collegesearch/index.html and www.xap.com and www.collegeconfidential.com

Chapter 9

- **Internship Listings:** www.monstertrak.com and www.internships.com
- **Employment Agencies for Part-Time or Full-Time Work:** www.officeteam.com and www.kellyservices.com and www.manpower.com and www.creativegroup.com and www.rhmr.com
- **General Employment Listings:** www.monstertrak.com and www.net-temps.com and www.craigslist.org and www.hotjobs.com and www.monster.com
- **Information About Textbook Costs:** www.MakeTextbooksAffordable.com

- **Lower-Priced Textbooks:** www.bookfinder.com and www.campusbookswap.com and www.half.com and www.walmart.com and www.textbookx.com and www.amazon.com and www.ebay.com and www.bigwords.com and www.barnesandnoble.com and www.booksoncampus.com and www.bookdonkey.com and www.scseller.com and www.calpirgstudents.org and www.bookcentral.com and www.cheapbooks.com and www.craigslist.org
- **Free Textbooks:** www.freeloadpress.com and www.text bookrevolution.org and www.gutenberg.org and www.gutenberg.org/browse/scores/top and http://books.google.com

Chapter 10
- **Loan Forgiveness:** http://www.finaid.com/loans/forgive ness.phtml
- **Consolidation of Direct Loans:** http://loanconsolidation.ed.gov/borrower/borrower.shtml
- **Other Consolidation Lenders:** http://www.finaid.com/loans/biglenders.phtml and http://www.finaid.com/loans/privateconsolidation.phtml and www.consolidation comparison.com
- **Federal Student Aid Ombudsman:** www.ombudsman.ed.gov
- **Federal Trade Commission Information About Credit for Consumers:** http://ftc.gov/bcp/conline/edcams/credit/coninfo.htm
- **Locating a Debt Advisor:** www.nfcc.org and http://www.debtadvice.org/takethefirststep/locator.html

- **Association of Independent Consumer Credit Counseling Agencies:** www.aiccca.org and http://aiccca.org/find.cfm
- **Finding a Personal Counselor:** http://www.campusblues.com/college_list.asp and http://www.psychologytoday.com/topics/ and http://therapists.psychologytoday.com/
- **Debt "Support Group":** www.debtorsanonymous.org

Chapter 11
- **Full List of College Accreditation Organizations:** http://www.chea.org/pdf/CHEA_USDE_AllAccred.pdf
- **Graduate School Directories:** www.gradschools.com and www.graduateguides.com and www.petersons.com/gradchannel
- **Graduate School Distance Learning Directories:** www.GraduateGuideDL.com and www.distance.gradschools.com

Appendix A
- **Apprenticeships and Other Career Training Opportunities:** http://www.careervoyages.gov and http://www.doleta.gov/atels_bat/fndprgm.cfm
- **Free Small Business Administration Training Programs:** www.sba.gov
- **The Learning Annex:** www.learningannex.com
- **Online Classes:** http://training.cyberu.com
- **Free College Class Materials:** http://open.yale.edu/courses/index.html and http://ocw.mit.edu/index.html and http://ocw.nd.edu and http://ocw.tufts.edu and http://ocw.uci.edu and http://www.uocwa.org and http://webcast.berkeley.edu and http://video.google.com/ucberkeley.html and http://openlearn.open.ac.uk and

http://www.apple.com/education/products/ipod/itunes_u.html
- **Tutors:** www.tutor.com and www.craigslist.com
- **Free Books:** www.gutenberg.org and www.gutenberg.org/browse/scores/top and http://books.google.com and www.freeloadpress.com and www.textbookrevolution.org
- **Free Online Encyclopedia:** www.wikipedia.com

REFERENCES

CHAPTER 1
1. For example: Leslie, L.L. (1990). Rates of return as informer of public policy. Higher Education, 20, 271-286
2. As explained in Chapter 2
3. As explained in Chapter 5
4. "National Postsecondary Student Aid Study (NPSAS)," National Center for Education Statistics; "Student loans—a life sentence," CNN/Money, May 2, 2006
5. "2004 CFS Planning and Paying for Higher Education Study," Collegiate Funding Services, October 2004
6. "Administrative petition to the Department of Education," The Project on Student Debt, May 4, 2006
7. "Degree Attainment Rates at American Colleges and Universities," UCLA Higher Education Research Institute, 2002
8. "College For All? Is there too much emphasis on getting a 4-year college degree?" U.S. Dept. of Education, January 1999
9. For example, "Big loans, bigger problems," State Public Interest Research Group, March 2001
10. "Salary Survey, Spring 2007," National Association of Colleges and Employers, April 2007
11. "Economic snapshots," Economic Policy Institute, March 14, 2004, based on data from the U.S. Bureau of Labor Statistics
12. *The End of Work*, Jeremy Rifkin, 2004
13. As explained in Chapter 5
14. Tracey King and Ellynne Bannon, "The Burden of Borrowing: A Report on the Rising Rates of Student Loan Debt," March 2002, The State PIRG's Higher Education Project
15. "2002 National Student Loan Survey," Nellie Mae, 2003
16. "2004 CFS Planning and Paying for Higher Education Study," Harris Interactive, October 2004
17. "2002 National Student Loan Survey," Nellie Mae, 2003

REFERENCES

18 "Don't leave college without it," Mother Jones, March/April 2002
19 "Consumer Bankruptcy Project," Harvard University, 2001
20 "The parent trap: Boomerang kids," U.S. News & World Report, December 12, 2005
21 U.S. Census Bureau, as cited in "Boomerang kids on the rise," The Biloxi Sun Herald, June 2006
22 "Your adult kids are back. Now what?" Money, December 29, 2006
23 "MonsterTRAK's entry-level job survey shows strong outlook, yet flat salaries," press release, April 5, 2006
24 "2002 National Student Loan Survey," Nellie Mae, 2003; "2004 CFS Planning and Paying for Higher Education Study," Harris Interactive, October 2004
25 "The College Debt Crunch," AllianceBernstein, May 26, 2006
26 "Paying Back, Not Giving Back: Student Debt's Negative Impact on Public Service Career Opportunities," The State PIRG's Higher Education Project, April 2006; "In Debt from Day One," Christian Science Monitor, March 9, 2004
27 "The College Debt Crunch," AllianceBernstein, May 26, 2006
28 "2002 National Student Loan Survey," Nellie Mae, 2003
29 "2002 National Student Loan Survey," Nellie Mae, 2003
30 "The College Debt Crunch," AllianceBernstein, May 26, 2006
31 "2002 National Student Loan Survey," Nellie Mae, 2003
32 "The College Debt Crunch," AllianceBernstein, May 26, 2006
33 "Anatomy of a credit score," BusinessWeek, November 28, 2005
34 As explained in Chapter 11
35 "Empty Promises: The Myth of College Access in America," The Advisory Committee on Student Financial Assistance, U.S. Department of Education, June 2002; Remarks of the Honorable George Miller, Chairman Designate, House Committee on Education and the Workforce, December 12, 2006 (http://www.house.gov/ed_workforce/newsroom/transcripts/GMremarks121206.pdf)
36 "Education Pays 2004," The College Board, 2005

37 College Board study, as cited in "Sticker shock," Inside Higher Ed, March 21, 2006
38 "2002 National Student Loan Survey," Nellie Mae, 2003
39 "2004 CFS Planning and Paying for Higher Education Study," Harris Interactive, October 2004
40 "The College Debt Crunch," AllianceBernstein, May 26, 2006
41 "Credit card debt imposes huge costs on many college students," press release, Consumer Federation of America, June 8, 1999
42 "Film renews focus on students' credit-card suicides," The Oklahoma City Journal Record, June 28, 2006
43 "Film renews focus on students' credit-card suicides," The Oklahoma City Journal Record, June 28, 2006
44 "Film renews focus on students' credit-card suicides," The Oklahoma City Journal Record, June 28, 2006
45 2006 NACUBO Endowment Study (National Association of College and University Business Officers)
46 2006 NACUBO Endowment Study (National Association of College and University Business Officers); amounts rounded to the nearest billion
47 2003 NACUBO Endowment Study (National Association of College and University Business Officers)
48 2005 NACUBO Endowment Study (National Association of College and University Business Officers)
49 "MIT fund tops Yale, erases tech loss with overseas, buyout bets," Bloomberg, December 4, 2006
50 "A good year for endowments," Inside Higher Ed, January 24, 2005; "The rich on the rise in endowments," Inside Higher Ed, January 22, 2007
51 "Fiduciary guidelines for foundation and endowment trustees," Smith Barney, 2004; 2003 NACUBO Endowment Study (National Association of College and University Business Officers)
52 "When $26 billion isn't enough," The Wall Street Journal, December 17-18, 2005

53 "Endowment envy," Inside Higher Ed, October 12, 2006
54 *Going Broke by Degree*, Richard Vedder, 2004; "Administrators' pay rises 3.5%, beating inflation for the 9th consecutive year," The Chronicle of Higher Education, February 2006; "Student compensation: Are students 'underpaid'?" Center for College Affordability and Productivity, December 2006
55 "2005-06 Administrative Compensation Survey," College and University Professional Association for Human Resources, 2006
56 "The Annual Report on the Economic Status of the Profession," AAUP, 2006-07.
57 "College presidents are hard-working, talented, and vastly overpaid," The Chronicle of Higher Education, May 7, 2004; "Study: More college presidents earning $500,000," Associated Press, November 20, 2006; "In tuition game, popularity rises with price," New York Times, December 12, 2006
58 "College presidents are hard-working, talented, and vastly overpaid," The Chronicle of Higher Education, May 7, 2004; "Study: More college presidents earning $500,000," Associated Press, November 20, 2006; "In tuition game, popularity rises with price," New York Times, December 12, 2006
59 "Study: More college presidents earning $500,000," Associated Press, November 20, 2006
60 "Study: More college presidents earning $500,000," Associated Press, November 20, 2006
61 "Teachers—Postsecondary," Occupational Outlook Handbook 2005, U.S. Department of Labor; "Who really benefits," The Chronicle of Higher Education, Jan. 25, 2005
62 "Bill would cap pay of university presidents," St. Petersburg Times, March 15, 2003
63 "College sports' $4 million man," Inside Higher Ed, January 11, 2007
64 "Salary pecking order," Inside Higher Ed," March 13, 2006

65 "Harvard fund managers paid more than $34 million," Associated Press, January 23, 2004; "Alumni blast high salaries of Harvard endowment's money managers," The Chronicle of Higher Education, February 6, 2004
66 "More small colleges dropping out," The New York Times, May 7, 2002
67 "Great expectations," Public Agenda, 2000
68 "The 2004 Chronicle Survey of Public Opinion on Higher Education," Chronicle of Higher Education, May 7, 2004; "Squeeze Play: How Parents and the Public Look at Higher Education Today," Public Agenda, June 2007
69 "Great expectations," Public Agenda, 2000
70 "The 2004 Chronicle Survey of Public Opinion on Higher Education," Chronicle of Higher Education, May 7, 2004; "Squeeze Play: How Parents and the Public Look at Higher Education Today," Public Agenda, June 2007
71 "The MetLife Survey of the American Teacher," MetLife, 2000
72 Newsweek/Kaplan College Guide, 2005
73 "Facts for Features: Back to School 2006-2007," press release, U.S. Census Bureau, August 2006
74 "Fall 2005 U.S. higher education enrollment trends survey signals overall credit stability," press release, Fitch Ratings, December 9, 2005

CHAPTER 2
75 "The most powerful people in the world of education in Washington aren't in an Ivory Tower," Washington Business Forward, July 1, 2002

76 "How We Do the Rankings," U.S. News and World Report, 2007 (http://www.usnews.com/usnews/edu/college/rankings/about/07rank_brief.php); "A Review of Measures Used in U.S. News & World Report's 'America's Best Colleges,'" The Center for Measuring University Performance, Summer 2002, http://mup.asu.edu/Gater 0702.pdf (viewed in 2007)

77 *College Rankings Exposed*, Paul Boyer, 2003

78 "UBC course enrollments manipulated," The Vancouver Sun, January 31, 2004

79 "Colleges boost donor numbers," The Wall Street Journal, March 2, 2007

80 "Glass floor: How colleges reject the top applicants—and boost their status," The Wall Street Journal, May 29, 2001

81 "How We Do the Rankings," U.S. News and World Report, 2007 (http://www.usnews.com/usnews/edu/college/rankings/about/07rank_brief.php)

82 "Is there life after rankings?" The Atlantic Monthly, November 2005

83 "College Rankings Reformed," Education Sector, September 22, 2006

84 "The cost of bucking college rankings," The Washington Post, March 11, 2007

85 "Would U.S. News make up fake data?" Inside Higher Ed, March 12, 2007

86 *College Rankings Exposed*, Paul Boyer, 2003

87 National Association for College Admission Counseling, as cited in *Newsweek/Kaplan College Guide*, 2005

88 "It's Only a Port of Call: Reflections on the State of Higher Education," Julie Johnson Kidd, in *Declining by Degrees*, edited by Richard Hersh and John Merrow, 2005

89 "The best class money can buy," The Atlantic Monthly, November 2005

90 "The Survey of College Marketing Programs," Research and Markets, 2007

91 "Our Clients," J.M. Lord & Associates, http://www.jmlord.com/frame/clients.html (viewed in 2007)
92 "Our Education Clients," Lipman Hearne, www.lipmanhearne.com/clients/education (viewed in 2007)
93 "The best class money can buy," The Atlantic Monthly, November 2005
94 "Symposium for the Marketing of Higher Education," American Marketing Association, http://www.marketingpower.com/aevent_event.php?Event_ID=24813 (viewed in 2007)
95 "The best class money can buy," The Atlantic Monthly, November 2005
96 "Welcome to Primary Research Group," Primary Research Group, http://primaryresearch.ecnext.com/ (viewed in 2007)
97 Trends and Tudes newsletter, Harris Interactive, January 2005
98 "The Survey of College Marketing Programs," Research and Markets, 2007
99 "Beaver College changes oft-derived name to Arcadia University," Associated Press, November 20, 2000; *Shakespeare, Einstein, and the Bottom Line*, David L. Kirp, 2004
100 "The competition for top undergraduates by America's colleges and universities," The Center for Measuring University Performance, May 2001, http://mup.asu.edu/gaterUG1.pdf (viewed in 2007)
101 "Recreation centers used to woo students," Associated Press, April 1, 2005
102 "Colleges get building fever," The Wall Street Journal, May 18, 2005
103 "Penn State wears Prada," Inside Higher Ed, June 9, 2006
104 "Penn State wears Prada," Inside Higher Ed, June 9, 2006
105 "College recruiters pitch Emory's name along 'final frontier': Pacific Northwest," The Emory Wheel, April 8, 2005
106 "The cost to compete," Sports Illustrated.com, January 19, 2005; "Serfs of the turf," Op-ed, The New York Times, November 11, 2007
107 "Schools making fans give more to keep best seats," USA Today, August 24, 2004

REFERENCES

108 "School logo-laden merchandise generates billions of dollars for universities," Silicon Valley/San Jose Business Journal, March 29, 2002

109 National Association of College Stores (www.nacs.org), as cited in "School logo-laden merchandise generates billions of dollars for universities," Silicon Valley/San Jose Business Journal, March 29, 2002

110 "What's in a name? Universities work to protect their logos and profit from them," The Business Journal of Kansas City, January 14, 2002

111 *Tuition Rising: Why College Costs So Much*, Ronald G. Ehrenberg, 2000

112 "School logo-laden merchandise generates billions of dollars for universities," Silicon Valley/San Jose Business Journal, March 29, 2002

113 "School logo-laden merchandise generates billions of dollars for universities," Silicon Valley/San Jose Business Journal, March 29, 2002

114 "School logo-laden merchandise generates billions of dollars for universities," Silicon Valley/San Jose Business Journal, March 29, 2002

115 Murphy, Robert G., and Gregory A. Trandel. "The relation between a university's football record and the size of its applicant pool," *Economics of Education Review*, 1994, volume 13: 265-70.

116 "The 'Flutie factor' is now received wisdom. But is it true?" Boston College Magazine, Spring 2003

117 "The 'Flutie factor' is now received wisdom. But is it true?" Boston College Magazine, Spring 2003

118 "Cost to compete higher for Gonzaga, Marquette," Sports Illustrated. com, January 18, 2005

119 "Score! Gonzaga University was struggling financially. Then it started winning basketball games," The Wall Street Journal, March 14, 2004

120 "Educational slam dunk?" The Wall Street Journal, March 30, 2006
121 "Score! Gonzaga University was struggling financially. Then it started winning basketball games," The Wall Street Journal, March 14, 2004
122 "Fired official blamed; Texas Tech admits violating dietary supplement rules," Associated Press, February 27, 2005; *Fall of the Ivory Tower*, George Charles Roche, 1994
123 "Intercollegiate Athletics," Albert J. Simone, Rochester Institute of Technology, March 16, 2004; "Many colleges bend rules to admit rich applicants," The Wall Street Journal, February 20, 2003; "76ers' Webber fined $100K," Associated Press, August 31, 2005
124 "Scandal at Houston: Ex-instructor, athlete accuse school of grade-fixing," Sports Illustrated, August 19, 2005; "Top grades and no class time for Auburn players," The New York Times, July 14, 2006
125 *Reclaiming the Game: College Sports and Educational Values*, William Bowen and Sarah Levin, 2003
126 "Grad rates increase slightly for Division I schools," Associated Press, September 27, 2006
127 "The All-Academic NCAA bracket," Inside Higher Ed, March 13, 2007
128 "Reading the Riot Act," University of Minnesota Magazine, September 8, 2003; "They got pretty rowdy," West Virginia MetroNews, March 25, 2005; "Alcohol advertising during college games a burning issue," Pittsburgh Post-Gazette, April 4, 2005
129 Nelson TF, Wechsler H, "School spirits: Alcohol and collegiate sports fans," Addictive Behaviors, 2003; 28(1): 1-11
130 Nelson TF, Wechsler H, "School spirits: Alcohol and collegiate sports fans," Addictive Behaviors, 2003; 28(1): 1-11
131 "Danger ahead!" New York Post, February 29, 2004; "Battery charges expected from Miami football recruit," The New York Times, February 9, 2004; "Bliss out," Sports Illustrated, Vol. 99, Issue 6, August 18, 2003; "WR leaving BYU; Player accused of lying to police will transfer," Associated Press, January 27, 2005

132	"ASU player is arrested in murder," The Arizona Republic, March 27, 2005
133	"Warrants: UConn players tried to return stolen computers," Connecticut Journal Inquirer, August 19, 2005
134	"Michigan State players could avoid charges in 'MacGyver' bomb incident," Associated Press, December 22, 2004
135	Crosset T., Benedict, J., & McDonald, M. "Male-student athletes reported for sexual assault: A survey of campus police and judicial affairs offices," Journal of Sport and Social Issues, 19 (2) 1995
136	Nelson TF, Wechsler H. School spirits: Alcohol and collegiate sports fans, Addictive Behaviors, 2003; 28(1): 1-11
137	"Hazed and confused," Inside Higher Ed, March 14, 2006; "On the web, college athletes acting badly," The New York Times, May 18, 2006
138	"The faculty bench," Op-ed, Inside Higher Ed, November 8, 2006
139	"The faculty bench," Op-ed, Inside Higher Ed, November 8, 2006
140	"Costs begin before college," USA Today, February 6, 2005
141	Research studies cited by FairTest, http://www.fairtest.org/univ/univproblems.htm; *Validity of high school grades in predicting student success beyond the freshman year*, Saul Geiser & Maria Veronica Santelices, University of California-Berkeley Center for Studies in Higher Education, June 2007
142	Research studies cited by FairTest (http://www.fairtest.org/univ/univproblems.htm); *The Case Against the SAT*, James Crouse and Dale Trusheim, 1988; "The best class money can buy," The Atlantic Monthly, November 2005; *Validity of high school grades in predicting student success beyond the freshman year*, Saul Geiser & Maria Veronica Santelices, University of California-Berkeley Center for Studies in Higher Education, June 2007
143	"They flubbed exams, got hired as executives of test companies," Bloomberg, November 3, 2006
144	"How much does it cost to buy your child in?" The Wall Street Journal, March 12, 2003

145 "Admissions preferences given to alumni children draws fire," The Wall Street Journal, January 13, 2003
146 "How much does it cost to buy your child in?" The Wall Street Journal, March 12, 2003; *The Price of Admission*, Daniel Golden, 2006; *Equity and Excellence in American Higher Education*, William Bowen, Martin Kurzweil, Eugene Tobin, 2006; "Access to the most selective private colleges by high-ability, low income students," Discussion Paper No. 69, Williams Project on the Economics of Higher Education, October 2005
147 "Bill would make colleges report legacies, early admissions," The Wall Street Journal, October 29, 2003
148 "Trends in College Pricing 2007," The College Board, October 2007
149 "Pell grants down, tuition up," Inside Higher Ed, October 25, 2006
150 "The top 10 most expensive colleges," CNN/Money, October 28, 2005
151 "Trends in College Pricing 2007," The College Board, October 2007
152 "Big, but not bad," The Chronicle of Higher Education, May 9, 2003
153 "Tuition & Fees," Colgate University, http://www.colgate.edu/DesktopDefault1.aspx?tabid=556 (viewed in 2007)
154 "In tuition game, popularity rises with price," The New York Times, December 11, 2005
155 "In tuition game, popularity rises with price," The New York Times, December 11, 2005
156 "Keeping (tuition) up with the Jones," Inside Higher Ed, January 24, 2007
157 "Keeping (tuition) up with the Jones," Inside Higher Ed, January 24, 2007
158 "A high price to pay," Newsday, March 21, 2004; "The College Cost Crisis: A Congressional Analysis of College Costs and Implications for America's Higher Education System," John Boehner and Howard McKeon, September 2003

159 *Going Broke By Degree*, Richard Vedder, 2004
160 U.S. Bureau of Labor Statistics; "Trends in College Pricing 2004," The College Board, 2004; "Trends in College Pricing 2005," The College Board, 2005; "Trends in College Pricing 2006," The College Board, 2006
161 "Trends in College Pricing 2007," The College Board, October 2007
162 "Trends in College Pricing 2007," The College Board, October 2007
163 "SOA students protest rising tuition costs," Columbia Daily Spectator, April 22, 2004; "Yale Students arrested in protest over admissions, financial aid policy," WTNH/Associated Press, February 24, 2005
164 "Pitt students face extra fee to pay college costs by credit card," Pittsburgh Post Gazette, April 19, 2004
165 "Student fees sit unused at UM," Baltimore Sun, March 27, 2004
166 "Colleges get building fever," The Wall Street Journal, May 18, 2005; "Trends in College Pricing 2007," The College Board, October 2007
167 "Public university students step into funding void," Associated Press, April 29, 2004
168 "Colleges get building fever," The Wall Street Journal, May 18, 2005
169 "Colleges get building fever," The Wall Street Journal, May 18, 2005
170 "Bursar institutes new fee policy," Indiana Daily Student, April 20, 2004
171 For example, The University of Texas at Dallas has a list of 48 mandatory and other fees in its Undergraduate Catalog (http://www.utdallas.edu/student/catalog/undcrgrad04/tuition-otherfees.html). In addition: "College graduation packs one final financial punch," Associated Press, May 3, 2006; "As support lags, colleges tack on student fees," The New York Times, September 4, 2007
172 "Student fees sit unused at UM," Baltimore Sun, March 27, 2004
173 *Fall of the Ivory Tower*, George Charles Roche, 1994; *U.S. v. Brown University, et al.*, 805 F.Supp. 288 (E.D. Pa.1992)
174 "College financial aid and antitrust action," National Bureau of Economic Research, November 2000

175 "Benevolent colluders? The effects of antitrust action on college financial aid and tuition," National Bureau of Economic Research Working Paper #7754, June 2000

176 www.568group.org

177 "Admission Trends Survey/State of College Admission," National Association for College Admission Counseling, 2005; "Enthusiasm trend up in college admissions," Associated Press, October 9, 2004

178 *Shakespeare, Einstein, and the Bottom Line*, David L. Kirp, 2004; "The best class money can buy," The Atlantic Monthly, November 2005

179 "The best class money can buy," The Atlantic Monthly, November 2005

180 "The best class money can buy," The Atlantic Monthly, November 2005

181 "Financial aid: How to get more," CNN/Money, March 31, 2004

182 "Pressure is on early admissions," USA Today, December 8, 2003

183 "New batch of Early Decision applicants sets records," The Tufts Daily, February 15, 2005

184 "The best class money can buy," The Atlantic Monthly, November 2005

185 "Fighting for financial aid," Student Leader, April 1, 2002, www.studentleader.com

186 "Fighting for financial aid," Student Leader, April 1, 2002, www.studentleader.com

187 "The best class money can buy," The Atlantic Monthly, November 2005; "The competition for top undergraduates by America's colleges and universities," The Center for Measuring University Performance, May 2001, http://mup.asu.edu/gaterUG1.pdf (viewed in 2007)

REFERENCES

188 "As merit-aid race escalates, wealthy often win," The Washington Post, April 19, 2005; *Tuition Rising*, Ronald Ehrenberg, 2002; "On sale now: Tuition discounting is increasingly common at colleges," The Wall Street Journal, May 16, 2002; "Universities giving less financial aid on basis of need," The New York Times, June 21, 1998

189 Lumina Foundation for Education, 2003, as cited in "As merit-aid race escalates, wealthy often win," The Washington Post, April 19, 2005

190 "Flagships flunked on access," Inside Higher Ed, November 21, 2006

191 "The best class money can buy," The Atlantic Monthly, November 2005

192 *Credit Card Nation*, Robert Manning, 2001

193 "Graduating Into Debt: Credit card marketing on Maryland college campuses," The Maryland Consumer Rights Coalition and Maryland Public Interest Research Group, February 19, 2004

194 "Marketing plastic: The new college try," BusinessWeek, October 15, 2007

195 "They're baaaaack: Card marketers on campus," Credit Card Management, May 27, 2003

196 "The dirty secret of campus credit cards," BusinessWeek.com, September 6, 2007

197 "Don't leave college without it," Mother Jones, March/April 2002

198 *Credit Card Nation*, Robert Manning, 2001

199 "Even cosier deals on campus," BusinessWeek, October 1, 2007

200 "Don't leave college without it," Mother Jones, March/April 2002

201 "Keep college from breaking the bank," CBS, August 8, 2006

202 "Room, Board & Bookies: The perils of student gambling," Focus on the Family, 2000

203 "Credit card chronicles," Credit Abuse Resistance Education, November 16, 2004; "Confessions of a credit-card pusher," Business Week.com, September 5, 2007

204 "Graduating Into Debt: Credit card marketing on Maryland college campuses," The Maryland Consumer Rights Coalition and Maryland Public Interest Research Group, February 19, 2004

205 "What you need to know about your financial aid office and their preferred lender list," MyRichUncle.com, http://myrichuncle.com/FinAidOffice.aspx (viewed in 2007); "Sallie Mae's success too costly?" CBS, May 7, 2006; "Lender/university entanglements," Inside Higher Ed, March 5, 2007; "Ask and ye shall receive," Inside Higher Ed, September 5, 2007; "Special Report: Student Loan Scandal," New America Foundation, http://www.newamerica.net/programs/education_policy/higher_ed_watch/student_loan_scandal

206 "Big money on campus," U.S. News and World Report, October 27, 2003

207 "Lender/university entanglements," Inside Higher Ed, March 5, 2007

208 "What you need to know about your financial aid office and their preferred lender list," MyRichUncle.com, http://myrichuncle.com/FinAidOffice.aspx (viewed in 2007); "When Sallie met Wall Street," *Fortune*, December 26, 2005; "Student loan xploited," The Village Voice, April 10, 2007; "Cuomo's smoking gun," Inside Higher Ed, April 5, 2007; "University rated lenders by perks," The Wall Street Journal, May 1, 2007

209 "Lenders' 2 tickets to paradise," Inside Higher Ed, October 24, 2006; "Offering perks, lenders court colleges' favor," The New York Times, October 24, 2006

210 "A blind eye," Higher Ed Watch Blog, New America Foundation, April 11, 2007; "Education department, on the case," Inside Higher Ed, July 10, 2007; "Permissible preferred lender lists," Inside Higher Ed, September 4, 2007

211 "More schools lend directly to students," The Wall Street Journal, September 8, 2005

212 "Big money on campus," U.S. News and World Report, October 27, 2003; "Sallie Mae's success too costly?" CBS, May 7, 2006

213	"Auditors: College loan program lacks oversight," Associated Press, January 25, 2005; "More schools lend directly to students," The Wall Street Journal, September 8, 2005
214	"Colleges find a way to keep profiting from loans," National Direct Student Loan Coalition, July 14, 2006
215	"Colleges find a way to keep profiting from loans," National Direct Student Loan Coalition, July 14, 2006
216	"Colleges playing tough on debt," The Boston Globe, November 19, 2006
217	"Colleges playing tough on debt," The Boston Globe, November 19, 2006
218	"Colleges playing tough on debt," The Boston Globe, November 19, 2006
219	*Fall of the Ivory Tower*, George Charles Roche, 1994; "Lender/university entanglements," Inside Higher Ed, March 5, 2007
220	"The literacy of America's college students," American Institutes for Research, January 2006
221	"National survey reveals gaps between students' perceived credit knowledge and real financial facts; more credit education needed," press release, Citigroup, March 17, 2005; "Big loans, bigger problems," State Public Interest Research Group, March 2001
222	"On-campus credit card solicitors pose danger," Yale Daily News, October 6, 1998
223	"The lure of easy credit leaves more students struggling with debt," The Chronicle of Higher Education, June 15, 2001
224	"Credit cards on campus," Consumer Federation of America, 1999
225	"The losing generation," Salon.com, February 21, 2006
226	"UC lengthens college stay," University of Cincinnati News Record, October 8, 2003
227	"Govy gridlock," The Dartmouth Online, February 24, 2005
228	"Seniors struggle to get crucial classes," Carolina Week, January 24, 2005

229 "Administration considers online wait list system," The GW Hatchet Online, September 30, 2004
230 "Registration period highlights budget problems," The Daily Campus, November 7, 2003
231 "MIS problems persist: Registration issues frustrate some students," The Oakland Post, November 28, 2001
232 "Higher education, higher bills," Detroit Free Press, August 9, 2005
233 "A battle over standards at for-profit colleges," The Wall Street Journal, September 30, 2005
234 "Does your B-school make the grade?" BusinessWeek, March 19, 2007
235 "A Matter of Degrees: Improving Graduation Rates in Four-Year Colleges and Universities," The Education Trust, May 2004; "College in 4 years? Try 5 or 6," CNN/Money, June 22, 2004
236 Williams College 2004-05 Class Agent Handbook
237 "College researchers dig up personal info on alumni as fundraising tool," The Morning Call, June 8, 2004; "Policy for release, access and distribution of alumni and donor information," Iowa State University Foundation
238 "College researchers dig up personal info on alumni as fundraising tool," The Morning Call, June 8, 2004; "Policy for release, access and distribution of alumni and donor information," Iowa State University Foundation
239 "When $26 billion isn't enough," The Wall Street Journal, December 17-18, 2005
240 Letter to the editor, The Wall Street Journal, January 9, 2006
241 "Annual giving," Princeton Alumni Weekly web exclusives, May 14, 2003, http://www.princeton.edu/~paw/archive_new/PAW02-03/15-0514/letters.html
242 "Poisoned ivy: Fight at Princeton escalates over use of a family's gift," The Wall Street Journal, February 7, 2006
243 "Made it!," Yale Alumni Magazine, October 1997

244 "Tufts Tomorrow collects $609 million in donations," The Tufts Daily, Sept. 16, 2002

245 "Voluntary Support of Education, 2006," Council for Aid to Education, February 2007

246 "Survey: College giving up sharply—especially to wealthiest schools," Associated Press, February 21, 2007

247 "2002-2003 Administrative Compensation Survey," College and University Professional Association for Human Resources, 2003

248 "Janitors' strike at U. of Miami escalates," Inside Higher Ed, March 3, 2006

249 University of Miami Faculty Manual, 2005-2006, iii

250 "Speaker says university officials see themselves as CEOs of a business," The Southern Illinoisan, September 8, 2005

251 "Court challenge on athletic aid," Inside Higher Ed, February 23, 2006; "Serfs of the turf," Op-ed, The New York Times, November 11, 2007

252 "Codes don't work," Inside Higher Ed, September 28, 2006; United Students Against Sweatshops (www.studentsagainstsweatshops.org)

253 As described in Chapter 4; "Campus cash-in: How American universities overcharge federal taxpayers for student labor," National Taxpayers Union, NTU Foundation Issue Brief 149, June 28, 2005

254 "Lobbying lawmakers, federal agencies wins universities goodies," USA Today, March 7, 2007

255 "The College Cost Crisis: A Congressional Analysis of College Costs and Implications for America's Higher Education System," John Boehner and Howard McKeon, September 2003

256 *Universities in the Marketplace*, Derek Bok, 2004

257 "Colleges seek a record number of patents," The Chronicle of Higher Education, December 3, 2004

258 "Inventions produced almost $1 billion for universities in 2002," The Chronicle of Higher Education, December 19, 2003

259 *Shakespeare, Einstein and the Bottom Line*, David L. Kirp, 2004

260 "Eureka! Universities such as Emory are reaping the benefits of marketing discoveries—from Google to Gatorade," Emory Magazine, Spring 2005

261 *Shakespeare, Einstein and the Bottom Line*, David L. Kirp, 2004

262 "Bill seeks access to tax-funded research," The Washington Post, May 3, 2006

263 "Lesser-known public colleges increase federal lobbying," The Chronicle of Higher Education, Oct. 22, 2004; "Lobbying to bring home the bacon," The Chronicle of Higher Education, Oct. 22, 2004

264 "Universities get free pass on new House ethics rules," March 7, 2007; "Lobbying lawmakers, federal agencies wins universities goodies," USA Today, March 7, 2007

265 "Anti-lobbying fever? Not in Higher Ed," Inside Higher Ed, December 21, 2006

266 "Anti-lobbying fever? Not in Higher Ed," Inside Higher Ed, December 21, 2006

267 *Lobbying for Higher Education: How Colleges and Universities Influence Federal Policy* (Vanderbilt Issues in Higher Education), Constance Ewing Cook, 1998

268 Posted to "Alma mater gets a clue," This Blog Sits at the Intersection of Anthropology and Economics (http://www.cultureby.com/trilogy/2005/06/alma_mater_gets.html) on June 16, 2005 by "Matt"

CHAPTER 3

269 "Special Report: College Housing," College Planning and Management magazine, June 2003 (http://www.peterli.com/global/pdfs/College Housing.pdf)

270 "Room Rates," University of Miami, 2007-08

271 "Room Rental Rates, Fall/Spring Semester 2007-2008," University of Florida

REFERENCES

272 "15th Annual Residence Hall Construction Report," American School & University, June 2004 (http://www.asumag.com/mag/406asu41.pdf)

273 For example, http://www.oregon.gov/DOR/STATS/docs/ExpR05-07/Chapter2.pdf; http://www.cga.ct.gov/2004/rpt/2004-R-0769.htm

274 *Realizing the Educational Potential of Residence Halls*, Charles Schroeder, Phyllis Mable, and Associates, 1994; "A Meta-Analysis of the Influence of College Residence Halls on Academic Performance," Journal of College Student Development v40 no5 (Sept./Oct. 1999): 551-61

275 Harvard University Student Handbook, 2004-2005 http://www.registrar.fas.harvard.edu/handbooks/student/chapter1/index.html

276 www.ed.gov/admins/lead/safety/crime/criminaloffenses/index.html

277 "On campus, creating an illusion by crime data," Philadelphia Inquirer, January 15, 2006

278 "Errors of admission?" Inside Higher Ed, May 18, 2006

279 "Alcohol advertising during college games a burning issue," Pittsburgh Post-Gazette, April 4, 2005

280 National Fire Protection Association (NFPA), as cited in "New fire-safety rules to affect WPI," Tech News, the student newspaper of Worcester Polytechnic Institute, November 14, 2000

281 "Experts say many residence halls don't have fire sprinklers," press release, Center for Campus Fire Safety, August 25, 2005

282 "Pain grips Seton Hall U: Students try to cope in wake of fatal fire," The New York Daily News, January 21, 2000

283 "Experts say many residence halls don't have fire sprinklers," press release, Center for Campus Fire Safety, August 25, 2005

284 "37% of Iowa dorm dwellers not protected by fire sprinklers," The Des Moines Register, February 4, 2007

285 "Where sprinklers are...and aren't," The Tennessean, October 2, 2003; "Sprinkler systems not required with Greek houses," The Daily Mississippian, August 26, 2005; "Harding takes proactive steps to reduce fire risks," The Daily Citizen, August 25, 2005

286 For example, "Assembly passes bill for dorm sprinklers," The New York Times, May 26, 2000
287 "Dormitory fires," U.S. Fire Administration Topical Fire Research Series, Vol. 1, Issue 14, March 2001/Revised December 2001
288 "Dining plan mulls reduction," The Duke Chronicle, February 12, 2004
289 "Dining Services—Frequently Asked Questions," University of Massachusetts Amherst, 2007; "FAQ's, Fiction and Urban Legend," Rutgers University, 2007; "Meal Plan FAQ," James Madison University, 2007
290 "Meal Plan Rates," University of Miami, 2007-08
291 "Meal Plan Rates," University of Miami, 2007-08
292 "Meal Memberships Fall 2007/Spring 2008," University of Florida
293 http://www.umass.edu/diningservices/faq.php
294 "Revised meal plan no improvement," The Daily Campus, March 23, 2005
295 "Weighing in on Pav food," The Cavalier Daily (The University of Virginia), Nov. 10, 1999
296 For example: "Dining mulls plan reduction," The Duke Chronicle, February 12, 2004; "Dining services gives students a raw deal," The Cavalier Daily, Oct 18, 2000; "Meal plans bite," College Heights Herald, August 20, 2002
297 "Dining provides good, bad qualities," Technician, November 10, 2004
298 "Dining provides good, bad qualities," Technician, November 10, 2004
299 "Digesting college life," iMPrint Magazine, November 2, 2005; viewed at www.imprintmagazine.org/2005/11/02/digesting-college-life/
300 "Digesting college life," iMPrint Magazine, November 2, 2005; viewed at www.imprintmagazine.org/2005/11/02/digesting-college-life/
301 "The Best 361 Colleges 2006," The Princeton Review, August 2005

302 "Other campuses: Freshman weight gain rises above myth status," Cornell University, January 14, 2005
303 "The freshman weight gain: a model for the study of the epidemic of obesity," International Journal of Obesity, November 2004
304 "Ohio University Dining Services Fun Facts," Ohio University, 2007
305 "Other campuses: Freshman weight gain rises above myth status," Cornell University, January 14, 2005
306 "Dining plan mulls reduction," The Duke Chronicle, February 12, 2004; "Dining services gives students a raw deal," The Cavalier Daily, Oct 18, 2000; "Meal plans bite," College Heights Herald, August 20, 2002
307 "Penn students hospitalized after possible food poisoning," Daily Pennsylvanian, Nov. 9, 1998
308 "Eat at your own risk: College cafeterias," www.cbsnewyork.com,, Sept 20, 2004
309 "Digesting college life," iMPrint Magazine, November 2, 2005, viewed at www.imprintmagazine.org/2005/11/02/digesting-college-life/
310 http://www.campusfood.com/default.asp?stay=1 (viewed in 2007)
311 "Reading, writing and revenue," Associated Press, January 15, 2004
312 "College newspapers have different policies on alcohol advertising," La Crosse Tribune, August 19, 2004
313 "Alcohol advertising during college games a burning issue," Pittsburgh Post-Gazette, April 4, 2005
314 "City to hold hearing on unpaid tickets," Boston College Heights, February 18, 2003, "Emory Policies: Financial Holds/Cancellation," Emory University, www.emory.edu/studentfinancials/Policies_FHC.htm (viewed in 2007); University of Florida 2005-06 Undergraduate Catalog; "Office of the Bursar: Frequently Asked Questions," Miami University in Ohio, www.units.muohio.edu/bur/faq (viewed in 2007); "No holds barred: Pay the bills or pay the price," Michigan State University, State News, 1998; "Orientation Guide," University of Virginia, 2006

315 "Orientation Guide," University of Virginia, 2006
316 "Caveat renter," Helena Independent Record, July 24, 2005
317 *Beer and Circus*, Murray Sperber, 2001
318 "Colleges try to contend with hovering parents," Associated Press, August 29, 2005
319 "Colleges try to contend with hovering parents," Associated Press, August 29, 2005
320 Colgate University Standard Fees 2005-06 (http://offices.colgate.edu/studentaccounts/annualfees.asp)
321 "Just for Parents," Colgate University, www.colgate.edu/DesktopDefault1.aspx?tabid=749&pgID=9000; "FinancingOptions," Colgate University, www.colgate.edu/desktopdefault1.aspx?tabid=1188
322 "Just for Parents," Colgate University, www.colgate.edu/DesktopDefault1.aspx?tabid=749&pgID=9000; "The Parent's Fund," Colgate University, www.colgatealumni.org/annualfund_parentsfund.htm
323 "Colleges ward off overinvolved parents," The Wall Street Journal, July 29, 2005

CHAPTER 4

324 Kansas State University 2004 Student Survey, http://www.ksu.edu/catl/GenEd/6StudentComments.htm (viewed in 2007)
325 Eastern Illinois University 2002 Alumni Survey of 1997 graduates, http://www.eiu.edu/~assess/alumni/02academics.doc (viewed in 2007)
326 "Choosing the Core," Inside Higher Ed, November 4, 2005
327 *ProfScam: Professors and the Demise of Higher Education*, Charles Sykes, 1988; *Shakespeare, Einstein, and the Bottom Line*, David L. Kirp, 2004
328 "Choosing the Core," Inside Higher Ed, November 4, 2005
329 "Bizarre college classes," The Princeton Review, www.princetonreview.com
330 "Higher education, higher bills," Detroit Free Press, August 9, 2005

331 "Budget cuts could worsen class overcrowding," The Daily Texan, February 25, 2003

332 "Myths and facts about Harvard," Harvard University Women's Swimming and Diving Team recruitment materials, 2005 (http://hcs.harvard.edu/~womswim/recruiting/myths.html

333 "Budget cuts could worsen class overcrowding," The Daily Texan, February 25, 2003

334 "Mass instruction or higher learning? The impact of class size in higher education," Bridget Terry Long and Eric Bettinger, 2005

335 "Instructional faculty and staff in higher education institutions who taught classes to undergraduates," National Center for Education Statistics, April 2000; "Background characteristics, work activities, and compensation of instructional faculty and staff," National Center for Education Statistics, December 2005

336 "Teachers-postsecondary," Occupational Outlook Handbook, U.S. Bureau of Labor Statistics, (http://stats.bls.gov/oco); *The Fall of the Ivory Tower*, George Charles Roche, 1994; *ProfScam: Professors and the Demise of Higher Education*, Charles Sykes, 1988

337 "Teachers-postsecondary," Occupational Outlook Handbook, U.S. Bureau of Labor Statistics, (http://stats.bls.gov/oco); "Office-hour habits of the North American professor," The Chronicle of Higher Education, May 13, 2003

338 "Instructional faculty and staff in higher education institutions who taught classes to undergraduates," National Center for Education Statistics, April 2000

339 "Instructional faculty and staff in higher education institutions who taught classes to undergraduates," National Center for Education Statistics, April 2000

340 "Reform tenure now: Addressing Florida's failed system," Foundation for Florida's Future, August 1, 1995; "Universities have lost focus on students when it comes to costs," The Daily Oakland Press, December 27, 2005

341 "Changing the incentives," Inside Higher Ed, January 19, 2006

342 *Going Broke by Degree*, Richard Vedder, 2004
343 "Just what the professor ordered," Op-Ed, The New York Times, September 16, 2005
344 "Reform tenure now: Addressing Florida's failed system," Foundation for Florida's Future, August 1, 1995
345 "Reform tenure now: Addressing Florida's failed system," Foundation for Florida's Future, August 1, 1995
346 "Adjunct faculty status debated," The Lafayette Online, November 12, 2004; "Teachers—Postsecondary," Occupational Outlook Handbook 2005, U.S. Department of Labor, 2005
347 "Instructional faculty and staff in higher education institutions who taught classes to undergraduates," National Center for Education Statistics, April 2000
348 "A balancing act: publish or teach," The Daily Bruin, February 17, 2005
349 "A balancing act: publish or teach," The Daily Bruin, February 17, 2005
350 "A balancing act: publish or teach," The Daily Bruin, February 17, 2005
351 "Teaching the 101," The Chronicle of Higher Education, September 8, 2004
352 "Teaching the 101," The Chronicle of Higher Education, September 8, 2004
353 *The Fall of the Ivory Tower*, George Charles Roche, 1994
354 *Shakespeare, Einstein, and the Bottom Line*, David L. Kirp, 2004
355 "Reform tenure now: Addressing Florida's failed system," Foundation for Florida's Future, August 1, 1995
356 "Clemson sets $150 million research goal," The Greenville News, November 22, 2002
357 "A balancing act: publish or teach," The Daily Bruin, February 17, 2005
358 "A balancing act: publish or teach," The Daily Bruin, February 17, 2005

References

359 "Living with myths: Undergraduate education in America," Change, 26(1), 28-32, 1994

360 "The relationship between research and teaching: a meta-analysis," Review of Educational Research, 66(4), 507-542, 1996

361 *What Matters in College? Four Critical Years Revisited*, AW Astin, 1993

362 "Adjunct faculty status debated," The Lafayette Online, November 12, 2004

363 "Part-time college teachers say unionizing imperils jobs," Chicago Tribune, August 28, 2000

364 "Fewer professors spend a full day on campus," Christian Science Monitor, February 24, 2004

365 "Professor of desperation," The Washington Post, July 21, 2002

366 "Fewer professors spend a full day on campus," Christian Science Monitor, February 24, 2004

367 *Imposters in the Temple: The Decline of the American University*, Martin Anderson, 1992

368 "Reform tenure now: Addressing Florida's failed system," Foundation for Florida's Future, August 1, 1995

369 *Imposters in the Temple: The Decline of the American University*, Martin Anderson, 1992

370 "Summers' storm warning," BusinessWeek, July 10, 2006

371 "Fewer professors spend a full day on campus," Christian Science Monitor, February 24, 2004

372 "The 1999 MLA Survey of Staffing in English and Foreign Language Departments," Modern Language Association, 1999

373 "The 1999 MLA Survey of Staffing in English and Foreign Language Departments," Modern Language Association, 1999

374 "Professor of desperation," The Washington Post, July 21, 2002

375 "Professor of desperation," The Washington Post, July 21, 2002; "Adjunct faculty status debated," The Lafayette Online, November 12, 2004; "Part-time college teachers say unionizing imperils jobs," Chicago Tribune, August 28, 2000

376 "Part-time college teachers say unionizing imperils jobs," Chicago Tribune, August 28, 2000
377 "Reform tenure now: Addressing Florida's failed system," Foundation for Florida's Future, August 1, 1995; "Serving time: The 6-year rule," Inside Higher Ed, June 22, 2005
378 "Professor of desperation," The Washington Post, July 21, 2002; "Fewer professors spend a full day on campus," Christian Science Monitor, February 24, 2004
379 "Adjunct faculty status debated," The Lafayette Online, November 12, 2004
380 *ProfScam: Professors and the Demise of Higher Education*, Charles Sykes, 1988
381 http://sacrate.com/database/search.asp?type=prof&prof=645, posted in 2003
382 Posting at (http://www.cultureby.com/trilogy/2005/06/alma_mater_gets.html), June 17, 2005 by "Supergenius"
383 "New research casts doubt on value of student evaluations of professors," The Chronicle of Higher Education, January 16, 1998
384 "Good teacher, bad teacher," The Notre Dame Saint Mary's College Observer, September 15, 2004
385 "New research casts doubt on value of student evaluations of professors," The Chronicle of Higher Education, January 16, 1998; "New questions on student evaluations," Inside Higher Ed, January 29, 2007;
386 "What is Tenure?" Jerz's Literacy Weblog, http://jerz.setonhill.edu/weblog/permalink.jsp?id=3129&embedComments=true, posting by Dennis Jerz on February 11, 2005
387 "Professors must speak properly," University of Central Florida, January 27, 2005
388 "Foreign TAs face communication breakdown," The Ohio State Lantern, October 13, 2004
389 "Instructors' accents make lessons hard, students say," San Francisco Chronicle, November 27, 1999

390 "Professors must speak properly," University of Central Florida, January 27, 2005
391 "Foreign TAs face communication breakdown," The Ohio State Lantern, October 13, 2004
392 "Instructors' accents make lessons hard, students say," San Francisco Chronicle, November 27, 1999
393 "Teach impediment: When the student can't understand the instructor, who is to blame?" The Chronicle of Higher Education, April 8, 2005
394 "Message from the Dean," University of Pennsylvania newsletter, January 2002; "Teach impediment: When the student can't understand the instructor, who is to blame?" The Chronicle of Higher Education, April 8, 2005; "Instructors' accents make lessons hard, students say," San Francisco Chronicle, November 27, 1999
395 "Teach impediment: When the student can't understand the instructor, who is to blame?" Chronicle of Higher Education, April 8, 2005
396 "Language-barrier bill planned," The Forum of Fargo-Moorhead, January 24, 2005
397 "Survey reveals pervasive political pressure in the classroom," press release, American Council of Trustees and Alumni, November 30, 2004
398 "Conservative students sue over academic freedom, " Associated Press, Dec. 20, 2004
399 For example, "The new PC," Russell Jacoby, The Nation, April 4, 2005
400 "Survey reveals pervasive political pressure in the classroom," press release, American Council of Trustees and Alumni, November 30, 2004
401 "Missouri St. settles suit with student over gay adoption issue," Associated Press, November 8, 2006
402 "On campus: Free speech for you but not for me?" USA Today, November 2, 2003

403 "Leaning left: Liberal bias seeping into students' college education," The LSU Daily Reveille, January 29, 2003
404 "Whose academic freedom?" Village Voice, December 17, 2004; "Witch hunt at UCLA," Los Angeles Times, January 22, 2006; "The new PC," The Nation, April 4, 2005
405 "On campus: Free speech for you but not for me?" USA Today, November 2, 2003
406 "Celebrity professors create buzz," Florida Times Union, February 18, 2003
407 "Desmond Tutu to teach one course at University of North Florida," Black Issues in Higher Education, December 19, 2002
408 'Visiting Professors of Journalism,' Princeton University, http://www.princeton.edu/~humcounc/visiting_professors_of_journalism.shtml (viewed on March 9, 2005)
409 "Celebrity professors create buzz," Florida Times Union, February 18, 2003
410 "Up, up and away," Inside Higher Ed, February 14, 2006; "Where all grades are above average," The Washington Post, January 28, 2003; "Grade inflation: It's not just an issue for the Ivy League," Carnegie Perspectives, June 2004; "Ivy League grade inflation," USA Today, February 7, 2002
411 "Princeton reining in grade inflation," Associated Press, September 20, 2005; "Making the grades," The New York Times, June 5, 1994; "ASU's business school getting tougher," East Valley Tribune, July 21, 2006; "Can tough grades be fair grades?" The New York Times, June 7, 2006; "Grade inflation: Devaluing B-schools' currency," BusinessWeek, April 19, 2005
412 http://www.goizueta.emory.edu/degree/undergra_adm_freshman.html (viewed in 2007)
413 "Does your B-school make the grade?" BusinessWeek, March 19, 2007

414 For example: "Can Emory College students take courses in the Business School?" http://www.college.emory.edu/current/support/fame/faq.html (viewed in 2007)

415 "Colleges impose restrictions on study-abroad programs," The Wall Street Journal, April 12, 2006

416 "In study abroad, gifts and money for universities," The New York Times, August 13, 2007

417 "Good teacher, bad teacher," The Notre Dame Saint Mary's College Observer, September 15, 2004

418 "Private Tutor List," Penn State University, www.math.psu.edu/UG/PrivateTutorList.htm (viewed in 2007)

419 "Private Tutor Index," University of Arizona, www.tutoring.arizona.edu/private_tutor_index.htm (viewed in 2007)

420 "Private Tutor List," Boise State University, http://tutoring.boisestate.edu/privatetutors.shtml (viewed in 2007)

421 "Private Tutors," Clemson University, www.clemson.edu/asc/private_tutoring.html (viewed in 2007)

422 "Private Tutors," Wayne State University, www.math.wayne.edu/~mtc/privtut.htm (viewed in 2007)

423 "Private Tutor Guideline," California State University, http://studentaffairs.csufresno.edu/lrc/private_tutor_guidelines.html (viewed in 2007)

424 "Private Tutor List," Western Washington University, http://www.wwu.edu/depts/tutorialcenter/Resources.htm (viewed in 2007)

425 "Overseas tutors help U.S. students online," USA Today, August 29, 2005

426 "Degree Attainment Rates at American Colleges and Universities," UCLA Higher Education Research Institute, 2002

427 U.S. Census data, as cited in "The college dropout boom," The New York Times, May 24, 2005

428 "College For All? Is there too much emphasis on getting a 4-year college degree?" U.S. Dept. of Education, January 1999

429 "Debate grows as colleges slip in graduations," The New York Times, September 15, 2006
430 "Class conscious," U.S. News & World Report, May 2, 2005
431 "Debate grows as colleges slip in graduations," The New York Times, September 15, 2006
432 "Debate grows as colleges slip in graduations," The New York Times, September 15, 2006
433 "Job Outlook 2004," NACE, 2003 (http://www.jobweb.com/joboutlook/2004outlook/JO04student.pdf)
434 "Job Outlook 2004," NACE, 2003 (http://www.jobweb.com/joboutlook/2004outlook/JO04student.pdf)
435 "Understanding employers' perceptions of college graduates," Change, May/June 1998 (http://www.stanford.edu/group/ncpi/documents/pdfs/lndmj98.pdf)
436 National Adult Literacy Survey, U.S. Department of Education, National Center for Education Statistics, 1992; Adult Literacy and Education in America, National Center for Education Statistics, 2001
437 "2003 National Assessment of Adult Literacy," U.S. Department of Education, 2005
438 "College students fall short in demonstrating the ICT literacy skills necessary for success in college and the workplace," press release, Educational Testing Service, November 14, 2006
439 "Wages and the university educated: A paradox resolved," Monthly Labor Review, July 1997
440 "They've got diplomas, but do they have skills," Software Development Times, September 1, 2005
441 "They've got diplomas, but do they have skills," Software Development Times, September 1, 2005
442 "They've got diplomas, but do they have skills," Software Development Times, September 1, 2005

443 "College Rankings Reformed: The Case for a New Order in Higher Education," Education Sector, September 22, 2006; "Is our students learning?" Washington Monthly, September 2006

444 "The measure of learning," U.S. News & World Report, March 12, 2007

445 "About the Commission," U.S. Department of Education, http://www.ed.gov/about/bdscomm/list/hiedfuture/about.html (viewed in 2007)

446 "A stinging first draft," Inside Higher Ed, June 27, 2006

447 "Commission report, take 2," Inside Higher Ed, July 17, 2006

448 "In focus: The Spellings Commission," Inside Higher Ed, http://insidehighered.com/news/focus/commission

449 "No college left behind?" Inside Higher Ed, February 15, 2006

450 "No college left behind?" Inside Higher Ed, February 15, 2006

451 "No college left behind?" Inside Higher Ed, February 15, 2006

452 David P. Hamilton, "Research Papers: Who's Uncited Now?" Science, January 4, 1991, p.25; letter to the editor of Science from David P. Pendlebury, Research Department, Institute for Scientific Information, February 9, 1991.

453 For example: the Journal of Wildlife Management (http://www.wildlife.org/publications/JWMguidelines05.pdf); the Journal of the Acoustical Society of America (http://asa.aip.org/jasa.html); the Journal of Dairy Science (http://adsa.org/jds/pgchg.html); the Journal of Cognitive Neuroscience (http://jocn.mitpress.org/misc/ifora.shtml), the Journal of Optical Engineering, the Journal of Electronic Imaging, and the Journal of Biomedical Optics (www.spie.org/app/Publications/index.cfm?fuseaction=journals&type=faq); the Biophysical Journal (www.biophysj.org/misc/ifora.shtml); and BioMed Central ($500 per article)

454 "MIT students pull prank on conference," Reuters, April 14, 2005

455 "Bigfoot research makes professor a campus outcast," Associated Press, November 3, 2006

456 *Going Broke by Degree*, Richard Vedder, 2004

457 "Research misbehavior may be widespread," United Press International, June 8, 2005; "Ethical problems in academic research," American Scientist, 1993, 81: 542-553; "The Columbia University 'miracle' study: Flawed and fraud," Skeptical Inquirer, September 2004; "A psychology professor resigns amid accusations of research fraud at Harvard," The Chronicle of Higher Education, August 10, 2001; "Research fraud investigation leads to departures from Northern Kentucky University," The Chronicle of Higher Education, September 19, 2003; "Researcher admits fraud in grant data," The Boston Globe, March 18, 2005

458 "When a mentor becomes a thief," The Chronicle of Higher Education, April 1, 2002

459 "Payola profs; for the right price, they'll betray our trust," Reader's Digest, July 2005; "At medical journals, writers paid by industry play big role," The Wall Street Journal, December 13, 2005

460 For an extensive discussion of this issue, see *University, Inc.: The Corporate Corruption of American Higher Education,* Jennifer Washburn, 2005 ;"University, Inc.: 10 things you should know about corporate corruption on campus," CampusProgress.org, 2005

461 *Imposters in the Temple,* Martin Anderson, 1992; *The Fall of the Ivory Tower,* George Charles Roche, 1994; Jeff Gotlieb, "Overcharge Estimate Climbs," San Jose Mercury News, November 15, 1991, p.B1; "Show us the money," Reader's Digest, May 2006

CHAPTER 5

462 Author's calculation based on "Trends in Student Aid 2007," The College Board, 2007

463 Note: The National Commission on the Cost of Higher Education also includes housing and food expenses in calculating students' total college costs.

464 "CollegePulse 2004," Harris Interactive, 2004; "Working Their Way Through College: Student Employment and its Impact on the College Experience," American Council on Education, 2006; "National average earnings by educational attainment," U.S. Census Bureau, Current Population Reports, P20-513, 1998 (adjusted for inflation to 2003 dollars): http://pubdb3.census.gov/macro/032005/perinc/new04_001.htm

465 For example: Day & Newburger (2002) The Big Payoff: Educational Attainment and Synthetic Estimates of Work-Life Earnings. (Current Population Reports, Special studies, P23-210). U.S. Census Bureau; "Education Pays 2004," The College Board, 2004; "College: An Investment in Yourself," Citibank, 2005, http://studentloan.citibank.com/slcsite/plancollege/investment.asp

466 For example: "Does college still pay?" The Economists' Voice, 2005, Volume 2, Issue 4; "Five Reasons to Skip College: A Reply," Productivity and Prosperity Project (P3), Arizona State University, May 2006

467 "Education Pays 2004," The College Board, 2005, (http://www.collegeboard.com/prod_downloads/press/cost04/EducationPays2004.pdf); "Survey: Most young adults have positive view of college," Associated Press, February 9, 2005

468 Author's calculation based on U.S. Census data in "Education Pays 2007," The College Board, 2007

469 "The short- and long-term career effects of graduating in a recession (Working Paper 12159)," National Bureau of Economic Research, April 2006

470 "Working on the double," The Wall Street Journal, November 1, 2005

471 *Generation Debt*, Anya Kamenetz, 2006, p.199

472 For full-time workers aged 25 and over; "Education Pays 2007," The College Board, 2007

473 "The tyranny of the diploma," Forbes, December 28, 1998

474 "Working on the double," The Wall Street Journal, November 1, 2005

475 *The End of Work*, Jeremy Rifkin, 1996; Michigan State University's Collegiate Employment Research Institute, 1993; U.S. Bureau of Labor Statistics, as cited in "Overeducated and underpaid," The New York Times, June 3, 1997
476 Monthly Labor Magazine, July 1992, as cited in *Success Without College*, Linda Lee, 2001
477 "Tough job market has undergrads knocking on grad schools' doors," Albuquerque Journal, August 16, 2005
478 "Tough job market has undergrads knocking on grad schools' doors," Albuquerque Journal, August 16, 2005
479 "Weighing the costs in public vs. private colleges," The New York Times, December 13, 2006
480 "Job outlook for college graduates," Occupational Outlook Quarterly, Winter 2004-05, U.S. Dept of Labor
481 "Economic snapshots," Economic Policy Institute, March 17, 2004 based on data from the U.S. Bureau of Labor Statistics
482 "Educated, experienced, and out of work," Economic Policy Institute, March 4, 2004
483 "Job Outlook Report 2005," National Association of Colleges and Employers, 2005
484 "Skirt the 'overqualified' stamp," USA Today, November 12, 2002
485 "College graduates aren't ready for the real world," Op-Ed, The Chronicle of Higher Education, February 18, 2005
486 "More new grads find job mobility is limited," College Journal from The Wall Street Journal, December 2, 2004
487 "More new grads find job mobility is limited," College Journal from The Wall Street Journal, December 2, 2004
488 "Behind 'shortage' of engineers: Employers grow more choosy," The Wall Street Journal, November 16, 2005; "The science education myth," Op-ed, BusinessWeek.com, October 26, 2007
489 "Behind 'shortage' of engineers: Employers grow more choosy," The Wall Street Journal, November 16, 2005
490 "College: The payoff shrinks," BusinessWeek, September 12, 2005

REFERENCES

491 "Youthquake," BusinessWeek, January 21, 2008

492 "The real reasons you're working so hard...and what you can do about it," BusinessWeek, October 3, 2005

493 "Watson Wyatt urges Congressional action, deliberate employer response to pension trends," press release, Watson Wyatt Worldwide, May 3, 2006

494 "Employee Health Benefits: 2005 Annual Survey," The Henry J. Kaiser Family Foundation, September 2005

495 For example: "Job outlook for college graduates," Occupational Outlook Quarterly, Winter 2004-05, U.S. Dept of Labor (http://www.bls.gov/opub/ooq/2004/winter/art02.pdf)

496 "How much is too much?" The Chronicle of Higher Education, October 21, 2005

497 For example, "College quality and the earnings of recent graduates," U.S. Department of Education, 2000

498 Dale, Stacy Berg and Alan B. Krueger. "Estimating the payoff to attending a more selective college: An application of selection on observables and unobservables," National Bureau of Economic Research, Quarterly Journal of Economics, 2002, v107(4,Nov), 1491-1527.

499 "The worthless Ivy League?" Newsweek, November 1, 1999

500 "A push for need-based aid," Inside Higher Ed, March 16, 2007

501 "Survey results detail what top entry level employers want most," press release, CollegeGrad.com, May 1, 2006

502 "Employers cite communication skills as key, but say many job seekers don't have them," press release, National Association of Colleges and Employers, April 26, 2006

503 "Any college will do," The Wall Street Journal, September 18, 2006

504 "Campus confidential," BusinessWeek, Sept 12, 2005; "Grade inflation: Devaluing B-schools' currency," BusinessWeek, April 19, 2005

505 "Stress test: Smarty grads find easy money in SAT prep for wealthy, nerved-up kids," Village Voice, April 28, 2005

506 For example: Dale, Stacy Berg and Alan B. Krueger. "Estimating the payoff to attending a more selective college: An application of selection on observables and unobservables," National Bureau of Economic Research, Quarterly Journal of Economics, 2002, v107(4,Nov), 1491-1527.; "College quality and the earnings of recent graduates," U.S. Department of Education, 2000

507 The 2004 Chronicle Survey of Public Opinion on Higher Education, The Chronicle of Higher Education, May 5, 2004

508 "On the Frontier of Adulthood," Institute of Social Research, University of Michigan, 2005; "The bank of mom and dad," The New York Times, April 20, 2006

509 For example, "Asset prices, consumption, and the business cycle," by John Y. Campbell, Chapter 19 in John Taylor and Michael Woodford eds. Handbook of Macroeconomics Vol. 1, 1999; "The Impact of Paying for College on Family Finances," Upromise, November 2000; *The Future for Investors*, Jeremy Siegel, 2005, p. 171

510 For example, $61,400 invested at 7% for 43 years becomes $905,202; $98,356 invested at 7% for 43 years becomes $1,450,033; and $160,000 invested at 7% for 43 years becomes $2,358,832 (after taxes and initial investments are subtracted)

511 "State Higher Education Finance FY 2005," State Higher Education Executive Officers, 2006

512 *Trends in Student Aid 2004*, The College Board, 2004

513 "State Higher Education Finance FY 2005," State Higher Education Executive Officers, 2006; "State spending continues to climb," Inside Higher Ed, December 8, 2006; "Rebound in Higher Ed support," Inside Higher Ed, March 8, 2007

514 "State spending continues to climb," Inside Higher Ed, December 8, 2006

515 *Going Broke by Degree*, Chapter 7, Richard Vedder, 2004

516 "State spending continues to climb," Inside Higher Ed, December 8, 2006; "Access, student aid and the new Democratic majority," Center for College Affordability and Productivity, November 15, 2006; *Going Broke by Degree*, Chapter 7, Richard Vedder, 2004

517 "The connection between government aid and college pricing," Journal of Student Financial Aid, 2003, Volume 33, Number 2

518 *Generation Debt*, Anya Kamenetz, 2006, p.23

519 *How to Think Like Benjamin Graham and Invest Like Warren Buffett*, Lawrence A. Cunningham, 2002

520 "AP Fact Sheet," The College Board, 2004

CHAPTER 6

521 "Gates Foundation adding to a school project," The New York Times, December 8, 2004; "Gates money to expand graduation/collegeread iness program," Seattle Post-Intelligencer, December 8, 2004

522 "Students with eye on college say aye to AP courses," St. Louis Post-Dispatch, April 10, 2004

523 "Missed Opportunities Revisited," Issue Brief, American Council on Education, February 2006

524 "College aid ripoffs," The Wall Street Journal, March 7, 2002

525 "List of Project ScholarScam defendants," Federal Trade Commission, http://www.ftc.gov/bcp/conline/edcams/scholarship/cases.htm (viewed in 2007)

526 "College aid ripoffs," The Wall Street Journal, March 7, 2004

527 "Scholarship Scams," Federal Trade Commission, http://www.ftc.gov/bcp/conline/edcams/scholarship/index (viewed in 2007)

528 "It's the season for scholarship scams," The Holland Sentinel, March 28, 2004

529 "FAFSA on the Web Worksheet," U.S. Dept of Education, www.fafsa.ed.gov/worksheet.htm (viewed in 2007)

530 "Paying for College: It Pays to Save," White House Initiative on Educational Excellence for Hispanic Americans, http://www.yesican.gov/secondary/paying/ (viewed in 2007)

531 "Why not to save for your kids' college years," AARP Bulletin, October 2004; "Tax policy and education policy: Collision or coordination?" by Susan Dynarski, Tax Policy and the Economy, v.18, 2004; "Today's lesson: Rethink college funds," The New York Times, September 24, 2005

532 "Why not to save for your kids' college years," AARP Bulletin, October 2004

533 "Why not to save for your kids' college years," AARP Bulletin, October 2004

534 "A lesson in saving for college," BusinessWeek, June 26, 2003

535 "How shopping can pay for college," The Wall Street Journal, September 23, 2004

536 Upromise Privacy Policy (http://www.upromise.com/corp/privacy.htm); BabyMint Privacy Policy (http://www.babymint.com/corp/CORP_PrivacyPolicy.aspxl)

537 "Sallie Mae completes acquisition of Upromise," press release, Upromise, August 23, 2006

538 "Vesdia announces divesture of BabyMint college savings program," press release, Vesdia, September 13, 2005

539 "Account Ownership: In Whose Name to Save?" FinAid.com, http://www.finaid.com/savings/accountownership.phtml

540 "Today's lesson: Rethink college funds," The New York Times, September 24, 2005

541 "3 fundamental lessons for maximizing college savings," AARP Bulletin Web Exclusive, October 2004

542 "A lesson in saving for college," BusinessWeek, June 26, 2003

543 "3 fundamental lessons for maximizing college savings," AARP Bulletin Web Exclusive, October 2004

544 Families and Work Institute, 2000, as cited in "Homework really does pay," Associated Press, August 5, 2005

545 "The College Debt Crunch," AllianceBernstein, May 26, 2006; "Working Their Way Through College: Student Employment and its Impact on the College Experience," American Council on Education, 2006

546 "A different income, a different college experience," Yale Daily News, January 25, 2005

547 For example: "Federal Work-Study Program: Receiving Payments," Georgia State University: http://www.gsu.edu/es/fwsp_receiving_payments.html (viewed in 2007)

548 "Federal Work Study Program Information," Massachusetts Service Alliance, 2004, http://www.mass-service.org/WorkStudy.shtml (viewed in 2006)

549 "Part-time college teachers say unionizing imperils jobs," Chicago Tribune, August 28, 2000; "Labor Board says graduate students at private universities have no right to unionize," The New York Times, July 16, 2004; "The recession and the academic job market," AWP Job List, The Association of Writers and Writing Programs, September 2002

550 "Education Tax Benefits," FinAid.com, http://finaid.com/otheraid/tax.phtml

551 "Harvard to waive fees for poor parents," The New York Times, March 1, 2004

552 "Rich student, poor student," Inside Higher Ed, March 16, 2006

553 "U-Va. acts to ease students' debt load," The Washington Post, February 7, 2004

554 "Bill calls for fixed tuition contracts," The Daily Camera, April 22, 2004; "Tuition rate issues still unresolved," Red and Black, June 22, 2006

555 "Financial aid: How to get more," CNN/Money, March 31, 2004

556 "Financial aid professionals at work in 1999-2000," National Association of Student Financial Aid Administrators (NASFAA), 2001

557 "Indebted to a diploma," The Decatur Daily, December 15, 2004

CHAPTER 7

558 "In debt from Day One," The Christian Science Monitor, March 9, 2004
559 "In debt from Day One," Christian Science Monitor, March 9, 2004
560 "Congress moves to cut college loan costs," Christian Science Monitor, January 16, 2007
561 "In debt from Day One," Christian Science Monitor, March 9, 2004
562 "Forget Yale—go State," The Washington Post, January 28, 2007
563 "National Postsecondary Student Aid Study (NPSAS)," National Center for Education Statistics, 2006; "Student loans—a life sentence," CNN/Money, May 2, 2006
564 "Fact Sheet: Republicans boost student aid, help millions of Americans go to college," Committee on Education and the Workforce, October 7, 2004
565 "Students relying more heavily on private lenders," press release, The College Board, October 2006
566 "Administrative petition to the Department of Education," The Project on Student Debt, May 4, 2006
567 "College students get wise about credit cards," press release, Nellie Mae, May 25, 2005
568 "Undergraduate Students and Credit Cards in 2004: An Analysis of Usage Rates and Trends," Nellie Mae, May 2005
569 "Quick facts about student debt," The Project on Student Debt, April 2006
570 Federal Trade Commission, as cited in "College credit," The OU Daily, January 28, 2005; "Undergraduate students and credit cards," Nellie Mae, 2002; "Don't leave college without it," Mother Jones, March/April 2002
571 "Credit card crackdown, Associated Press, Nov 24. 2004
572 "Graduating Into Debt: Credit card marketing on Maryland college campuses," The Maryland Consumer Rights Coalition and Maryland Public Interest Research Group, February 19, 2004

References

573 "Politicians offer lecture on high debt," Houston Chronicle, February 19, 2005

574 This 30-year loan has a total cost of $123.47 per month (including principal and interest), leading to a total cost of $1,482 over one year, $7,408 over 5 years, $14,816 over 10 years, $29,633 over 20 years, and $44,450 over 30 years, as determined by using a loan calculator like the one at www.bankrate.com

575 "How to escape card debt," Gannett News Service, January 2, 2007

576 "Your late fees, their millions," Village Voice, January 24, 2006

577 "Sallie Mae's success too costly?" CBS, May 7, 2006

578 National Postsecondary Student Aid Study (NPSAS), National Center for Education Statistics, 2002; "The Burden of Borrowing," The State PIRG's Higher Education Project, March 2002; "How much college debt is too much?" MSN Money, http://moneycentral.msn.com/content/CollegeandFamily/Cutcollegecosts/P36836.asp (webpage viewed in 2007)

579 "2002 National Student Loan Survey," Nellie Mae, 2003

580 "College on credit: How borrowers perceive their education debt," Nellie Mae National Student Loan Survey, February 6, 2003

581 "Thirty and broke," BusinessWeek, November 14, 2005

582 "The Fortune 500," Fortune, April 2005

583 "Sallie Mae's fee-based businesses exceed $1 billion; managed loans grow 16 percent to $142 billion," press release, Sallie Mae, January 18, 2007

584 "Expired: How a credit king was cut off," The New York Times, March 7, 2004

585 "Fee Income 2003," CardWeb, http://www.cardweb.com/cardflash/2004/january/I2a.xcml

586 "Your mi$ery is their profit," Village Voice, November 2, 2004

587 "Do as I say, not as I do," Inside Higher Ed, December 21, 2006

588 *Generation Debt*, Anya Kamenetz, 2006, p.18

589 "The lure of easy credit leaves more students struggling with debt," The Chronicle of Higher Education, June 15, 2001

590 "Collegiate Funding Services acquires Youth Media and Marketing Networks," press release, Collegiate Funding Services, April 26, 2004
591 "Nelnet acquires Peterson's," press release, NelNet/Peterson's, July 27, 2006
592 "In a merger of student-loan giants, Sallie Mae will buy much of USA Group," The Chronicle of Higher Education, June 23, 2000; "Banks double student loan volume by infiltrating financial aid packaging business," Higher Ed Watch Blog, New America Foundation, April 19, 2007
593 "2004 CFS Planning and Paying for Higher Education Study," Collegiate Funding Services, October 2004; "Sallie Mae launches new 'Be Debt Smart' campaign to educate students, parents, and graduates on managing debt and understanding credit," press release, Sallie Mae, February 14, 2007; "2002 National Student Loan Survey," Nellie Mae, 2003; "National survey reveals gaps between students' perceived credit knowledge and real financial facts; more credit education needed," press release, Citigroup, March 17, 2005
594 "The lure of easy credit leaves more students struggling with debt," The Chronicle of Higher Education, June 15, 2001
595 "Film renews focus on students' credit-card suicides," The Oklahoma City Journal Record, June 28, 2006
596 "Lenders misusing student database," The Washington Post, April 15, 2007
597 "Lawmakers again target maligned student loan subsidy," The Washington Post, December 30, 2005; "Dems: make student loans friendly," Fortune, November 2006; "Lender overcharged U.S. $1 billion, audit finds," Inside Higher Ed, October 2, 2006
598 "The problem with Boehner," Op-ed, The Seattle Times, January 12, 2006
599 "A bid for better student loans," Op-ed, The Washington Post, February 5, 2007
600 *The Credit Card Industry: A History*, Lewis Mandell, 1990

601 "Borrowing to Make Ends Meet: The Growth of Credit Card Debt in the '90s," Demos, September 2003; *Credit Card Nation*, Robert Manning, 2001

602 "Consumer groups ask Congress to rein in credit card companies' most punitive tactics," press release, January 24, 2007

603 "Consumer groups ask Congress to rein in credit card companies' most punitive tactics," press release, ACORN and other top consumer groups, January 24, 2007; "Majoring in credit-card debt," BusinessWeek.com, September 4, 2007

604 "Lending a hand: A report on the lobbying expenditures and political contributions of the five largest student loan corporations," The State PIRG's Higher Education Project, October 2002

605 "The problem with Boehner," Op-ed, The Seattle Times, January 12, 2006

606 "Shady Sallie," Village Voice, January 13, 2006

607 "The unkindest cuts," TomPaine.com, January 12, 2006

608 "Newly bankrupt raking in piles of credit offers," The New York Times, December 11, 2005

609 *The Two-Income Trap*, Elizabeth Warren and Amelia Warren Tyagi, 2003

610 "Sallie Mae's success too costly?" CBS, May 7, 2006

611 "U.S. gets tough on failure to repay student loans," The Wall Street Journal, January 10, 2005

612 "Sallie Mae's success too costly?" CBS, May 7, 2006

613 "Sen. Levin holds hearing on credit card practices," press release, senator Carl Levin, March 7, 2007

614 "indieWIRE INTERVIEW: James Scurlock, director of 'Maxed Out,'" indieWIRE, March 11, 2007

615 Author's re-calculation, based on the formula at http://www.moneychimp.com/articles/finworks/fmmortgage.htm

616 Based on author's re-calculation of the formula at http://www.moneychimp.com/articles/finworks/fmmortgage.htm

617 *Positive Illusions*, Shelly Taylor, 1989

618 "Big loans, bigger problems," State Public Interest Research Group, March 2001
619 "Student Loans," FinAid, http://finaid.com/loans/studentloan.phtml; "Funding Your Education, 2005-2006," U.S. Department of Education (http://studentaid.ed.gov/students/attachments/siteresources/fund_ed_high.pdf)
620 "For grads only: Payback time," CNN/Money, 2005
621 "Student loan math," The Washington Post, February 17, 2005; "Straight Talk on Student Loans," Robert Shireman, Center for Studies in Higher Education, UC Berkeley, October 2004; "Robbing Joe College to pay Sallie Mae," Op-ed, The New York Times, December 12, 2005
622 "Student loan math," The Washington Post, February 17, 2005
623 "Big money on campus," U.S. News & World Report, October 27, 2003; "What you need to know about your financial aid office and their preferred lender list," MyRichUncle.com, http://myrichuncle.com/FinAidOffice.aspx (viewed in 2007); "Sallie Mae's success too costly?" CBS, May 7, 2006; "Lender/university entanglements," Inside Higher Ed, March 5, 2007
624 "When Sallie met Wall Street," Fortune, December 26, 2005
625 "Who Borrows Private Loans?" Issue Brief, American Council on Education, August 2007
626 "Colleges: Too close to lenders?" BusinessWeek, February 26, 2007
627 "Film renews focus on students' credit-card suicides," The Oklahoma City Journal Record, June 28, 2006
628 "Don't fall into credit card hole," USA Today, May 10, 2002
629 "Anatomy of a credit score," BusinessWeek, November 28, 2005

CHAPTER 8

630 *How College Affects Students*, Ernest T. Pascarella & Patrick T. Terenzini, 2005; "College Rankings Reformed: The Case for a New Order in Higher Education," Education Sector, September 22, 2006; "Is our students learning?" Washington Monthly, September 2006

REFERENCES

631 "The Best 357 Colleges," The Princeton Review, 2005
632 Based on data from the Education Trust websites (www.edtrust.org and www.collegeresults.org), which in turn is based on data reported by the schools to the U.S. Dept of Education. This data only includes students who enrolled in colleges in 1996 or 1997.
633 "A flood of crimson ink," Op-ed, The Wall Street Journal, April 29, 2005
634 "Who needs Harvard?" Time, August 21, 2006
635 "Grade inflation: Devaluing B-schools' currency," BusinessWeek, April 19, 2005; "Princeton becomes first to formally combat grade inflation," USA Today, April 26, 2004; "Does your B-school make the grade?" BusinessWeek, March 19, 2007
636 "Does your B-school make the grade?" BusinessWeek, March 19, 2007
637 "Who needs Harvard?" Time, August 21, 2006
638 "Who needs Harvard?" Time, August 21, 2006
639 "Does your B-school make the grade?" BusinessWeek, March 19, 2007
640 "Who needs Harvard?" Time, August 21, 2006
641 "History of the Ivy League," Ivysport, http://www.ivysport.com/history.php (website viewed in 2007); "What is the origin of the term 'Ivy league,'" Princeton University, http://www.princeton.edu/mudd/news/faq/topics/ivy_league.shtml
642 "Dean Cain '88 joins team to document Ivy League football," The Daily Princetonian, September 9, 2004
643 "Salary Survey," National Association of Colleges and Employers, July 2006
644 "Salary Survey," National Association of Colleges and Employers, July 2006

645 For example: "College quality and future earnings: where should you send your child to college?" American Economic Review, Vol. 79, No. 2, 1989, by E. James, N. Alsalam, and J. Conaty; "College quality and the earnings of recent graduates," U.S. Department of Education, 2000; Dale, Stacy Berg and Alan B. Krueger. "Estimating the payoff to attending a more selective college: An application of selection on observables and unobservables," National Bureau of Economic Research, Quarterly Journal of Economics, 2002, v107(4,Nov), 1491-1527.

646 "Survey results detail what top entry level employers want most," press release, CollegeGrad.com, May 1, 2006

647 "New survey results detail what top employers want most," press release, CollegeGrad.com, May 2, 2005

648 1999-2000 National Postsecondary Student Aid Study, National Center for Education Statistics, 2000

649 "Top 10 most popular majors," The Princeton Review, http://www.princetonreview.com/college/research/articles/majors/popular.asp (website viewed in 2007)

650 "Paying by the program," Inside Higher Ed, March 26, 2007

651 "The Chronicle Survey of Public Opinion on Higher Education," The Chronicle of Higher Education, May 7, 2004

652 For example: "Bigger is better for some undergrads," USA Today, February 6, 2002

653 "Considering a college honors program," National Association for College Admission Counseling, Jan/Feb 2003, http://www.nacacnet.org/MemberPortal/News/StepsNewsletter/considering_college_honors-program.htm

654 "New building will gather humanities departments under one roof," press release, Georgia State University, September 29, 2005

655 http://en.wikipedia.org/wiki/Georgia_State_University

656 "Any college will do," The Wall Street Journal, September 18, 2006

657 "Forget Yale—go State," The Washington Post, January 28, 2007

658 "Full-Time Undergraduate Tuition, Fees and Other Expenses for Fall 2007 & Spring 2008," University of Maryland Office of the Bursar, www.umd.edu/bursar

659 "Tuition help for college can be found in unusual places," Chicago Tribune, August 28, 2005

660 *Higher Ed, Inc.*, Richard Ruch, 2001

661 "Funding worries for community colleges," Associated Press, April 8, 2005

662 "Growth of for-profit colleges moderates," Inside Higher Ed, December 13, 3005

663 For example: "Continuing studies," The Weekly Standard, December 7, 2005

664 "Harvard for less: Extension courses' new allure," The New York Times, November 18, 2005

665 "Harvard for less: Extension courses' new allure," The New York Times, November 18, 2005

666 "Harvard for less: Extension courses' new allure," The New York Times, November 18, 2005

667 "Traditional colleges court online learners for new revenue," Boston Business Journal, November 28, 2003

668 For example: "For-profit college: Costly lesson," CBS News, January 30, 2005

669 For example: "The profit chase," Slate, November 16, 2005; "For-profit college: Costly lesson," CBS News, January 30, 2005

670 *Higher Ed, Inc.*, Richard Ruch, 2001

671 "A battle over standards at for-profit colleges," The Wall Street Journal, September 30, 2005

672 "Degrees@StateU.edu," The Wall Street Journal, May 9, 2006

673 "Students prefer online courses," Associated Press, January 13, 2006

674 "Engaged Learning: 2006 Annual Report," National Survey of Student Engagement, November 2006

675 "Traditional colleges court online learners for new revenue," Boston Business Journal, Nov 28, 2003

676 "Making the Grade: Online Education in the United States, 2006, the 2006 Sloan Survey of Online Learning," The Sloan Consortium, November 2006

677 "Online degrees more acceptable in the workplace, according to new Vault survey, press release, Vault, October 19, 2005

678 "Online degrees more acceptable in the workplace, according to new Vault survey, press release, Vault, October 19, 2005

679 "Online degrees more acceptable in the workplace, according to new Vault survey, press release, Vault, October 19, 2005

680 "Online degrees more acceptable in the workplace, according to new Vault survey, press release, Vault, October 19, 2005

681 "Who would hire an online grad," MSN Encarta, 2007, http://encarta.msn.com/elearning_article_whowouldhire_archive/Who_would_hire_an_online_grad.html (website viewed in 2007)

682 "Trends in College Pricing 2006," The College Board, 2006

683 "Junior colleges get some respect," BusinessWeek Online, July 30, 2006; "Community college can be a springboard," Pittsburgh Post-Gazette, March 7, 2004

684 "Background characteristics, work activities, and compensation of instructional faculty and staff," National Center for Education Statistics, December 2005

685 "Junior colleges get some respect," BusinessWeek Online, July 30, 2006

686 *2007 National Student Satisfaction-Priorities Report*, Noel-Levitz, 2007

687 For example: "Job outlook for people who don't have a bachelor's degree," Occupational Outlook Quarterly, Winter 2004-05, U.S. Bureau of Labor Statistics

688 "Cognitive effects of community colleges and four-year colleges," Community College Journal, Jan. 1996, by E. Pascarella, M. Edison, A. Nora, L. Hagedorn, and P. Terenzini

689 "Academic intensity, attendance patterns, and bachelor's degree attainment," U.S. Department of Education, 1999
690 "Median usual weekly earnings of employed full-time wage and salary workers 25 years and over by educational attainment and sex, 2005 annual averages," Current Population Survey, U.S. Department of Labor, Bureau of Labor Statistics, 2006
691 "Facing down the 'snob factor,'" Inside Higher Ed, May 5, 2006
692 "Forget Yale—go State," The Washington Post, January 28, 2007
693 "Junior colleges get some respect," BusinessWeek Online, July 30, 2006
694 *Great Careers in 2 Years*, Paul Phifer, 2003
695 "College graduates now turning to trade school," The Columbus Dispatch, May 27, 2007
696 "College acceptance rates: How many get in?" USA Today, November 8, 2006
697 "State of College Admission," National Association for College Admission Counseling, May 2006
698 "Who needs Harvard?" Time, August 21, 2006
699 Thomas Nixon, as cited in "City gives FDNY an F over phony diplomas," AM-NY, February 1, 2007
700 *Colleges That Change Lives*, Loren Pope, 1996, revised in 2006
701 "Who needs Harvard?" Time, August 21, 2006
702 "Who needs Harvard?" Time, August 21, 2006
703 "Good match, reach, safety: What are my chances?" The Princeton Review, http://www.princetonreview.com/college/research/articles/find/MatchReachSafety.asp (viewed in 2007)
704 "Good match, reach, safety: What are my chances?" The Princeton Review, http://www.princetonreview.com/college/research/articles/find/MatchReachSafety.asp (viewed in 2007)
705 "What price college admission?" BusinessWeek, June 19, 2006

706 "The college dropout boom," New York Times, May 24, 2005; "Graduating Into Debt: Credit card marketing on Maryland college campuses," Maryland Consumer Rights Coalition and Maryland Public Interest Research Group, February 19, 2004

707 "Weighing the costs in public vs. private colleges," The New York Times, December 13, 2006

708 "The lure of easy credit leaves more students struggling with debt," The Chronicle of Higher Education, June 15, 2001

709 "Any college will do," The Wall Street Journal, September 18, 2006

710 "Path to the corner office often starts at a state school," CareerJournal.com, September 25, 2006

CHAPTER 9

711 "Community college can be a springboard," Pittsburgh Post-Gazette, March 7, 2004

712 "2004 brings a significantly brighter job outlook," press release, Experience, Inc., April 5, 2004; "More students interning this summer, says new Vault survey," press release, Vault, April 25, 2006

713 "More students interning this summer, says new Vault survey," press release, Vault, April 25, 2006

714 "Ripoff 101: How the current practices of the publishing industry drive up the cost of college textbooks," California and Oregon Student Public Interest Research Groups, January 2004; "Group wants textbooks costs kept in line," USA Today, Feb. 2, 2004

715 "Ripoff 101: How the current practices of the publishing industry drive up the cost of college textbooks," California and Oregon Student Public Interest Research Groups, January 2004

716 "Ripoff 101: How the current practices of the publishing industry drive up the cost of college textbooks," California and Oregon Student Public Interest Research Groups, January 2004

717 "Ripoff 101: How the current practices of the publishing industry drive up the cost of college textbooks," California and Oregon Student Public Interest Research Groups, January 2004

REFERENCES

718 "Ripoff 101: How the current practices of the publishing industry drive up the cost of college textbooks," California and Oregon Student Public Interest Research Groups, January 2004

719 "Selling out: a textbook example," The Chronicle of Higher Education, June 27, 2003

720 "A textbook problem: Cost," Democrat and Chronicle, March 15, 2004

721 "Book Industry Trends 2005," Book Industry Study Group, 2005, pp. 189-190

722 "A textbook problem: Cost," Democrat and Chronicle, March 15, 2004; "Where the new textbook dollar goes," National Association of College Stores, 2004

723 As listed at "Make Textbooks Affordable," www.maketextbooksaffordable.com

724 "A textbook problem: Cost," Democrat and Chronicle, March 15, 2004

725 "College Textbooks: Enhanced offerings appear to drive recent price increases," United States Government Accountability Office, July 2005

726 "Bills to lower textbook prices reach state Senate," The California Aggie, May 25, 2004

727 "Textbook rentals may be new option for CA colleges," The California Aggie, April 21, 2004

728 "Textbook piracy takes toll in Mexico," The Boston Globe, June 1, 2004

729 "Scanning the globe for Organic Chemistry," U.S. News and World Report, April 19, 2004

730 "A textbook problem: Cost," Democrat and Chronicle, March 15, 2004

731 "Phi Beta Kappa and others battle less-prestigious groups for image and money," The Press-Enterprise, March 15, 2004

732 "Phi Beta Kappa and others battle less-prestigious groups for image and money," The Press-Enterprise, March 15, 2004

733 "Accolades, for a price," The Cavalier Daily, March 22, 2002
734 "Accolades, for a price," The Cavalier Daily, March 22, 2002
735 "Phi Beta Kappa and others battle less-prestigious groups for image and money," The Press-Enterprise, March 15, 2004
736 "The 360 Youth Network: College," Alloy Media + Marketing, http://www.alloymarketing.com/media/college/index.html (viewed in 2007)

CHAPTER 10
737 Assuming a starting balance of $23,000, at 8% annual interest, over 30 years
738 "Big loans, bigger problems," State Public Interest Research Group, March 2001
739 "Big loans, bigger problems," State Public Interest Research Group, March 2001
740 "Bracing for the bankruptcy bill," CNN/Money, March 9, 2005; "Not necessarily a fresh start," BusinessWeek, July 11, 2005
741 "Debt 'counselors' hit for $100M scam," Reuters, March 30, 2005
742 "Debt 'counselors' hit for $100M scam," Reuters, March 30, 2005
743 "Credit counseling: A business rife with bad guys," BusinessWeek, July 11, 2005
744 "Debt 'counselors' hit for $100M scam," Reuters, March 30, 2005

CHAPTER 11
745 "Tough job market has undergrads knocking on grad schools' doors," Albuquerque Journal, August 16, 2005
746 "Tough job market has undergrads knocking on grad schools' doors," Albuquerque Journal, August 16, 2005
747 For example: "In debt from Day One," Christian Science Monitor, March 9, 2004
748 "Lesson for students: The best debt is none," The Washington Post, September 24, 2006

REFERENCES 319

749 "Master's degrees abound as universities and students see a windfall," New York Times, September 12, 2007

750 "Getting noticed," BusinessWeek SmallBiz, Winter 2005

751 "Making medical education relevant," The Chronicle of Higher Education, January 13, 2006

752 Study conducted by the Association of American Law Schools, and cited in "Goofing off in law school," Inside Higher Ed, January 3, 2006; "Third-year law school: Jury's out on its value," Associated Press, August 10, 2005

753 "Educating Lawyers: Preparation for the Profession of Law," Carnegie Foundation for the Advancement of Teaching, January 2007

754 "In battle against attrition, law schools revamp old strategy," The Boston Globe, May 9, 2006

755 "Bar Exam Central," Law.com, http://www.law.com/special/students/barexam/ (viewed in 2007)

756 "Where's the 'B' in B-Schools?" Op-ed, BusinessWeek, November 27, 2006

757 Graduate Management Admission Council survey, as cited in "Is the M.B.A. obsolete?" U.S. News & World Report, April 11, 2005

758 "Who needs the real world?" BusinessWeek, February 13, 2006

759 "Grade inflation: Devaluing B-schools' currency," BusinessWeek, April 9, 2005

760 "Campus confidential," BusinessWeek, September 12, 2005

761 "What makes grad students graduate?" Inside Higher Ed, Dec 6, 2005

762 "Doctor Dropout," The Chronicle of Higher Education, January 16, 2004

763 "Doctor Dropout," The Chronicle of Higher Education, January 16, 2004

764 *Three Magic Letters: Getting to Ph.D.*, Michael Nettles and Catherine Millett, 2006

765 "What makes grad students graduate?" Inside Higher Ed, Dec 6, 2005

766 *Getting What You Came For: The Smart Students' Guide to Earning a Master's or Ph.D.*, Robert Peters, 1997
767 *Imposters in the Temple*, Martin Anderson, 1992
768 "Doctor Dropout," The Chronicle of Higher Education, January 16, 2004
769 "Doctor Dropout," The Chronicle of Higher Education, January 16, 2004
770 "Doctor Dropout," The Chronicle of Higher Education, January 16, 2004
771 "Doctor Dropout," The Chronicle of Higher Education, January 16, 2004
772 "Doctor Dropout," The Chronicle of Higher Education, January 16, 2004
773 "Doctor Dropout," The Chronicle of Higher Education, January 16, 2004
774 "What makes grad students graduate?" Inside Higher Ed, Dec 6, 2005
775 For example, California Board of Psychology, www.psychboard.ca.gov/admin/feeschedule.htm ($40 licensing exam application fee; $500 EPPP licensing exam fee; $129 California Jurisprudence & Professional Ethics exam fee; $400 license fee; plus study materials, tutoring, $410 biannual renewal fee, and continuing education costs)
776 "Medical School Graduation Questionnaire," Association of American Medical Colleges, 2006; "Higher Ed's high finance," BusinessWeek, June 7, 2005
777 "Medical School Graduation Questionnaire," Association of American Medical Colleges, 2006
778 "Medical School Graduation Questionnaire," Association of American Medical Colleges, 2006
779 *America's Best Graduate Schools*, U.S. News & World Report, 2007
780 *America's Best Graduate Schools*, U.S. News & World Report, 2007

REFERENCES

781 "High-priced student loans spell trouble," Associated Press, October 1, 2007

782 "Student loans—a life sentence," CNNMoney, May 1, 2006

783 "Big jobs that pay badly," CNN/Money, August 17, 2005

784 "Social Work Salaries and Careers," Princeton Review, http://www.princetonreview.com/grad/research/programProfiles/salariescareers.asp?programid=64 (viewed in 2007)

785 "Teachers—preschool, kindergarten, elementary, middle, and secondary," Occupational Outlook Handbook 2006-07, U.S. Department of Labor

786 "First Year Starting Salary—National Average," Physicians Search, http://www.physicianssearch.com/physician/salary1.html (viewed in 2007)

787 "Pediatric training and job market trends: results from the American Academy of Pediatrics Third-Year Resident Survey, 1997-2002," Pediatrics, October 2003

788 "MGMA Physician Compensation and Production Survey," Medical Group Management Association, 2005

789 "Pay, working conditions for rural docs vary by practice," Physician Compensation Report, December 2003

790 "Time to Degree of U.S. Research Doctorate Recipients," National Science Foundation, 2006

791 "Doctor Dropout," The Chronicle of Higher Education, January 16, 2004; "Exploring ways to shorten the ascent to a Ph.D.," The New York Times, October 3, 2007

792 Stanford University/Rand Corporation study, cited in "Doctorate surplus in science, engineering is ongoing, researchers say," press release, Stanford University, June 5, 1995; "Are we training too many scientists?" The Scientists, September 2006

793 "So you want to go to grad school?" Thomas H. Benton, The Chronicle of Higher Education, June 3, 2003; "Wanted: Really smart suckers," The Village Voice, April 27, 2004; "Hard case: Job market wanes for U.S. lawyers," Wall Street Journal, September 24, 2007

794 U.S. Labor Department, as cited in "The attorney, unemployed," The National Law Journal, April 10, 2003
795 "Do we need more lawyers?" Inside Higher Ed, March 27, 2007
796 "MBA applicants are MIA," BusinessWeek, April 18, 2005
797 "Status of the American Public School Teacher," 2003, National Education Association
798 "The postdoc trap," Monitor on Psychology, May 2000
799 The American Psychological Association's most recent Doctorate Employment Survey (conducted in 2003 and available at http://research.apa.org/des03.html).
800 The American Psychological Association's most recent Doctorate Employment Survey (conducted in 2003 and available at http://research.apa.org/des03.html).
801 "Some clinical psychology students' growing debt burden triggers response from training programs," APA Monitor, February 1999
802 "Some clinical psychology students' growing debt burden triggers response from training programs," APA Monitor, February 1999
803 "Some clinical psychology students' growing debt burden triggers response from training programs," APA Monitor, February 1999
804 "Some clinical psychology students' growing debt burden triggers response from training programs," APA Monitor, February 1999
805 "Some clinical psychology students' growing debt burden triggers response from training programs," APA Monitor, February 1999
806 "Some clinical psychology students' growing debt burden triggers response from training programs," APA Monitor, February 1999
807 "Some clinical psychology students' growing debt burden triggers response from training programs," APA Monitor, February 1999
808 "Some clinical psychology students' growing debt burden triggers response from training programs," APA Monitor, February 1999
809 "The Ethical Principles of Psychologists and Code of Conduct," American Psychological Association, 2002
810 "Medical School Tuition and Young Physician Indebtedness," Association of Medical Colleges, March 23, 2004

811 "In debt from Day One," Christian Science Monitor, March 9, 2004
812 "The best B-schools of 2006," BusinessWeek, October 23, 2006
813 "Do online MBAs make the grade?" BusinessWeek Online, August 18, 2005
814 "B-Schools with a niche," BusinessWeek, Sept 5, 2005
815 "The best B schools," BusinessWeek, October 23, 2006
816 "What's an MBA really worth," BusinessWeek, September 23, 2003
817 "For Gen X, it's Paradise Lost," BusinessWeek.com, June 30, 2003
818 "Who says a lawyer needs law school?" Associated Press, Sept 21, 2005
819 "Hedge funds and private equity alter career calculus," New York Times, September 16, 2007

APPENDIX A

820 "The college dropout boom," New York Times, May 24, 2005
821 "Famous professionals who don't have college degrees," http://realitytv.about.com/od/theapprentice/a/nodegrees.htm
822 "Success without a college degree," CareerBuilder.com, November 3, 2006
823 http://www.barnesandnobleinc.com/our_company/management_team/leonard_riggio/leonard_riggio.html
824 "Is it worth it?" The Daily Texan, October 7, 2004
825 "Finding career success without a college degree," The Times-Picayune, March 24, 2005
826 http://www.galegroup.com/free_resources/bhm/bio/simmons_r.htm
827 "Why you can't ignore Kanye," Time, August 21, 2005
828 *The American Presidency*, Alan Brinkley & Davis Dyer, 2004
829 "The 400 Richest Americans," Forbes, September 2005; "Money Trails," The New York Times, September 25, 2005
830 1995 US Trust survey, as cited in "Workers need skills, not college," Investor's Business Daily, April 15, 1997

831 "More than half of executives would start career over in different industry, Korn/Ferry survey finds," press release, Korn/Ferry International, October 10, 2005

832 Dale, Stacy Berg and Alan B. Krueger. "Estimating the payoff to attending a more selective college: An application of selection on observables and unobservables," National Bureau of Economic Research, Quarterly Journal of Economics, 2002, v107(4,Nov), 1491-1527; "College quality and future earnings: Where should you send your child to college," James, Alsalam, & Conaty, American Economic Review, Vol. 79, No. 2, 1989

833 "College quality and the earnings of recent college graduates," National Center for Education Statistics, August 2000

834 "Job outlook for people who don't have a bachelor's degree," Occupational Outlook Quarterly, Winter 2004-05, US Dept of Labor (http://www.bls.gov/opub/ooq/2004/winter/art01.htm)

835 "Economic Snapshots; Jobs in the future: No boom in the need for college graduates," Economic Policy Institute, July 21, 2004

836 "The dirty little secret of credential inflation," Op-ed, The Chronicle of Higher Education, September 27, 2002

837 *Success Without College*, Linda Lee, 2001

838 *The 300 Best Jobs That Don't Require a Four-Year Degree*, J. Michael Farr, LaVerne Ludden & Laurance Shatkin, 2006

839 "Job outlook for people who don't have a bachelor's degree," Occupational Outlook Quarterly, Winter 2004-05, US Dept of Labor (http://www.bls.gov/opub/ooq/2004/winter/art01.htm)

840 "Job outlook for people who don't have a bachelor's degree," Occupational Outlook Quarterly, Winter 2004-05, US Dept of Labor (http://www.bls.gov/opub/ooq/2004/winter/art01.htm)

841 "The falling-down professions," New York Times, January 6, 2008

842 "College isn't for everyone," USA Today, June 15, 2004

INDEX

A

ABC's of Getting Out of Debt, The (Sutton), 217
ABD (All But Dissertation), 234
accreditation, 186
ACT
 bias of, 26
 fee waivers, 189
activity fees, 31
adjuncts, 73
admissions process
 criteria for, 26
 general, 25–27
admit-deny, 35
Advanced Placement (AP), 119
Alford, Debbie, 42, 192–93
Allen, Woody, 245
Alloy, Inc., 206
American Association of Collegiate Registrars and Admissions Officers (AACRAO), 19
American Association of University Professors, 50
American Council on Education, 50
American Marketing Association, 19
America's Top Jobs for People Without College (Farr), 253
America's Top 100 Jobs for People Without a Four-Year Degree (Krannich and Krannich), 253
AmeriDebt, Inc., 217–18
Amherst College, endowment, 8
Amp Agency, 206
Anderson, Justin, 142
Anderson, Tamara, 236
Angelou, Maya, 245

application
 fees, 25–26
 process, 185–89
 rejection of, 191–92
Arcadia University, 19
Arizona State University
 cost by major, 173
 grade inflation, 82
 sports programs, 24
Arnold, Lee, 46
Associate's degree, 180–83
Association of College Honor Societies, 205
Association of Independent Consumer Credit Counseling Agencies, 218
athletic fees, 31
Austin College, student loan kickbacks, 40
Austin, Jane, 245

B

Babson College, work study, 133
BabyMint, 129–30
bachelor's degree, 180, 183
"bait and switch" trap, 82–83, 137–38
bankruptcy, 3
Barker, James, 72
Bayh-Dole Act, 49–50
Baylor University, sports programs, 21, 24
Beaver College. *See* Arcadia University
Beeman, Dean Richard, 78
Behar, Trevor, 59
Bell, Alexander Graham, 245
Bennington College, tuition and fees, 28

Berklee College of Music, 166
Best Colleges, The (The Princeton Review), 188, 197
Better Budget Financial Services, Inc., 217
Better Business Bureau, 125, 218
Biggs, Danielle, 235
Bill and Melinda Gates Foundation, 119
Blevins, Andy, 244
Bloom, Julie, 78
Boehner, John, 151
Bohman, Roger, 71
Boise State University, private tutoring, 84
Bok, Derek, 15
Bonner, Neal W., 112
"boomerang kids," 3
Borjas, George, 78
Boston College
  financial hold, 63
  sports programs, 22
Boston University
  campus renovations, 20
  debt collector, 41
  grade inflation, 82
  work study, 133
Bowen, Roger, 79
Brandeis College, work study, 133
Brandon, Emily, 36
Branson, Richard, 245
Brigham Young University
  credit cards, 39
  sports programs, 22
Brooklyn College, complaints about instructors, 77
Brown University, completion time, 166
Bucknell University, tuition and fees, 28
Buffett, Warren, 111, 116
Bureau of Labor Statistics (U.S.), 152
Burton, Kasis, 60
BusinessWeek, 1, 107–108, 218, 242

C

California State University, private tutoring, 84
campus renovations, 19–20
Career Assistance Planning (CAP), 124
Career College Association, 175
career issues
  dream careers, 4, 142–43
  effect of college costs, 109–11
  employers, 111
  family background, 110
  job availability, 105–107
  non-college path, 250–53
  salaries, 2, 100–103, 105, 107–108, 169–70
  success without college, 248–50
Carnegie Mellon University, electives at, 68
Case Western Reserve University, student loan kickbacks, 40
Cedar Crest College, fundraising, 45
Center for Campus Fire Safety, 56
Chany, Kalman, 34
Chase, William, 11–12
Chronicle of Higher Education, 203
Citibank, 149
class fees, 31
Clemson University, private tutoring, 84
Cleveland State University, campus renovations, 19–20

coaches salaries, 11
Coalition for Consumer Bankruptcy Debtor Education, 163
cognitive dissonance, 26–27
Cole, Kristin, 230
Colgate University
  customer service, 63–65
  tuition and fees, 28, 29
College Board, 119, 148
College Board Book of Majors, The (The College Board), 172
college debt. *See* debt
College Majors Handbook with Real Career Paths and Payoffs (Fogg, Harrington, and Harrington), 172
College Navigator, 188
College Parents of America, 51, 126–27
College Results, 188
college selection, 165–69
CollegePulse, 19
Colleges That Change Lives (Pope), 187
Collegiate Assistance Services, 124
Collegiate Funding Services, 130, 149
Collegiate Learning Assessment (CLA), 88
Collegiate Licensing Company, 22
Collinge, Alan, 146
Collins, Randall, 247–48
Columbia University
  completion time, 166
  endowment, 9
  for-profit programs, 175
  research patents, 49
  rising costs, 31
  use of teaching assistants, 73
  transferring credits, 195
  tuition and fees, 28
Combs, Sean "P. Diddy," 246
Commission on the Future of Higher Education, 88–89
Committee on Education (U.S.), 141
Complete Book of Colleges, The (Princeton Review), 197
construction fees, 31
Consumer Credit Counseling Service of New York, 163
Consumers for Responsible Credit Solutions (CRCS), 162
continuing education programs, 176, 251
Cookson, Willy, 105
Cooper, William, 30
Cornell University
  completion time, 166
  endowment, 9
cost of college
  and alternative investments, 112–14
  effect on careers, 109–11
  emotional damage of, 5–6
  financial value of, 98–100
  and free classes, 118–19
  general, 1
  and hidden charges, 94–97
  immediate costs, 95
  by major, 173
  opportunity costs, 95
  "real college value" formula, 100
  real costs of, 96–97
  saving for, 128–32
  and student loans, 94–96
  tax benefits of, 134–35
  and unemployment, 106–107
Council on Higher Education Accreditation, 186

coursecasting, 251
Coverdell plans, 129
Creative Group, The, 199
Credit Abuse Resistance Education Program, 163
Credit Card Nation, 163
credit cards
    and debt, 1
    deregulation of, 150
    and fees, 31
    general, 160–64
    marketing of, 38–39, 42
Cronkite, Walter, 245
CSS/PROFILE aid applications, 122
Cummings, Catherine, 39
curriculum, 67
Curtis, John, 73
customer service, 62–65, 201–202

D

Dartmouth University, grade inflation, 82
dean salaries, 9
debt
    appropriate level, 152–56
    counseling, 217–18
    credit and debt information, 163–64
    general, 144–47
    graduate school, 229–30
    interest, 145–46, 154
    repayment period, 153–54
    unmanageable loan debt, 147
    credit cards, 144–45
Debt Management Foundation Services, Inc., 217
Debtors Anonymous, 219–20
Deco Consulting Services, 124
degree options, 180–85
Dell, Michael, 245

Denecke, Daniel, 228
DeSales University, fundraising, 45
Desroches, Steve, 231
developmental admissions, 27
Dickson, Tom, 76
Diffley, Peter, 225
Direct Loans, 140, 158
division I sports schools *v.* other schools, 179–80
Doctor of Psychology (PsyD) degree, 236–38
doctoral degrees, 233–34
donation jackpots, 47
dormitories. *See* housing
dropping out of college, 2, 84–85, 104
dual enrollment, 119
Duke, Jared, 60, 61
Duke University
    coursecasting, 251
    developmental admissions, 27
    electives, 67
    endowment, 7
    meal plans, 57
Dynarski, Susan, 128, 131

E

early college, 119
early decision trap, 34–35
earmarks, 49
Edison, Thomas, 245
education, quality of, 87–89
Education Sector, 17
electives, 67–68
Emerson College, work study, 133
Emory University
    "bait and switch" trap, 82–83
    developmental admissions, 27
    endowment, 7
    financial hold, 63
    for-profit programs, 175

housing costs, 55
ratings, 16
recruitment practices, 20
endowments, 7–9
    investment managers, 11
    investment returns of, 8
enrollment management, 18
Erickson, Justin R., 192
"Estimating the Payoff to Attending a More Selective College," 110
Everything College Major Text Book, The (Nadler), 172
Expected Family Contribution (EFC), 125–27, 131
exploiting enthusiasm, 34
extension programs, 176

F

Farber, Philip, 237
Faulkner, William, 245
Federal Family Education Loan Program (FFEL), 158
Federal loans, 157
Federal Student Aid Guide, 127
Federal Student Aid Ombudsman, 216
Federal Trade Commission (U.S.), 218
FinAid, 123, 127, 131, 160
financial aid
    admit-deny, 35
    applying for, 121–23
    and "bait and switch" trap, 82–83, 137–38
    evaluating offers of, 135–36
    Expected Family Contribution (EFC), 125–27
    general, 32–42
    government investment in, 139–41
    negotiating for, 138–39
    packages, 132–35
    preferential packaging, 36–38
    scams with, 124–25
    types of, 120–21
financial hold, 63
568 Group, 33
529 savings plans, 129
fixed tuition plans, 137–38
food strategies and costs, 57–62, 197–98
four-year trap, 42–44
Fox, Angel, 142
Frank, Robert, 248
Franklin and Marshall College, ratings, 16
Free Application for Federal Student Aid (FAFSA), 122, 127
free college classes, 118–19
Freeload Press, 204
Freeman, David, 167
Friis, Janus, 246
fundraising, 44–47
Furtado, Maria, 187

G

Gallery of Best Resumes for People Without a Four-Year Degree (Farr), 253
Gallop, Lance, 76, 83–84
Gap-Year Advantage, The (Haigler and Nelson), 116
Gates, Bill, 244–45
Gates Foundation. *See* Bill and Melinda Gates Foundation
Geffen, David, 246
general class requirements, 66–67
Generation Debt, 163
Generation Debt (Kamenetz), 1
Generation Debt (Ulrich), 217

George Mason University, sports programs, 23
George Washington University
 class availability, 43–44
 fixed tuition plans, 137
 tuition and fees, 28
Georgetown University
 electives, 67
 sports programs, 22
Georgia State University, new programs, 174
Glenn, John, 245
Golde, Chris, 226
Golden Key, 205
Gonzaga University, sports programs, 21, 22, 23
Google, 204
government spending, 48–51, 114–15
grade deflation, 81–82
grade inflation, 167
grade non-disclosure, 224
graduate school
 cost of, 222
 and debt, 229–30
 dropout risk in, 225–28
 effective strategies with, 238–43
 general, 221–22
 and low average salaries, 231–35
 as risky investment, 228–35
graduates
 literacy level of, 86–87
 success of, 86–87
graduation fees, 32
Gragg, Joel, 178
Grande, Bette, 78
 grants, 120, 132
Great Books of the Western World (Encyclopedia Britannica), 252

Grinnell College, endowment, 8, 30
Gutenberg, 204

H
Haley, Alex, 245
Hampshire College, grading policy, 167
Harding University, student loan kickbacks, 40
Harrington, Bryon, 59–60
Harvard University
 business program, 224
 class size, 68
 curriculum changes, 67
 developmental admissions, 27
 endowment, 7–9
 financial aid, 136
 for-profit programs, 175
 grade inflation, 82
 grade non-disclosure, 224
 housing costs, 55
 student debt, 229
 use of teaching assistants, 73
 work study, 133
Hawkins, David, 35
Heilker, Paul, 203
Hemmendinger, David, 87
Hemmingway, Ernest, 245
Higher Education Scholarship Program, 124
honor societies, 205–206
Hope Scholarship Credit, 134
housing
 costs of, 53–57
 options for, 196–97
 room and board expenses, 28–29

How to Choose a College Major (Andrews), 172

Huizenga, Wayne, 245
hybrid schools, 119

I
Independent Scholar's Handbook, The (Gross), 253
Indiana University
　electives, 67
　tuition reimbursement, 32
Inside Higher Ed, 69
Institute for College Access and Success, The, 163
instructors
　and part-time status, 73–74
　ratings of, 76–77
　skills of, 75–77
internet resources, 257–65
Internship Bible, The (Princeton Review), 199
internships and fees, 31, 198–200
Iona College, meal plans, 198
Iowa State University
　fundraising, 45
　cost by major, 173
IRA, 129

J
J.M. Lord & Associates, Inc., 18
James Madison University, meal plan, 57–58
Jennings, Peter, 245
Jerz, Dennis, 77
Job Outlook 2004, 86
Jobs, Steve, 245
Jones, Marilee, 187
Jump$tart Coalition for Personal Financial Literacy, 163

K
Kamenetz, Anya, 42, 163

Kaufman, Roger, 46
Kelly Services, 199
Kenyon College, tuition and fees, 28
Kroc, Ray, 245
Krueger, Bill, 170
Kubasak, Marc, 71

L
Lafley, A.G., 193
Landgraf, Kurt, 26
late fees, 32
Laude, David, 68
Leakey, Richard, 245
Learning Annex, The, 251
legacy admissions, 27
Lehigh University, fundraising, 45
Levin, Carl, 151
Levine, Mel, 107
Lifetime Learning Credit, 134
Lilienthal, Heidi, 237
Lipman Hearne, 19
Liu, Min, 78
loans. *See* student loans
lobbyists, 50
Loesburg, Jonathan, 74
Lovitts, Barbara, 227, 228
Loyola College, meal plans, 198
Lutes, Kyle, 87

M
Maguire Associates, 19
majors
　general, 169–73
　and starting salaries, 169–70
Make Textbooks Affordable, 204
Mandl, Michael, 49–50
Mann, Christine, 46
Manpower, Inc., 199
market research, 19

marketing strategies
  and credit cards, 38–39
  by financial institutions, 38–42
  general, 18–20, 206
  and use of sports, 21–25
Massa, Robert, 110
Massachusetts Institute of
  Technology (MIT), engineering
  program, 166
Maxed Out (Scurlock), 151–52
MBNA, 148
McDevitt, Douglas, 182
McGinnis, Tom, 174
McGoff, Chris, 182
McIntyre, Warren, 131
meal plans, 57, 197
media fees, 32
medical school, 232–33
Megill, Colin, 58
Meldrum, Jeffrey, 90
merchandizing
  and sports programs, 21–22
  and sweatshops, 48
merit aid, 37, 121
Miami-Dade College, new
  programs, 174
Miami University (Ohio)
  financial aid, 136
  financial hold, 63
Michigan State University
  financial aid, 136
  financial hold, 63
  lender program, 40
  selling lists, 39
  sports programs, 24
  student loan kickbacks, 40
Middle States Association of
  Colleges and Schools, 186
Mitchell, Stephen A., 66–67

Money Book for the Young,
  Fabulous & Broke, The
  (Orman), 217
Monster.com
Montgomery, Trevor, 142–43
Moravian College, fundraising, 45
Morgan, Noah, 44, 68
Moyer, Sean, 6
MTV, 20
Muhlenberg College
  electives, 67
  fundraising, 45
Muldowney, Tom, 128
Mullen, Patty, 237
Munier, Craig, 40
My Rich Uncle, 160
Myers, Michele Tolela, 17
myths about college, 1, 7, 43, 53,
  55, 56, 57, 59, 60, 67, 69, 70,
  71, 72, 75, 77, 79, 81, 84, 98,
  100, 104, 105, 106, 109, 114,
  165, 170, 212, 231, 244, 247,
  250

N

Nassirian, Barmak, 150
National Association of Colleges
  and Employers, 152
National Association of Student
  Financial Aid Administrators,
  123
National Center for Education
  Statistics, 247
National Collegiate Athletic
  Association (NCAA), 50
National Consumer Council, 217
National Council of Higher
  Education Loan Programs, 150
National Council on Economic
  Education, 163

National Foundation for Credit Counseling, 218
National Grant Foundation, 124
National Scholarship Foundation, 124
National Survey of Student Engagement (NSSE), 88
Neal, Anne, 80
need aid, 121
Neff, Thomas, 193
Nellie Mae, 149
Nelnet, 149
New England Association of Schools and Colleges, 186
New York Medical College, student debt, 229
New York Times, The, 109, 250
New York University
application fees, 25
film studies program, 166
Newsweek, 110
Nichols, Paige, 147
Noel-Levitz, 19, 149
non-profit schools *v.* for-profit schools, 175–78
North Central Association of Colleges and Schools, 186
North Idaho College, meal plans, 198
Northeastern University
debt collector, 41
work study, 133
Northwest Commission on Colleges and Universities, 186
Northwestern University
completion time, 166
endowment, 7
merchandizing, 21–22
Nova Southeastern University, lender program, 40

O

Oakland University, class availability, 44
Odogbili, Gloria, 241
Office Team, 199
Ohio State University
campus renovations, 19
complaints about instructors, 77
sports-related violence, 24
use of teaching assistants, 73
Ohio University, food services, 60
Oklahoma State University, lender program, 41
ombudsperson, 202
on-campus housing. *See* housing
O'Neill, Peggy, 63
online programs *v.* traditional programs, 178–79
Orfield, Gary, 85
Orr, Everett, 143
Osgood, Russell, 30
outsourcing, 107

P

Parent Loans for Undergraduate Students. *See* PLUS loans
Park, Suki, 27
parking fees, 31
Parnes, Lydia, 218
"Paying for College: It Pays to Save," 128
Pell Grants, 120
Pennsylvania State University
campus renovations, 20
endowment, 8
private tutoring, 84
online programs, 178
Perkins loans, 157
Peters, Robert, 226

Peterson's College Planner, 123, 127, 149
Peterson's Graduate Schools in the U.S. (Peterson's), 243
Peterson's Guide to Online Learning (Peterson's), 179
Phi Beta Kappa, 205
Phi Kappa Phi, 205
Pike, Patricia, 236
PIRGs' Higher Education Project, 123
Plunkett, Travis, 148
PLUS loans, 157
Pool, Mitzi, 6
Pope, Loren, 168, 187
positive illusion, 156–57
preferential packaging, 36–38
pre-paid tuition plans, 129
president salaries, 9–12
price fixing, 33–34
Prikazsky, Nina, 149
Primary Research Group, 19
Princeton Review, The, 60
Princeton Review Guide to College Majors, The (Princeton Review), 172
Princeton University
 developmental admissions, 27
 endowment, 8
 financial aid, 136
 grade inflation, 82
 use of teaching assistants, 73
private college *v.* public colleges, 173–75
private loans, 158–59
professional admission counseling, 189–90
professors
 perks for, 10
 political beliefs of, 79–80
 and priority of research, 70–73
 ratings of, 76–77
 and sabbaticals, 70
 salaries of, 9
 skills of, 75–77
 and tenure system, 70–71
 and time spent teaching, 69–73
 See also instructors
profiteering, 12–13
ProfScam (Sykes), 75–76
Project on Student Debt, 51, 163
Project ScholarScam, 124
Providence University, sports programs, 21
Purdue University, sports-related violence, 24

R

Rahmat-Samii, Yahya, 71, 72
Rakoff, Todd, 223
rating system, 15–18
Ray, Rachel, 246
Ready or Not, Here Life Comes (Levine), 107
recruitment officers, 20
Reichard, Gary W., 222
Rennie, Drummond, 91
research, value of, 89–92
Revenue Management (Cross), 37
Rice University
 endowment, 7
 financial aid, 136
Riggio, Leonard, 246
Robert Half International, 199
Robertson, William, 46
Robinson, Perry, 74
Rochester Institute of Technology, meal plans, 198
Roderick, Melissa, 85
room and board expenses. *See* housing
Rothkopf, Arthur, 16

Rubin, Donald, 78
Ruch, Richard, 175
Ruiz, Peofilo, 72
Russell, Jenny, 105–106
Rutgers University
   hands-on training, 241
   meal plans, 57–58
   president salary, 10
   sports programs, 24

S
Sallie Mae, 130, 148, 149
San Diego State University, hands-on training, 241
Sanborne, Jill, 103
Sarah Lawrence College
   grading policy, 167
   tuition and fees, 28
Sarnoff, David, 245
Sarwack, Susan, 77–78
SAT
   bias of, 26
   fee waivers, 189
Saving for College, 131
saving for college, 128–32
Schaeffer, Bob, 17
Schlueter, June, 73
Schmalensee, Richard, 223
scholarships, 120, 132
school-as-lender programs, 40–42
Scurlock, James, 151–52
Sebold, Sean, 128
"Self-Directed Search," 172
Seton Hall University
   dormitory fire, 56
   student loan kickbacks, 40
Sgro, Tony, 39
Shaw, Richard, 42
Shaw, Terri, 151
Shulman, Lee, 89
Sickler, Eric, 20
Siegel, Jeremy, 113
Siegel, Lewis, 228
Silva, Jose, 85
Simmons, Russell, 246
Sirianni, Mike, 36
Slavitt, Gabriel, 167
Slinkski, Raymond, 181
Small Business Administration, 250
Smith College, and work study, 133
Soltan, Margaret, 25
Southern Association of Colleges and Schools, 186
Spellings, Margaret, 88
Sperber, Murray, 63
Spielberg, Steven, 245
sports programs
   general, 21–25
   and merchandising, 21–22
St. Joe's University, sports programs, 21
Stafford loans, 137, 157–58
Stanford University
   business program, 224
   completion time, 166
   coursecasting, 251
   developmental admissions, 27
   endowment, 7–9
   fundraising, 47
   grade inflation, 82
   grade non-disclosure, 224
state fees, 32
State Public Interest Research Groups, 51
Steir, Max, 143
Sternberg, Robert J., 89
Strapped (Draut), 1
"Strong Interest Inventory," 172
Student Aid Incorporated, 124

Student Aid Report (SAR), 123, 126
Student Assistance Services, 124
Student Debt Alert, 163
Student Financial Services. *See* Student Assistance Services
"Student Guide to Financial Aid," 123
Student Loan Advocates and Volunteer Exchange, 163
Student Loan Justice, 163
Student Loan Justice Testimonial Website, 147
Student Loan Servicing Alliance, 150
Student Loan Watch/Higher Ed Watch, 163
student loans
 and bankruptcy, 216–17
 consolidation lenders, 211–12
 consolidation of, 209–11
 debt deferment, 215
 debt problems and assistance, 213–17
 forbearance, 215–16
 forgiven or cancelled, 208
 general, 2–3, 132–33, 144, 157–59
 lenders, 39–40, 150–51, 159–60
 loan grace period, 208–209
 loan origination fees, 146
 prepayment of, 212
 private loans, 158–59
 refinance of, 216
 repayment strategies, 212–13
 total cost of, 94–96
StudentLoanJustice.org, 146
study abroad programs, 83
Success Without College (Lee), 248, 253

Summers, Larry, 73–74
Swarthmore College, endowment, 8
Sykes, Charles, 75–76
Syracuse University, sports programs, 21

T
Tarantino, Quentin, 245
tax benefits, 121, 134–35
teaching assistants (TAs), 73–74
Technical and Vocational Schools (Peterson's), 184
technical degree, 183–84
technology or administrative fees, 31
Teitelbaum, Michael S., 227
tenure system, 70–71, 77, 92–93
Terhune, Jim, 64
textbook companies, 202–205
Textbook Revolution, 204
Thatch, Robert, 227–28
300 Best Jobs Without a Four-Year Degree (Farr, Ludden, and Shatkin), 253
360 Youth, 206
Tinto, Vincent, 85
Top 100 Careers Without a Four-Year Degree (Farr), 253
Totenberg, Nina, 245
Trinity College, tuition and fees, 28
Troy University, online programs, 178
Truman, Harry S., 246
Truth About Credit, The, 163
Tufts University, donation jackpots, 46
tuition
 fees, 28–31
 fixed plans, 137–38

reimbursement, 120–21
remission, 120
tips, 194–96
waivers, 120
Turner, Ted, 245
tutors, 251–52
Tutu, Desmond, 81
Twain, Mark, 243
202 High Paying Jobs You Can Land Without a College Degree (Rich), 253
Two-Year Colleges 2006 (Peterson's), 183

U
Ultimate College Guide, 188
unemployment, 106–107
United States Student Association, 50
University of Akron, campus renovations, 19–20
University of Arizona, private tutoring, 84
University of California (Berkeley)
 complaints about instructors, 77
 coursecasting, 251
 use of teaching assistants, 73
University of California, endowment, 7–8
University of California (Los Angeles), student loan kickbacks, 40
University of Chicago
 endowment, 7
 grade non-disclosure, 224
 student debt, 229
University of Colorado
 construction fees, 31–32
 sports-related violence, 24

University of Connecticut
 class availability, 44
 sports programs, 21
 sports-related violence, 24
University of Delaware, president's salary, 10
University of Florida
 financial hold, 63
 housing costs, 54
 meal plans, 58
University of Georgia, fundraising, 45
University of Houston, class size, 68
University of Illinois
 cost by major, 173
 lender program, 41
 online programs, 178
University of Iowa, "bait and switch" trap, 82–83
University of Kansas
 cost by major, 173
 merchandizing, 21
 sports programs, 21
University of Maryland
 application fees, 25
 bank marketing, 39
 fees, 32
 for-profit programs, 175
 lender program, 41
 online programs, 178
 sports-related violence, 24
 tuition, 174
University of Massachusetts
 campus renovations, 20
 meal plans, 57–58
 online programs, 176, 178
 use of teaching assistants, 73
 work study, 133
University of Miami
 application fees, 25

food services, 58
for-profit programs, 175
housing costs, 53–54, 55
janitorial pay, 48
sports programs, 21
University of Michigan
    campus renovations, 20
    complaints about instructors, 77
    developmental admissions, 27
    endowment, 8
    president's salary, 10
    selling lists, 39
    sports programs, 21
University of Minnesota
    endowment, 8
    hands-on training, 241
    lender program, 41
    sports-related violence, 24
University of Nebraska, student loan kickbacks, 40
University of North Carolina
    application fees, 25
    class availability, 43
    endowment, 8
    financial aid, 136
University of Notre Dame
    developmental admissions, 27
    endowment, 7
University of Oklahoma, selling lists, 39
University of Pennsylvania
    developmental admissions, 27
    endowment, 9
    food services, 61
    lender program, 40
    transferring credits, 195
    Wharton School of Business, 224, 241–42
University of Phoenix, lender program, 40
University of Pittsburgh, lender program, 41
University of Puget Sound, fundraising, 45
University of Richmond, tuition and fees, 28
University of Rochester, business program, 224
University of Tennessee, selling lists, 39
University of Texas
    application fees, 25
    endowment, 7
    business program, 224
University of Vermont
    Coca-Cola, 62
    lender program, 41
University of Virginia
    endowment, 9
    financial aid, 136
    financial hold, 63
University of Washington, use of teaching assistants, 73
University of Wisconsin (Madison)
    donation jackpots, 46
    cost by major, 173
    sports programs, 24
unrealistic optimism, 156–57
Upromise 129–30
Ursinus College, tuition and fees, 30
U.S. News and World Report, 15–17

V

Vassar College, tuition and fees, 28
Vaughn, Bill, 28
Vedder, Richard, 91, 114–15
visiting professors, 81
Vogel, Mitch, 73

Volvovski, Vicky, 60

W
Wake Forest University, sports programs, 21
Wall Street Journal, The, 83, 105, 133, 166
Ward, David, 92
Warren, Elizabeth, 41, 149, 151, 160
Washington State University, online programs, 178
Washington University
 business program, 224
 endowment, 7
 for-profit programs, 175
 ratings, 18
Wayne State University, private tutoring, 84
Webster University, lender program, 40
Wesleyan University
 tuition and fees, 28
 work study, 133
West, Kanye, 246
West Virginia University
 sports programs, 21
 sports-related violence, 24
Western Association of Colleges and Schools, 186
Western Washington University, private tutoring, 84
Wharton School of Business. *See* University of Pennsylvania
What Color is Your Parachute? (Bolles), 172
What Color is Your Parachute for Teens? (Bolles), 172
Williams College
 electives, 68
 endowment, 7–8
 fundraising, 44–45
Wilson, Kim, 142
Wintour, Anna, 246
Wohlert, Amy, 221
Wolff, Alexis, 133
Woodbury, Robert, 16
work-study, 121, 133–34
workers' wages, 47–48
Workforce Committee (U.S.), 141
Wright Brothers, 245

X
Xavier University, sports programs, 21

Y
Yale University
 donation jackpots, 47
 endowment, 7–9
 ratings, 18
 rising costs, 31
 use of teaching assistants, 73
Young Money, 163
Youngstown State University, campus renovations, 20
Youth Media and Marketing Networks, 149

Z
Zottola, Paul-Henry, 230

Notes:

Notes:

ABOUT THE AUTHOR

Marc Scheer, Ph.D., is a researcher, career counselor, and educational consultant who lives in New York City. He has counseled students at public and private colleges and universities around the country, and he has managed a wide range of educational, financial, and investment studies for large research and media firms. Dr. Scheer completed his Ph.D. in counseling psychology. For more information, visit http://NoSuckerLeftBehind.blogspot.com